The Nearly Men

Lloyd Bonson

First Edition Published by Stanhope Books 2013

www.stanhopebooks.com

Cover design by Lloyd Bonson
Back Cover photograph © Williams F1

ISBN-13: 978-1-909893-02-3

Dedication:

For those who should be here, but are not
To love ones we miss, you are never forgot
Friends and family, no longer here
We always remember you, you are always near

Lloyd Bonson – April 2012

Contents

4

Preface

I had always planned to write a follow-up to 'One Hit Wonders', researching much of the content for this book at the same time. Having looked at those who had won a single Grand Prix, I was naturally curious about those that hadn't. The drivers who tittered on the edge of victory, only the have it pulled away from underneath them.

Many names such as Chris Amon and Martin Brundle fill the immediate thoughts of anyone asked to name such drivers, yet the likes of Casare Perdisa and Teo Fabi may be a little more unfamiliar.

What is even more surprising, are the names that don't make it to this list, drivers who tasted success in other disciplines such as Le Mans or IndyCar, yet couldn't achieve success in Formula One. One of the most notable names here would be Derek Bell or Henri Pescaolo; although there are a whole host of others.

Once again it seemed only fair that the Indianapolis 500 and Formula Two events which counted towards the World Championship to be included, as their records form part of the statistics.

Lloyd Bonson

Cliff Allison
World Championship Years Active: 1958 – 1961
World Championship Teams: Lotus, Scuderia Centro Sud, Ferrari,
UDT Laystall

Henry Clifford Allison was born on the 8th February 1932 in Brough, Westmorland (now the county of Cumbria). Like many of his contemporaries, he started his racing career in Formula 3 racing a Cooper-JAP in 1952; he managed third in his heat at Kirkcaldy in April of that year.

Some good placing's followed in 1953 including fifth at Oulton, second at Brough and a further second at Charterhall. The following year Cliff took wins at Cadwell Park and Bo'ness and fifth at Crystal Palace, now in a Cooper Mk VIII. This was followed by Fourth in the Redex Trophy and had now caught the eye of Colin Chapman and given the chance to race for Team Lotus. Allison won the performance prize driving a 744cc Lotus in the 1957 24 Hours of Le Mans, and the following year the Lotus of Allison and Chapman placed 6th in the 12 Hours of Sebring endurance race for sports cars.

Alongside Graham Hill, Allison gave Team Lotus their Formula One debut at the 1958 Monaco Grand Prix. He was forced to make numerous pit stops during the 1958 Monaco Grand Prix race, but his Lotus finished 6th, 12 laps behind race winner Maurice Trintgnant. Allison came in 4th with his Lotus in the 1958 Grand Prix of Europe at Spa-Francorchamps, more than 4 minutes behind victor Tony Brooks. He had no sense of the glory that was to follow for Lotus, but said: "I always reckoned that Colin had the ability to design a winning car. But what worried me was that it might kill me before that happened! I had all sorts of problems with Lotuses. They were all very, very light"

His efforts in the underdeveloped Lotus caught the attentions of Enzo Ferrari and he was offered a drive with Scuderia Ferrari for 1959. This gave him a mixed season of Sports Car and Single Seat racing for the season.

At Monaco Grand Prix the Ferrari factory team fielded truncated versions of the cars they ran in future grand prix races, their long sleek snouts were cut away to allow more air into the cooling systems. German driver Wolfgang von Trips lost control of his Porsche in a bend where the street was steeply inclined to Casino. Allison's Ferrari crashed into him as he spun. The Lotus of Bruce Halford came next into the blind curve and became part of the wreck and none of the three cars would continue.

Allison teamed up with Dan Gurney in one of three team Ferrari cars that competed in the 1000 km Nürburgring race, and was paired with Jean Behra in a Ferrari which finished 2nd in the 12 Hours of Sebring.

Fifth place at the Italian Grand Prix that year was his best single seater result, but Allison had done enough to remain with Ferrari for the following season.

In February 1960, the Grand Prix circus headed to Argentina for the opening round of the season. Bruce McLaren's Cooper won the race, yet Allison showed his class in by dragging his outdated front-engined Ferrari home second. He appeared to be the man of the moment; yet two accidents in May would have a profound effect on his future.

Allison skidded off the road during practice for the Targa Florio Sicily during the early part of the month. His Ferrari was travelling at around 100 mph when a tyre burst. The car crashed into a scrub forest, destroying itself and most of what it touched. When the accident happened he was nearing the end of a five mile straight by the sea, the only very fast stretch of road in the event. Allison escaped from the wreck without a scratch, but his face held an expression of fear.

He then suffered a major crash behind the wheel of his Ferrari while practicing for the 1960 Monaco Grand Prix. His Ferrari slammed into a straw barrier. He was unconscious when he was taken to a hospital. Allison sustained a broken left arm, rib fractures, facial cuts, and a concussion. When he awoke from a 16-day coma he found he could speak French, which was odd since he had understood not a word of the language previously.

It took him almost the rest of the year to recover from his injuries. He came back in 1961 driving a Lotus for the private UDT-Laystall team. At Spa he crashed heavily at the fast Blanchemont turning, which ended his career as he suffered broken legs and spent two years recovering.

Allison had reached the end of his yellow-brick road. It took him a long time to get over the bitter frustration and disappointment that he had been left behind. He went quietly back to Brough to work in his father's Grand Prix Motors garage business, occasionally driving the local school bus in his later years.

It was only when he made occasional visits to Formula One races in the Nineties that he came to realise that people still remembered him. During an interview at Monaco in 1992 he admitted: "I don't want to sound big-headed, but at the time of the accident in Monte Carlo, I knew I was already driving as quickly as the other drivers in Ferrari, and probably a little bit quicker." He would have been perfectly suited to the "Sharknose" Ferrari in which Phil Hill won his 1961 crown.

Allison started to participate in historic racing events and demonstrations, once sharing a Lotus with the historic racer Malcolm Ricketts on a re-run of the famed Mille Miglia. At one checkpoint he was personally sought out and congratulated by Luca di Montezemolo, the president of Ferrari. That, and the reception he got on his return to the F1 paddocks, did not compensate for Cliff Allison's lost career, but one of the finest fellows in the sport quietly admitted that he was overcome to discover that he had not been forgotten.

Cliff Allison passed away in his home town of Brough, on 7th April 2005.

At the end of his World Championship career, Allison had competed in 18 Grand Prix races gaining one podium position. He had scored 11 World Championship points.

George Amick
World Championship Years Active: 1957 – 1958
World Championship Teams: Snowberger, Epperly

George Amick was born on the 24th October 1924 in Oregon, USA. He started racing Midgets in 1955, taking four podiums from the nine races he entered. The following year was more prolific for the racer, taking part in 65 races, four of which he won.

For 1957 he moved up to the USAC National Championship and attempted to enter the Indy 500. However his outdated Snowberger chassis was no-where near competitive enough and he failed to qualify for the event.

As such, his rookie appearance at the Indianapolis 500 came in 1958. Amick was assigned a "lay-down" roadster commissioned by car owner Norm Demler, designed by Quinn Epperly, and built by master Indianapolis chief mechanic George Salih. Amick found himself running a comfortable second to leader Jimmy Bryan with just 20 laps remaining. Demler and Salih felt Amick was in a position to catch Bryan and perhaps even win, but decided against pushing their rookie driver into a potentially fatal mistake and Amick came home an easy second.

He was second in the USAC championship that year and felt comfortable going for the championship the following season. The opening race of 1959 was a 100-mile race at the Daytona Speedway, where Amick was involved in a fatal accident. Major open-wheel racing would not return to the track for many years.

At the end of his World Championship career, Amick had been entered in two Grand Prix races gaining one podium position. He had scored 6 World Championship points.

Chris Amon
World Championship Years Active: 1963-1976
World Championship Teams: Reg Parnell Racing, Ian Raby Racing, Cooper, Amon, Ferrari, March, Matra, Tecno, Tyrrell, BRM, Ensign, Wolf

The only child of a wealthy sheep farmer, Christopher Arthur Amon was born on the 20th July 1943 in Bulls, New Zealand. On leaving school, he persuaded his father to buy him an Austin A40 Special, which he entered in some minor local races and hillclimbs. He progressed to a 1.5 litre Cooper and then an old 2.5L Maserati 250F, but only began to gain a solid reputation when he drove the Cooper-Climax T51 which Bruce McLaren had used to win his maiden Grand Prix.

For 1962 Amon entered the Cooper for the New Zealand winter series. His own attempts were hampered by mechanical problems. However, Scuderia Veloce entered him in a similar car at Lakeside, where he performed well in challenging conditions. At that race English driver Reg Parnell was watching and he persuaded Amon to come to England and race for his team.

For the 1963 Formula One season the Parnell team were using one year old Lola Mk4A chassis, powered by 1962 spec Climax V8 engines. Amon was teamed with the very experienced Maurice Trintignant for the first race of the season at Monaco and his Grand Prix career started with what was to become typical bad luck: Trintignant's Climax developed a misfire, so he took over Amon's car.

At the Belgian Grand Prix Amon he retired after nine laps after an oil fire ended his race. He continued to experience mechanical problems at the Dutch, Mexican and German Grands Prix. His best results of the year were seventh at the French and British Grands Prix. Parnell was nonetheless impressed with Amon's results in what was regarded as less-than-competitive machinery and promoted him to team leader.

Reg Parnell died from peritonitis in January 1964 and his son Tim took over the team. In a series of pre-season races in Britain and Italy, Amon recorded three fifth places at Snetterton, Silverstone and Syracuse.

However, he failed to qualify for the first F1 race of the season, the Monaco GP. His luck appeared to change at the next race, the Dutch GP, where he scored his first World Championship points. The rest of his season, however, was blighted by mechanical problems.

The Parnell team were offered BRM engines for 1965, on the proviso that Richard Attwood was its regular driver. Reluctantly, Parnell agreed and Attwood took Amon's place. Spotting an opportunity, Bruce McLaren quickly signed Amon for his new McLaren team, but when no second McLaren F1 car materialised, Amon could only drive in CanAm races.

At the French GP Amon rejoined Parnell to stand in for an injured Attwood. For the British Grand Prix at Silverstone, he was entered to drive a second Brabham-BRM run by Ian Raby, but the car never materialised. At the German GP Amon mechanical failure again forced an early retirement. His last drive before Attwood's return, a non-championship race in Enna, Sicily, also ended in retirement.

During 1966 Amon continued to race for McLaren in CanAm. He was intended to drive the second McLaren M2B but yet again the team never made the intended expansion to two cars. However, an opportunity arose to drive for the Cooper F1 team after Richie Ginther left them for Honda. Amon drove for Cooper at the French GP and was scheduled to drive for them for the rest of the season, until the more successful John Surtees left Ferrari to join Cooper and Amon found himself dropped.

Despite his lacklustre Grand Prix career, Amon did score his biggest success to date when he partnered Bruce McLaren in a 7-litreFord GT40 Mark II at the 1966 Le Mans 24-hour race, spearheading a formation finish. He subsequently received an invitation to meet Enzo Ferrari in Maranello, where he signed to race for Ferrari in 1967 alongside Lorenzo Bandini, Mike Parkes and Ludovico Scarfiotti.

Amon's first year with Ferrari did not begin well, whilst driving to Brands Hatch for the pre-season F1 Race of Champions, he crashed his road car and had to withdraw. Tragedy then struck the Ferrari team when Bandini died following a crash during the 1967 Monaco Grand Prix,

Parkes broke both his legs at the Belgian Grand Prix and Scarfiotti went into temporary retirement.

This left Amon as Ferrari's only driver for the rest of the season, until joined by Jonathan Williams for the final race in Mexico. At the end of 1967, Amon had achieved three third places and finished fourth in the Drivers' Championship.

His Ferrari contract also included sports car racing and he began 1967 by winning the Daytona 24 Hours and 1000km Monza events with Bandini in the 4-litre Ferrari 330-P4. He finished the year partnering Jackie Stewart to a second place at the BOAC 500, which sealed the manufacturer's world championship for Ferrari by one point over Porsche.

1968 was the year aerodynamics first played a significant role in F1 car design and early on Amon worked with Ferrari engineer Mauro Forghieri to place aerofoils on the Ferrari 312. He won the first two rounds of the Tasman Series but lost the series to Jim Clark.

After the first race of the F1 season in South Africa, Amon achieved pole positions in three of the following four races. However, due to ever-present mechanical problems he only scored a single Championship point from them. Throughout the rest of the season he never qualified lower than fifth place although victory still eluded him

At the British Grand Prux, he duelled to the line with Jo Siffert's Lotus 49B and in Canada he dominated the race despite a malfunctioning clutch. Seventeen laps from the chequered flag, , his car's transmission failed. From all of those promising starts that season he was only able to finish five races.

Amon's appalling run of failures continued into 1969. Despite six starts within the top six of the grid, he was only able to achieve a third-place at the Dutch GP. The Ferrari V12 engine was unreliable and although it's Flat-12 replacement had proven very fast in testing, it had suffered many mechanical breakages.

For Amon, there was no guarantee it would be any more dependable than the V12, so although the new engine was clearly more powerful, he decided to leave Ferrari for a Cosworth DFV powered team. In an ironic twist of fate the new flat-12 engine would become one of the best F1 engines of the 1970s, and the car he was due to drive in 1970, the Ferrari 312B would take four victories!

For the 1970 Formula One season, Amon joined Jo Siffert at the newly formed March team. Amon won the pre-season Silverstone International Trophy, but once the F1 season began he found himself prevented from converting good qualifying positions into good results. He qualified second behind Stewart's Tyrrell March for the season-opening South African Grand Prix only for his own March to overheat within fourteen laps. Amon then qualified sixth for the Spanish Grand Prix only for his March's Ford-Cosworth DFV engine to expire within ten laps. He qualified and ran second in the Monaco Grand Prix until his suspension failed twenty laps from the finish.

His second in the Belgian Grand Prix finally gave the March works team their first points finish, but after qualifying fourth for the next race, the Dutch Grand Prix, his car's clutch broke after just one lap. Amon duplicated his Belgian result in France, but thereafter only achieved one further result of note in the year, a third place Canada.

By the end of the year, disagreements with March co-founders Max Mosley and Robin Herd meant that Amon had decided to move to former world champions Matra. By 1971 the Matra team, was not what it was. Ken Tyrell had left to run his own team the previous season and Matra's V12 engine was heavy. Despite this Amon once again scored a pre-season victory, this time at the Argentine Grand Prix. Once the F1 season had begun, he managed a third-place at the Spanish GP and scored a couple of fifth places in the South African and French GPs.

His run of bad luck followed him. He had a major accident at the Nürburgring which put him out for the following race in Austria. At the Monza he qualified in pole position and despite a poor start to the race looked as if he would capitalise on it. Once again it was not to be, the visor on his helmet became detached and Amon had to slow to avoid risking a major accident. He finished the race in sixth place, scoring just one Championship point.

He stuck with Matra for the following year and achieved a handful of points-scoring finishes, but only one podium appearance, at the French GP. It was here he achieved the fifth and final pole position of his career and was leading the race until loose stones from the surface on the Clermont-Ferrand circuit, caused a puncture forced him to pit. He charged back through the field, annihilating the circuit's lap record to finish third.

Matra decided to end their participation in F1 at the end of 1972, so Amon found himself looking to return to March as a driver for 1973. The place, was given to Jean-Pierre Jarier, for financial reasons. Amon therefore signed for a team with a good reputation in the lower formulae, Tecno.

Unfortunately, the team went from bad to worse and wasn't able to field the Tecno PA123/6 until the fifth GP of the season, the Belgian GP. Amon managed to finish in sixth position, but was unhappy with the car. By the time of the Austrian GP, four races from the end of the season, Amon's patience had run out and he left the team.

Tyrrell offered Amon a drive in their third car for the last two races of the season. After a mediocre first outing at the Canadian GP, he and Jackie Stewart withdrew from the United States GP, following the death of their teammate François Cevert during qualifying.

For the 1974 F1 season Amon teamed up with Gordon Fowell to design a car for his new Chris Amon Racing team. Structurally, the design proved to be weak and was not ready for an F1 appearance until the fourth race of the season, the Spanish GP. Amon was only able to qualify 23rd and was forced to retire after 22 laps due to brake issues.

Following further work and testing, Amon returned for the Monaco GP and qualified twentieth, but, thanks to mechanical problems, he was unable to start the race. Further problems meant Amon was not able to reappear until the Italian GP, but this time he was unable to qualify.

Chris Amon in his Amon-Ford AM01 during qualifying at Monaco

Unfortunately for Amon and Fowell, that sealed the fate of both the car and Chris Amon Racing, leaving Amon to drive the season's last two races with the faltering BRM team, although there were no drives on the table for 1975. However, a chance meeting with Morris Nunn of Ensign led to two GP drives in the Ensign N175 at the Austrian and Italian GPs, with a full time drive the following year.

Ensign's first race of the 1976 season was the South African GP where Amon qualified 18th and finished 14th. Thereafter results began to improve, with Amon finishing fifth in the Spanish GP; and then qualifying eighth for the Belgian GP. More points seemed likely from the race until his car lost a wheel 19 laps from the finish and Amon was lucky to escape unhurt from the ensuing accident.

Amon's skill enabled him to score an incredible 3rd grid position start for the Swedish GP. During the race it looked as if he would join Tyrrell drivers Jody Scheckter and Patrick Depailler on the podium, until suspension failure threw him from the track on the 38th lap.

He returned for the British GP, where he was running 4th in the race when his engine developed a water leak. Rather than risk losing an engine, his team called him in to retire.

At the German GP problems dogged his attempts to qualify well, but it was Niki Lauda's now famous crash during the second lap of the race that had a far greater impact. He refused to take part in the restart and he was fired from the team. Amon declared his retirement from the sport and returned to New Zealand.

Walter Wolf contacted Amon and persuaded him to drive for his Wolf team in the North American races near the end of the season. However, Amon was involved in a heavy collision with another car and once again was lucky to walk away unharmed. He didn't then take part in either the Canadian or United States GPs.

Amon turned down an offer of a fulltime F1 drive for 1977, but did attempt a return to CanAm racing in 1977 with a Wolf-Dallara WD1. However, after only one race he quit, saying "I'm just not enjoying this anymore".

His place in Wolf's Can-Am team was taken by the young and then unknown Canadian driver, called Gilles Villeneuve, whom Amon would later recommend to Enzo Ferrari.

Amon returned once again to New Zealand, this time to retire from F1 motor racing for good, and is still regarded to be one of the best Formula One drivers never to win a championship Grand Prix. His reputation for bad luck was such that fellow driver Mario Andretti once joked that "if he became an undertaker, people would stop dying".

Back in New Zealand he farmed and then began doing tests for a local motoring TV programme. He helped Toyota New Zealand develop their cars and competed on occasion in Toyota machinery in events such as the EnergyWise Rally in 2004.

There is now a Toyota Amon Cup, awarded to the winner of the Toyota Racing Series in New Zealand and in 2007 Amon lent his name to the Chris Amon International Scholarship to support Kiwi drivers in their quest to further their careers in International single-seater racing.

At the end of his World Championship career, Amon had been entered in 108 Grand Prix races standing on the podium 11 times. He had scored 83 World Championship points

Bob Anderson
World Championship Years Active: 1963-1967
World Championship Teams: DW Racing

Robert "Bob" Anderson was born in Hendon, London on the 19th May 1931. He competed in Grand Prix motorcycle racing , was a two-time winner of the North West 200 race in Northern Ireland and finished second on his debut at the Isle of Man TT on a Norton 500cc.

After several seasons in motorcycle racing, he switched to car racing in 1961, when he ran a Formula Junior Lola in a race at Snetterton. He continued to race cars and eventually became a Team Lotus Formula Junior driver, winning a race at Montlhéry and finishing second at Monaco.

In 1963 he bought a Lola Mk4 Formula One car, and raced under the guise of DW Racing Enterprises. The team was small, so small in fact, that it composed of Bob and a small team of mechanics. Despite this hindrance he took the flexible little Lola to victory in the non-Championship Rome Grand Prix in that first year.

For the following years he ran private Brabham cars under the same banner, with his best result a third place in the 1964 Austrian Grand Prix. He was awarded the von Trips Memorial Trophy as the most successful private entrant of 1964.

In 1967, whilst testing at Silverstone, he suffered an accident in which he slid off the track in wet conditions and hit a marshal's post. Anderson suffered serious chest and neck injuries and died later in Northampton General Hospital.

At the end of his World Championship career, Anderson had been entered in 29 Grand Prix, stepping on the podium once. He had scored 8 World Championship points.

Michael Andretti
World Championship Years Active: 1993
World Championship Teams: McLaren

When your father has successfully competed in just about every form of motor racing imaginable, making a career decision must be pretty though. Yet that was the situation facing Michael Mario Andretti.

The eldest son of racing ledgend Mario Andretti, was born 5th October 1962 and started racing in 1980, driving a Formula Vee car in Local SCCA events.

In 1981 he won six of the 11 Super Vee races and won the championship and moved up to Formula Atlantic, winning the Championship in 1983. In the same year he joined his father and Philippe Alliot in the Porsche Kremer Racing Team, taking third place in the Le Mans 24 Hours, driving a Porsche 956. This would prove to be his best result in the famous endurance event.

For 1984 he moved up again, this time to CART IndyCars, where he scored five third place finishes and ended the season in seventh overall. In the Indianapolis 500, he finished fifth and shared the Rookie of the Year award with Roberto Guerrero. The 1986 Long Beach round of the Indycar championship would see Michael take the first of 42 CART wins – only his farther and A.J. Foyt have scored more IndyCar victories.

Unfortunately for Michael, his family's bad luck at Indy held through for him. In 1991, he led with twelve laps remaining, but finished second to Rick Mears. In 1992, he dominated the race, leading a full four-fifths of the laps, but, with eleven laps remaining, his fuel pump failed. He also dropped out while leading the Indy 500 in 1989, 1995 and 2003 and currently holds the record for most laps led in the Indy 500 without having achieved a victory.

Andretti achieved major title success by winning the 1991 CART/PPG IndyCar World Series for Newman/Haas Racing, taking victory in 8 of 17 races. He won all five of the road courses that season which caught the eye of Ron Denis and the McLaren Formula One team.

He signed the drive for the team in September 1992, when they were still utilising powerful Honda engines. Unfortunately, the 1993 season was not a success. Honda had pulled out for Formula One leaving McLaren little option but to use the 'customer' Ford Cosworth engines. These were 2 specifications behind the 'works' units used by the Benetton team.

It was also unfortunate for Andretti that testing was being restricted, particularly over the Grand Prix weekend giving him little chance to learn the circuits. It meant he never got to grips with highly technical aspects which he was not used to in the technologically simpler IndyCars, such as active suspension and traction control. Combined with an unstable team – Ayrton Senna was driving on a race-by-race basis with Mika Hakkenen waiting in the wings – and Michael's insistence to commute from the US meant the season was always going be difficult.

Andretti failed to shine in the 1993 McLaren

A string of collisions meant that he only completed three laps in his first three races and three points-scoring finishes, including a third place at Monza, were perceived as too little, too late. He left the team and the series by mutual agreement after that race and he would never sit in a Formula 1 car again.

After McLaren replaced Andretti with Häkkinen, Michael returned to the CART series for 1994 and drove for Chip Ganassi, where he once again proved very successful. He won his very first race back in the series at Surfers Paradise, having led every lap along the way.

In 1995 he returned to Newman/Haas Racing, replacing Nigel Mansell. He finished as runner-up to Jimmy Vasser in 1996 and more race wins followed in the years to come, but his 1991 championship success remained his only title in CART/IndyCar racing.

He took his 42nd and final Indycar victory Long Beach in 2002. This was ironic as the track as the scene of his first victory 16 years earlier.

After competing in the 2003 Indianapolis 500, Andretti retired from full-time IndyCar racing. He led the race for 28 of the opening 94 laps before a throttle linkage failure put him out of contention once again. That year he bought into the "Team Green" squad turning into Andretti Green Racing and for 2003. Tony Kanaan won the 2004 IndyCar Series Championship for Andretti Green Racing and the following year Dan Wheldon won the Indy 500, and the Championship for the team. In 2007, Scotland's Dario Franchitti also won the Indianapolis 500 and the IndyCar Series title for AGR.

Andretti returned to the driver's seat for the 2006 Indianapolis 500 in a one-time effort to assist the development of his son, Marco, an IndyCar rookie for the '06 season. Michael led the race with four laps to go, before falling to second behind his son a lap later. He went on to finish third, while Marco only just missed out on the 500 victory after he was passed just before the start/finish line on the last lap by three-time Indycar champion Sam Hornish, Jr.

After qualifying his car in 11th place for the 2007 Indianapolis 500, Andretti went on to finish 13th. He then announced that this would be his last Indy 500 as a driver.

With his family name there was always going to be much expected of Michael, and he certainly performed better than any other Andretti, apart from his father. Had he have moved to McLaren a year earlier when they were still a dominant force things might have been different.

At the end of his World Championship career, Michael Andretti had started 13 Grand Prix races with just one podium to his name. He had scored 7 World Championship points.

Peter Arundell
World Championship Years Active: 1963-1966
World Championship Teams: Lotus

Peter Arundell was born on the 18th November 1933 in Ilford, Essex. He became a professional racing driver after finishing his time in the Royal Air Force, competing mainly in MG, Elva and Lotus cars.

He won an early Formula Junior race held in England, the John Davy Trophy at the Boxing Day Brands Hatch meeting in an Elva-D.K.W. in 1959. In 1962 he won the British Formula Junior championship in a Lotus 22, and also in 1963 in a Lotus 27. He also won the Monaco Formula Junior race in 1961 and 1962.

In 1963 he won the last Formula Junior race held in England, the Anglo-European Formula Junior Trophy in a Lotus 27-Ford. This incredible string of success led to Arundell being accused of using illegal engines, although this was never proved.

By now he was member of Team Lotus and joined their Formula One team in 1964, marking the start of his World Championship career with two podium finishes. He was regarded as a strong prospect for the future and a great supporting driver for World Champion Jim Clark.

Whilst taking part in Formula 2 at Reims in 1964, he had a spin and was hit at high speed by Richie Ginther; Arundell was thrown from the car in the impact, which resulted in him missing most of the 1965 season.

Lotus boss Colin Chapman saved his place in the team for 1966, with Arundell taking third on his comeback in the non-championship South African Grand Prix at East London on 1 January 1966. However, he did not enjoy any further success, mainly due to the uncompetitive BRM H16 engine Lotus were using at the time, and he retired from Formula One at the end of the season.

He retired from racing altogether in 1969, and later moved to Florida, where he set up the software company Mystique who were notorious for their adult themed video games of the early 1980's.

Peter passed away on the 16th June 2009.

At the end of his World Championship career, Peter Arundell had started 11 Grand Prix races and finished on the podium twice. He had scored 12 World Championship points

Richard Attwood
World Championship Years Active: 1964-1969
World Championship Teams: BRM, Reg Parnell, Cooper, Lotus

Richard James David "Dickie" Attwood was born on the 4th April 1940 in Wolverhampton, Staffordshire. Motoring was in his blood, his father was a motor trader and a young Richard started his working career as an apprentice at sports car manufacturer Jaguar, which wetted his appetite for racing.

His first race was in 1960 at the wheel of a Triumph TR3. For 1961 he joined the Midlands Racing Partnership to drive for them in club-level Formula Junior events, and continued in this role until the end of 1962. In 1963 the team expanded into the international arena, and Attwood immediately grabbed motorsport headlines when he won the Monaco Grand Prix FJ support race, in a Lola Mk5a. At the end of the season he won the inaugural Grovewood Award, voted for by a Guild of Motoring Writers panel.

On the back of this success, MRP decided to step up to the Formula Two class for 1964. Attwood won in Vienna and took second places in the Pau Grand Prix, Eifelrennen and Albi Grand Prix. This was at a time when top-line Grand Prix drivers were an integral part of the F2 series and at Pau he was only beaten by reigning Formula One World Champion Jim Clark driving a full-works Lotus.

Attwood's performances in Formula 2 prompted Alfred Owen, the proprietor of BRM, to offer him an opportunity in his works Formula One team. His first outing for the team was in the non-Championship News of the World Trophy race, at Goodwood, in which he took the BRM P57 to fourth place, the first non-Lotus finisher and the only car to end on the same lap as Colin Chapman's fleet winners.

Attwood's second F1 outing was in the 1964 British Grand Prix, driving BRM's experimental four wheel drive P67 model. Having been the project's test driver Attwood did manage to qualify the overweight car, albeit in last place on the grid. However, as the car was principally intended as a rolling test bed, BRM decided to withdraw the P67 prior to the race itself, costing Attwood his first World Championship start.

During 1964, he was also approached by the Ford GT prototype project team. The car would evolve into the Ford GT40, and Attwood became one of the first drivers to take the iconic car onto a race track. He shared a GT40 with Jo Schlesser in the 1964 24 Hours of Le Mans, but was forced to retire due to the car catching fire.

His first major international sports car victory came at the 1964 Rand 9 Hours race in South Africa, driving David Piper's Ferrari P2. It was with David Piper that Attwood developed perhaps his longest lasting professional relationship; driving Piper's green Ferraris on many occasions over the following five years.

Tim Parnell signed Attwood to his privateer Reg Parnell Racing team for 1965, driving a formerly class-leading Lotus 25. Unfortunately for Attwood, by 1965 the chassis was past its best, and fitted with the BRM motor it was distinctly uncompetitive. Although generally reliable, Attwood only managed to pick up a pair of 6th-place points finishes towards the end of the season.

In 1966 Attwood headed to Australia and New Zealand as a part of BRM's Tasman Series squad. His Tasman performances were very promising; including a win at Levin, yet his growing success in sports cars meant he sat out the majority of the 1966 and 1967 F1 seasons.

His only appearance came as a substitute for works-Cooper driver Pedro Rodríguez at the 1967 Canadian Grand Prix, bringing the Cooper-Maserati home in 10th place. During 1966 he maintained his run of form in F2, taking victory in the Rome Grand Prix and a second 2nd place at Pau in 1966, but concentrated firmly on sports cars in 1967.

After Mike Spence's untimely death during the 1968 Indianapolis 500 race Attwood rejoined the BRM works team, now run by Parnell, as his replacement. Attwood's first race on his return was perhaps his most spectacular, taking fastest lap in the 1968 Monaco Grand Prix, on his way to a strong second-place finish behind Graham Hill's works Lotus.

However, results declined through the remainder of the season, and four races from the end Attwood was himself replaced by Bobby Unser.

Always something of a Monaco specialist, it was in the principality that Richard Attwood made his final Formula One start. Colin Chapman brought in the Brit as substitute for the injured Jochen Rindt, driving the Lotus 49B in 1969. He finished in a respectable fourth-place. Although this was his last F1 drive, he did appear at the 1969 German Grand Prix in an F2 Brabham for Frank Williams. This was at a time when F2 cars were eligible to enter the German Grand Prix World Championship round mainly due to the length of the Nurburgring Nordschliffe circuit. Attwood finished 6th overall, and second in the F2 class.

Having driven privateer Porsches, for the 1969 World Sportscar Championship season Dickie Attwood was signed to the Porsche works team. Commonly paired with fellow Brit Vic Elford, the season's highlights were a pair of second places, driving the Porsche 908, in the BOAC 500 (the drivers' home race at Brands Hatch) and the Watkins Glen 6h race. Later in the season Attwood was again involved in the development of an iconic sports racing car: the Porsche 917. The Elford/Attwood pairing took their 917LH up to 327 laps in the 1969 24 Hours of Le Mans, but the car suffered a gearbox failure with only two hours to go, after leading for a substantial portion of the race.

Attwood subsequently went on to win the Le Mans 24 Hours in 1970 with a Porsche 917K, along with Hans Herrmann. Hermann and Attwood also took second place in the 1970 Nürburgring race, this time back in a 908. Driving with Herbie Müller once more in a Porsche 917 he finished second in the 1971 24 Hours of Le Mans, this time for the John Wyer privateer team. At the end of the season, after also winning the 1000km Zeltweg race, Attwood retired from motorsport.

Richard Attwood came out of retirement briefly in 1984, as a part of the moribund Aston Martin Nimrod Le Mans project. Following his car's failure to finish in the 1984 24 Hours of Le Mans race, Attwood retired from front line racing for good.

Today he is still very active in historic motorsport, often making memorable appearances at the Goodwood Festival of Speed, among many yearly excursions.

At the end of his World Championship career, Richard Attwood had been entered in 17 Grand Prix races finishing on the podium once. He had scored 11 World Championship points

Attwood's last competitive Formula 1 drive was with Lotus

Manny Ayulo
World Championship Years Active: 1951-1955
World Championship Teams: Kurtis Kraft, Kuzma, Lesovsky

Manuel Ayulo was born on the 20th October 1921 in Burbank, California. His efforts, along with those of friend and teammate Jack McGrath, helped establish track roadsters as viable race cars at USAC events such as the Indianapolis 500 – in fact he and Jack shared a drive in the 1951 event finishing in third place.

His other Indy 500 results were disappointing, but for 1955 he would be racing a new Kurtis Kraft chassis. However, during practise he crashed his car into a concrete wall and was killed. At the time of the crash, it was found that Ayulo was not wearing his seat belt and that he was carrying wrenches in his pockets.

At the end of his World Championship career, Manny Ayulo had been entered in five Grand Prix races finishing on the podium once. He had scored 2 World Championship points

Jean Behra
World Championship Years Active: 1952-1959
World Championship Teams: Gordini, Maserati, BRM, Ferrari

Born in Nice, France on the 16th February 1921, Jean Marie Behra raced motorcycles for Moto-Guzzi prior to changing to sports cars and Grand rix racing. Behra began driving cars competitively in 1952.

Behra was racing a Gordini in the Pan-American road race in 1952. He won the first stage of the five-day race from Mexico's southern border to the United States border at Ciudad Juárez near El Paso. He started 19th and finished with a time of 3 hours, 41 minutes, and 44 seconds. On the second day of competition Behra crashed his car on a curve approximately fifty miles from Puebla.

In 1954 Behra won the non-championship Grand Prix of Pau, in a six-cylinder Gordini. He finished 180 metres ahead of Maurice Trintignant after having to make many pit stops due to mechanical trouble.

He repeated his success at the Grand Prix de Pau for a second consecutive year, this time at the wheel of a Maserati. Alberto Ascari led until the 19th lap but dropped back after brake failure. A crowd of 50,000 watched as only eleven of sixteen starters finished the race.

Behra teamed up with Luigi Musso were for the 1,008 kilometre super-Cortemaggiori Grand Prix at Monza, Italy. Sharing a 3-litre Maserati, they won the race and established course and lap records for 6.3 kilometre track.

He earned the pole position for a Grand Prix at Rouen, France in July 1956. His Maserati was clocked at an average speed of nearly 97 miles per hour around the twisting track.

In 1957 Behra yet again won the Pau Grand Prix. However he was increasingly frustrated that the Pau event was never considered for a World Championship spot. Behra was injured while testing a car for the Mille Miglia, yet recovered to race a Maserati in the 24 hours of Le Mans.

For 1958, Behra drove mixture of Porches', Maserati's and BRM's, again combining single seat and sports car racing. Behra won the 6th Rouen Grand Prix, although this was yet another –non-championship race. Altogether he scored wins in 8 straight European races in 1958.

Behra finished 4th at Riverside International Raceway in a small Porsche RSK. He then made a quick exit and took an airplane to Europe, where he left for the Grand Prix of Morocco at Casablanca. He was in such a hurry that he left Riverside, California in an ambulance to catch his flight.

In 1959 he moved to Ferrari where he partnered with Tony Brooks. Behra won a 200-mile international race of Formula One cars at Aintree, in April 1959. However, when he retired in the French Grand Prix at Reims after a piston failure, Behra was involved in a strong discussion in a restaurant in which he punched team manager Romolo Tavoni. On hearing of this, Enzo Ferrari instantly dismissed him from the team.

Within weeks he crashed his Porsche RSK in rainy weather in the sports car race at AVUS, in Berlin, Germany.The sports car race featured entries of cars under 1,500 c.c. engine capacity.

After three laps Behra was third behind Wolfgang von Trips and Bonnier, who eventually finished one and two. The AVUS used a strip of the Autobahn 2.5 miles in length. The north and south bound lanes were fifty feet apart. At one end was a hairpin turn which drivers negotiated at around 30 mph. At the other end was a 30-foot high, steeply banked loop. Behra lost control in the pouring rain. His Porsche began to fishtail and the car kept going higher and higher up the slick, steep bank. Then the Porsche spun and went over the top of the banking, with its nose pointing toward the sky. It landed heavily on its side on top of the banking. Behra was thrown out and for a fleeting moment he could be seen against the background of the sky, with his arms outstretched as though attempting to fly. He impacted one of eight flagpoles arranged at the summit of the embankment which bore the flags of the competing nations.

Behra came down into trees and rolled into a street. A doctor arrived from a Red Cross ambulance and on examination shook his head. A hospital bulletin stated that Behra broke most of his ribs in addition to the skull fracture which killed him.

Behra was buried in Nice, France six days after the crash in which he died. In between there were three funeral services. 3,000 mourners in Nice lined the streets from wall to wall. The first funeral service was in Berlin, followed by another in Paris.

During his World Championship career, Jean Behra had been entered in 53 Grand Prix races earning nine podium finishes. He had scored 51 World Championship points

Eric Bernard
World Championship Years Active: 1989-1994
World Championship Teams: Larrousse, Ligier, Lotus

Eric Bernard was born on the 24th August 1964 in Martigues, near Marseille, France. Spurred on by the exploits of countryman Alain Prost, he started karting in 1976 and in the seven years that followed, won four French titles. He studied agriculture but only chose the course because it allowed him plenty of spare time to test karts.

In 1983 he attended racing school at Paul Ricard and was one of the finalists at the Volant Elf competition. He beat Jean Alesi and Bertrand Gachot to the prize, earning himself a fully sponsored drive in Formula Renault for 1984. He finished sixth in the series, but won the following year, and entered French Formula Three in 1986. In 1988 he entered Formula 3000 and was an impressive newcomer to the series.

In 1989, he was called up to the French Larrousse team for the French Grand Prix, replacing Yannick Dalmas. On his debut, he ran as high as 5th place, and was still in 7th when his Lamborghini V12 engine failed a few laps from the end. Bernard stood in again at the following British Grand Prix, before returning to Formula 3000.

He was rewarded with a full-season drive for Larrousse in 1990. He took his first point for 6th place at the Monaco Grand Prix, and his best result came at Silverstone in the British Grand Prix, where he took 4th place.

Bernard elected to stay on at Larrousse for the 1991 season, but the team were in trouble, losing their Lamborghini engines and a majority of their sponsors, and then having their 1990 points stripped by the FIA.

In spite of this Bernard took 6th place in the Mexican Grand Prix, yet slipped back down the field, failing to qualify for the first time in his career at the Portuguese Grand Prix. Worse was to come, however, when Bernard broke his leg in the first practice session for the Japanese Grand Prix.

Bernard fought back to fitness, and after a year's recovery his old sponsors Elf managed to get him into a test driver seat for the Ligier team. The two-year testing contract paid off and 1994 saw Bernard promoted to a race seat, alongside rookie Olivier Panis. Sadly for Bernard, Panis largely outpaced him, and the team's Renault V10 engine was counterweighted by the team using a "B"-spec version of the 1993 JS39 chassis. Bernard took third place in the high-attrition German Grand Prix, but by the European Grand Prix he was dropped in order to accommodate Johnny Herbert.

He was engaged by Herbert's previous team, Team Lotus, to fill the seat at the European GP, but it was to be his last F1 drive, with Mika Salo taking over later in the season.

For 1995, he was linked to a return to Larrousse, but the team folded before the season began after failing to agree terms to merge with the underfunded DAMS F1 project. Since then, Bernard has moved to sportscar racing.

At the end of his World Championship career, Eric Bernard had been entered in 47 Grand Prix races finishing on the podium once scoring 10 World Championship points

Tony Bettenhausen
World Championship Years Active: 1950-1960
World Championship Teams: Kurtis Kraft, Deidt, Kuzma, Epperly, Watson

Melvin Eugene Bettenhausen was born on the 12th September 1916 in Tinley Park, Illinois. At school he was nicknamed "Tunney" after heavyweight boxing champion Gene Tunney. "Tunney" later became "Tony" and the name stuck.

Bettenhausen was part of the midget car "Chicago Gang" with Emil Andres, Cowboy O'Rourke, Paul Russo, Jimmy Snyder, and Wally Zale. They toured tracks in the Midwest and East Coast of the United States, sometimes racing as often as six nights a week.

He drove in the AAA and USAC Championship Car series, racing in the 1941 and 1946-1961 seasons with 121 starts, including 14 in the Indianapolis 500. He finished in the top ten 74 times, with 21 victories.

He won the National Championship in 1951 after recording eight victories and two second place finishes in fourteen events. He announced his retirement from all racing but the Indianapolis 500 after the season.

He decided to return full-time for the 1954 season. He was involved in a midget car wreck in Chicago, suffering head injuries after striking a concrete wall. He was in critical condition for several days, suffering a concussion, a scalp wound and a hole near the eye that required a piece out of a thigh bone to fill it.

He prearranged to co-drive with "Chicago Gang" friend Paul Russo in the 1955 Indianapolis 500. They finished second. This would prove to be his best finish in the Indy 500.

In 1958 he became the only driver to win the national championship without a win. He was assured the title with a second place finish at Phoenix.

Tony miraculously survived a crash in 1959, tore up his car, and got another ride. His $30,000 race car hit the outside wall and the inside rail of the 2nd turn to slide 33 feet into the infield - upside-down.

On May 12, 1961, Tony was in high spirits after some fast laps he'd ran two days prior. He called his wife Valerie to make plans for the family to join him in Indy the next day. That afternoon, Tony's friend and fellow racer Paul Russo was complaining about the setup of his racer and Tony offered to test it out.

About 5000 spectators saw his car roar down the main straight, plunge into the outside wall of the track, and roll 325 feet along the barrier snapping metal poles and ripping fencing from its moorings. The car came to rest upside down outside the track in a grassy plot between the wall and Grandstand A, its tail consumed by flame.

He was killed instantly when the car hit the wall. USAC ruled the accident was caused by mechanical trouble. An inexpensive anchor bolt fell off the front radius rod support, permitting the front axle to twist and misalign the front wheels when the brakes were applied, which forced the car into the wall.

During his World Championship career, Tony Bettenhausen had competed in 11 Grand Prix finishing on the podium once scoring 11 World Championship points

Lucien Bianchi
World Championship Years Active: 1959-1968
World Championship Teams: ENB, UDT Laystall, Reg Parnell, Scuderia Centro Sud, Cooper

On the 10th November 1934 Luciano Bianchi was born in Milan, Italy. The son of an Alfa Romeo Grand Prix mechanic, Lucien was surrounded by cars and racing from a young age. The Bianchi family moved to Belgium when Lucien was 12 years old.

Lucien Bianchi's first race event was at the Alpine Rally in 1951. He won the 1957, 1958 and 1959 Tour de France before entering Formula One in 1959. He drove various cars under the banner of the Equipe National Belge (ENB) team, including a Cooper T51, a Lotus 18 and an Emeryson, yet only scored a single point with the team.

After a couple of races for the UDT Laystall team in 1961, he returned to ENB. In 1963 he competed in the Belgian Grand Prix in Reg Parnell's Lola Mk4 and was back in 1965 for Scuderia Centro Sud.

He finally secured a more regular drive in Formula One in 1968, with the Cooper-BRM team, although success was elusive despite a bright start. Bianchi managed his best Formula One performance, finishing third at the 1968 Monaco Grand Prix, in his first race for Cooper.

Bianchi also raced touring cars, sports cars and rally cars, being successful in all disciplines, his biggest victories coming in the 1968 Le Mans 24 Hours, behind the wheel of a Ford GT40 with Pedro Rodríguez. He was killed when his Alfa Romeo T33 spun into a telegraph pole during testing for Le Mans in 1969.

During his World Championship career, Lucien Bianchi had been entered in 19 Grand Prix finishing on the podium once. He had scored 6 World Championship points

Mark Blundell
World Championship Years Active: 1991-1995
World Championship Teams: Brabham, Ligier, Tyrell, McLaren

Mark Blundell was born in Barnet, London, on the 8th April 1966. At the age of 14, Blundell was racing motocross bikes across England. When it was legal for him to do so on his 17th birthday, he made the switch to four wheels in Britain's Formula Ford. In his first season he placed second in both British Junior Formula Ford Championships.

The following season proved that 1984 had been no fluke, as Mark took the Esso British and Champion of Snetterton FF1600 crowns. The next year, he upgraded his ride to the more powerful FF2000 category, and promptly won the BBC Grandstand series. He even returned to FF1600 for the European Championship racing, taking pole, and finishing fourth overall. With 1986 came another championship in FF2000, this time the European title.

At this point in his career, Blundell decided it was time to take his continuing success, and move on to international racing. He bypassed the traditional stepping stone of Formula 3 and joined TOMS-Toyota in Formula 3000. Despite having to cope with an underfunded and underpowered car, he showed incredible talent and strung together a series of promising results, including a number of race wins.

1987 meant a switch to the works Lola team in F3000, at that time one of the biggest teams in the series. In a closely contested season, Blundell managed a very respectable sixth place in the final standings.

The following year, he made a deal with the sports car team at Nissan, landing a factory seat. He also managed a test drive with the Williams Formula One team. By 1990, Blundell had abandoned F3000 to concentrate on sports cars. That same year, he earned pole position at the prestigious Le Mans 24 Hours race driving a Nissan R90CK. Not only was he a massive 6.040 seconds clear of 2nd place, but he became the youngest driver to ever achieve pole position at Le Mans.

The year 1991 marked the biggest step forward in Mark Blundell's racing career , his Formula One debut. His debut season saw a sixth place in

Belgium with the Brabham Yamaha team. He also maintained his testing deal with Williams. The increasing decline of the Brabham team saw the unfortunate Blundell cast onto the F1 sidelines the following season, but he was able to pick up a full-time testing role with McLaren that would stand him in good stead for the future. He was far from idle between tests, either, racing sportscars for the factory Peugeot outfit, and adding a race victory to his earlier pole position at the Le Mans 24hrs.

1993 saw the return of Mark Blundell to the pinnacle of motorsport. A drive with Ligier netted him his first two podium finishes in South Africa and Germany. He finished tenth in the final World Championship standings. It was a one-year deal with Ligier, however, and in 1994 he signed with Tyrrell.

It was not as successful a year as '93, and Blundell managed only one podium finish in the 1994 Spanish Grand Prix, which was the last F1 podium finish for Tyrrell. At the end of the season, owing to lack of sponsorship, Tyrrell released him.

This would prove to be a blessing in disguise, as the retirement of Nigel Mansell meant a return to McLaren for Blundell, this time, in a race seat. Teamed with future two-time world champion Mika Häkkinen, Blundell recorded five points finishes and once again took tenth in the final standings. 1995 also saw continued success in sports cars with a fourth place showing in Le Mans, but was Mark Blundell's final year in Formula One, as the signing of David Coulthard by McLaren meant that Mark would have to find a job somewhere else.

Out of Formula One, Blundell moved to the U.S. and joined the CART racing team PacWest Racing, with fellow former F1 driver Maurício Gugelmin of Brazil alongside. A huge crash in the early stages of the season in Rio meant Mark had to sit out for several races owing to injury. Despite this, Mark was third in the rookie standings with three top six finishes in the U.S. 500, Detroit Grand Prix, and Michigan International Speedway races.

1997 was a breakout year, and Blundell recorded race victories in Portland, Toronto, and Fontana en route to sixth in the championship.

That year he was also named British Driver of the Year by Autosport magazine.

A disappointing season in 1998 left a bewildered Blundell languishing further down the points standings than he would have liked, and injury early in 1999 - after a massive crash in testing left him with broken vertebrae and he again wound up outside the top 20.

Retained by PacWest for a fifth straight season, Mark Blundell again contested the CART Champcar series in 2000, partnered by Brazilian Mauricio Gugelmin. It was a tough year though and Mark only scored 18 points and slumped to 21st in the championship standings. His teammate Gugelmin in comparison scored 39 and was classified 17th.

In 2001 Mark Blundell and PacWest agreed to an amicable split. With the CART scene no longer holding competitive prospects, Blundell switched his attentions back to a European base. Racing wise though the Brit was not able to undertake a full season of racing due to the MB/PW agreement and MB, thus concentrated on his MG Le Mans program.

Despite not finishing the 24 Hours of Le Mans the MG Lola EX257 impressed on it's debut, qualifying one-two in the LMP675 class and before both cars retired - one after four and a half hours and the other just after the 12-hour mark - the MG had reached as high as third overall within two hours of the start of the race and also established the fastest wet weather lap, with a blistering third fastest time overall.

Since 2001, Blundell's racing involvement has steadily declined, with only the occasional event. He did test a Dale Coyne Champ Car to help prepare Darren Manning for a one-off in the first CART race in Britain at Rockingham, and raced in the British round of the World Rally Championship, "I enjoyed my first experience in a rally car although it was pretty hairy at times," he said, "I've now got total respect for the rally drivers."

2003 saw great success in sports cars. Along with Johnny Herbert and David Brabham, he finished second at the 24 Hours of Le Mans, completing a 1-2 sweep by Bentley. He also finished third at the 12 Hours of Sebring, finishing top among the Bentleys.

Off-track, Blundell joined ITV television in Britain as an analyst during the Formula One season. This position lasted until the end of the 2008 F1 season when ITV lost coverage to the BBC.

Blundell also spends time running a management company, 2MB Sports Management, who handle the contracts of such people as McLaren test driver Gary Paffett and British Formula Three champion and Indycar driver Mike Conway. The name refers to the fact that it was founded by Blundell and former team-mate Martin Brundle, who stepped down from the company in January 2009.

In 2012 Blundell joined the Anglo-American United Autosports team to spearhead the Pro/Am crew in the six-round Blancpain Endurance Series.

After 63 races, Blundell achieved 3 podiums, and scored a total of 32 championship points.

Felice Bonetto
World Championship Years Active: 1950-1953
World Championship Teams: Maserati, Scuderia Milano, Alfa Romeo

As an Italian racing driver, driving for Maserati, much was expected of Felice Bonetto, but he was unable to deliver. Born on the 9th June 1903 in Manerbio, near Brescia, Italy, he enjoyed a brief Formula One career, including a win in the non-Championship Portuguese Grand Prix in 1953.

Bonetto finished second in the Formula Two Monza Grand Prix in 1949, before making his Formula One debut at the Swiss Grand Prix the following year. He drove a works Alfa Romeo in 1951, finishing third in the Italian Grand Prix. A move to sports cars followed, but he returned to Formula One at the end of 1952 and was going well in the works Maserati in 1953.

At the 1953 Dutch Grand Prix, Bonetto was forced to hand his car over to team leader José Froilán González, who could score some important championship points. This netted Bonetto his second podium place and shared points.

Bonetto also had some success in sports car racing, he finished 2nd at the 1949 Mille Miglia and won the 1952 Targa Florio, until his fatal accident while driving a Lancia on the 1953 Carrera Panamericana This was a race that he was leading, when he left the road after jumping uneven pavement before colliding with a lamp-post.

Felice Bonetto is buried at the Italian section of Mexico City's Dolores Cemetery; he scored 17.5 points in 16 races finishing on the podium twice.

Johnny Boyd
World Championship Years Active: 1955-1960
World Championship Teams: Kurtis Kraft, Epperly

Johnny Boyd was born on 19th August, 1926 in Fresno, California. He was the Bay Cities Outdoor Midget Champion in 1951, and raced in the AAA and USAC Championship Car series from 1954 to 1966 with 56 starts, although never won a race.

Boyd qualified for the Indianapolis 500 for the first time in 1955 but finished 29th after being involved in an accident that killed driver Bill Vukovich. In a dozen starts, his best race was in 1958, when he led 18 laps and finished 3rd. In total, he finished in the Top 10 at the 500 five times.

Boyd retired as a driver after failing to qualify for the Indy 500 and Milwaukee race in 1967. He died of cancer at age 77 in his hometown of Fresno.

During his World Championship career, Jonny Boyd appeared in 6 races, finishing on the podium once, scoring four points.

Martin Brundle
World Championship Years Active: 1984-1996
World Championship Teams: Tyrell, Zakspeed, Williams, Brabham, Ligier, McLaren, Jordan

Probably one of the most famous 'Nearly Men', Martin John Brundle was born on the 1st June 1959 in King's Lynn, Norfolk. He began his racing career at the age of 12, competing in grass track racing, in the Norfolk village of Pott Row. In 1975, he moved to Hot Rod racing and received 'Star grade' status.

In 1979, he started racing single seaters with Formula Ford. He also forged a name for himself in saloon car racing, driving Tom Walkinshaw's BMW race cars, achieving second against a field of international drivers at Snetterton. He won the BMW championship in 1980 and partnered Sir Stirling Moss in the BP/Audi team of 1981, racing an Audi 80 in the British Saloon Car Championship.

In 1982, he moved up to Formula 3 achieving five poles and two wins in his debut season. He won the Grovewood Award as the most promising Commonwealth driver. He famously contested the British Formula Three Championship with Ayrton Senna in 1983, finishing a close second, and the two progressed to Formula One the next year.

His Formula One career began with Tyrrell in 1984. He put in a number of aggressive and fast drives, finishing fifth in his first race at Brazil and then second at Detroit. Then Tyrrell were disqualified from the world championship in 1984 because of a technical infringement involving lead in the water, wiping his achievements for that season from the record books.

For the next two seasons he remained with Tyrrell, but without a works engine supply the team struggled. In 1987 he switched to Zakspeed, but managed only two points, which would prove to be the only ones in the team's history.

Four years of F1 racing for underfunded teams led him to seek a new challenge, and so he competed in the 1988 World Sportscar Championship for Jaguar, winning the title with a record points haul. He also won the Daytona 24 Hours the same year and became the test driver for Williams, standing in for Nigel Mansell at the 1988 Belgian Grand Prix, after Mansell was struck down with chickenpox.

Brundle standing in for Nigel Mansell at the 1988 Belgian GP

In 1989 he returned to F1 full-time with the returning Brabham squad, but the former champions were unable to recapture their early 1980s success and Brundle opted to move back into the sports car arena for 1990. Victory at Le Mans came that year rejuvenated his career, but still a top-line race seat in Formula One eluded him.

As well as contesting races in sports prototypes, Brundle also contested the American IROC series in 1990, taking a victory at the temporary circuit at Burke Lakefront Airport. That was the only IROC victory for a British driver, and Brundle finished 3rd in the overall standings.

In 1991 he rejoined Brabham, but the squad had fallen even further down the grid and results were sparse. For 1992 he switched to Benetton.

It was a productive season, with a strong finish to the year. He came close to a win at Canada, where having overtaken Schumacher and closing on leader Gerhard Berger, the transmission failed.

He never outqualified team-mate Michael Schumacher, but made up places with excellent starts (sixth to third at Silverstone), outraced the German at Imola, Montreal, Magny-Cours and Silverstone, and scored a notable second place at Monza.

At Spa, Brundle went by when Schumacher went off the track. Schumacher noticed blisters on his team-mate's tyres on his return to the circuit and came in for slicks, a move that won him the race. Had Brundle not been distracted he would have pitted as planned at the end of that lap, with victory the most likely result.

To the shock of the F1 paddock, Brundle found himself dropped from Benetton for 1993, Italian Riccardo Patrese taking his place. He came very close to a seat with world champions Williams, but in the end Damon Hill got the drive instead.

Still in demand within F1, Brundle raced for Ligier in 1993. More points finishes and a fine third at Imola were achieved in a car without active suspension. Brundle was the most successful driver who did not have an active suspension system in his car and Ligier were the most successful team without active suspension.

For 1994 Brundle was in the frame for the vacant McLaren seat alongside Mika Häkkinen. McLaren were hopeful of re-signing Alain Prost, who had retired at the end of 1993 after winning his fourth championship title. Brundle eventually got the drive, beating out McLaren test driver Philippe Alliot. He was confirmed less than two weeks before the season-opening 1994 Brazilian Grand Prix.

Joining the team was a case of bad timing in many ways. McLaren were on a downturn and throughout 1994 were unable to win. The team's Peugeot engines were unreliable, as was to be expected from a debuting engine supplier. At Silverstone Brundle's engine appeared to explode just as the starting lights turned green. In reality the culprit was a clutch that cracked spilling its lubricants on top of the hot engine causing a spectacular fire. Nevertheless, when the car was reliable, Brundle put in strong performances that season, most notably at Monaco where he finished second to Schumacher.

Having had poor luck and with Mansell signed to McLaren for 1995, Brundle once more raced for Ligier that year, although not for the full season. To appease Mugen-Honda he had to share the second seat with Aguri Suzuki, a move denounced by many commentators and fans. He impressed however, a strong fourth at Magny-Cours and what would be his last F1 podium, at Spa, being the highlights.

In 1996 he teamed up with Rubens Barrichello at Jordan and enjoyed a good season, despite a slow start and a spectacular crash at Melbourne's inaugural GP, with regular points, fourth his best result. He finished fifth in the 1996 Japanese Grand Prix, which was his last Grand Prix in Formula One.

Brundle had hoped to stay in F1 beyond 1996, but could not find a seat. He was offered a seat at Sauber in 1997 following the dropping of Nicola Larini, but decided against it. Brundle did however return to Le Mans. Drives for Nissan, Toyota and Bentley impressed, but a second victory failed to materialise.

Having largely retired from motor racing, Brundle became a highly regarded commentator on British television network ITV, whom he joined when they began Formula One coverage in 1997, initially alongside Murray Walker, and from 2002 James Allen. Brundle joined the BBC's commentary team alongside Jonathan Legard when they won the rights to show F1 from 2009. Before the start of the 2011 season, the BBC announced that Brundle was being promoted to lead commentator and would be joined by fellow former F1 driver, David Coulthard. He signed for Sky Sports' coverage at the end of 2011 following the BBC's decision to relinquish their rights to show half of the following season's races live due to budgetary constraints.

For his television work Brundle has won the RTS Television Sports Award for best Sports Pundit in 1998, 1999, 2005 and 2006.

In 2008 he came out of racing retirement to drive in the Formula Palmer Audi Championship alongside his son Alex, who was a series regular. He scored three top-eight finishes from the three races in which he took part.

Brundle came out of retirement again to race for United Autosports in the 2011 Daytona 24 Hours, sharing a Ford-powered Riley with Zak Brown, Mark Patterson and former Ligier and Brabham teammate Blundell; the team finished fourth overall.

Brundle has made antoher return the Le Mans endurance race, this time partnering his son Alex in a Zytek-Nissan LMP2 car in the 2012 event. As this was his first appearance at the race for over a decade, he trained hard to get back into the right physical condition. The Brundle's drove well and finished 15th overall.

Martin Brundle achieved 9 podiums, and scored a total of 98 championship points. He holds the dubious distinction of having the longest Formula One career, which spanned 158 Grand Prix starts, without a race victory, a pole position or a fastest lap.

Ivan Capelli
World Championship Years Active: 1985-1993
World Championship Teams: Tyrell, AGS, March, Leyton House,
Ferrari, Jordan

Ivan Franco Capelli was born in Milan on 24th May, 1963.He began his career as a kart driver when he was 15 years old, and after four years he moved to the Italian Formula Three Championship, where he won the championship in 1983. After that he moved with the Coloni team to the European Formula Three Championship, and here he was the champion again in 1984.

In 1985 he graduated to the European Formula 3000 Championship with a Genoa Racing March-Cosworth and won one race. The same year he debuted in Formula 1, driving a Tyrrell at the European Grand Prix, and finished fourth in Australia. Despite this, he was not picked up for a full time F1 drive in 1986.

For 1986 he returned to the Formula 3000 Championship, still with Genoa Racing, and also raced a BMW in the European Touring Car Championship. He also raced a couple of times in F1 with the AGS team. Meanwhile, Cesare Garibaldi, the boss of Genoa Racing, was working with Robin Herd of March to create a new F1 team - with Capelli as a core component in their plans. By now, Capelli and Garibaldi had an almost father-son relationship.

For 1987 Capelli was F1 full-time with the March team, led by Garibaldi and running Herd's new chassis with a Cosworth V8 normally aspirated engine. Capelli also continued with BMW touring cars for the Schnitzer team, as the March budget was tight, so tight in fact that they raced at the Belgian Grand Prix with a detuned 3.3 litre sports car engine rather than the full 3.5l F1 unit. The Schnitzer team had works status with BMW, allowing him to be on the German company's payroll.

Capelli scored the F1 team's first point with 6th at the Monaco Grand Prix and March's return to F1 was generally seen as competent, professional and promising for the future. On to 1988, and Capelli had a new weapon at his disposal, a new March chassis designed by Adrian Newey, allied to the Judd V8 engine.

March had hoped to be the favoured development partner for this engine but found themselves sharing it with Williams and Ligier, both of whom had lost their engine deals. Capelli was also joined in the team by British F3 Champion, Brazilian Maurício Gugelmin. Together, they made a strong team, and March was the revelation of the year. At Spa-Francorchamps he scored his first podium with a third place behind the McLaren's of Ayrton Senna and Alain Prost and at Suzuka he made a piece of history by being the driver of the only naturally aspirated car to lead a Grand Prix in a season of turbo dominance.

However, the momentum was not maintained. March were in financial problems and sponsor, Leyton House, acquired a controlling interest in the team. Although Gugelmin finished 3rd in his home race at Jacarepaguá in 1989, this was done in the 1988 car. The definitive 1989 Leyton House March was a disappointment, and neither driver troubled the leading cars for the rest of the year. However, the team spirit remained intact despite the death of Garibaldi in a car crash.

1990 started off little better. Newey's new car had excellent aerodynamics but was intolerant of bumps. Things were so bad that on the notoriously bumpy Mexico City track neither driver could make the car work and both failed to qualify. But at Paul Ricard in France at the very next race, Capelli led Gugelmin in a Leyton House 1-2 deep into the race. Gugelmin retired and Capelli was overtaken close to the end by Prost, and finished second. Revisions to the car had made it more competitive, but in truth it was the billiard table-smooth track which allowed the result. Despite some promising showings at Silverstone and Hockenheim, the remainder of the year was unfulfilling.

In 1991, Leyton House was responsible not only for chassis development but also bankrolled the ambitious Ilmor V10 engine programme. With so many new ingredients, results were again thin on the ground although Capelli often qualified and raced well. When Leyton House's owner Akira Akagi was arrested in connection with the Fuji Bank fraud, the team was in a precarious state. Capelli had signed for Scuderia Ferrari for the '92 season, so he voluntarily stepped down, allowing pay driver Karl Wendlinger to finish the season and personally paid to attend the races he missed to offer support to the team and advice to his rookie substitute.

In 1992, Capelli became the first Italian to driver for Ferrari since Michele Alboreto in 1988. The Scuderia had gone through a tough time in 1991, but with a new car, the F92A, expectations were high. The new car was not competitive and before the season began Capelli was showing his disappointment. A driver who enjoyed the convivial atmosphere of a family-type team, he struggled to integrate with the bureaucratic structure of early 90s Ferrari. Losing motivation, the team in turn lost confidence in him and his teammate Jean Alesi gained the upper hand. Capelli was sacked before the season's end.

This experience seemingly broke his spirit, but those who had worked with him at March still had faith, notably Ian Phillips, then Jordan team manager. Taking a Jordan seat for 1993 alongside a young Rubens Barrichello, Capelli failed to rediscover the spark that not long ago had marked him as a champion of the future. After failing to qualify for the second race in Brazil, he left the team by mutual consent. Capelli was distraught and Jordan was disappointed too - they knew Capelli had the ability, but he just couldn't muster it up any longer. His F1 career was over.

Following F1, he raced a Nissan Primera with mixed results in German Supertouring for BMS Scuderia Italia and later took part in the Trofeo Maserati one-make series. He also became an F1 commentator on Italian TV station Rai 1 and remains a popular personality in the F1 paddock.

At the end of his Formula One carrier, Ivan Capelli had been entered in 98 Grand Prix, scoring 31 points and 3 podium finishes.

Duane Carter
World Championship Years Active: 1950-1960
World Championship Teams: Stevens, Deidt, Lesovsky, Kurtis Kraft, Kuzma

Duane Carter was born on the 5th May 1913 in Frenso, California, and started racing midgets at the dirt track in the west side of Fresno while attending University. In 1939, he was a consistent winner on the Nutley board track with future journalist Chris Economaki was his unofficial crew chief. He won the 1940 Detroit VFW Motor Speedway title and the 1942 championship at Sportsman Park in Cleveland. He moved up to the sprint cars, and won the 1950 Midwest division.

He made 47 starts in the AAA and USAC Championship Car series, between 1948and 1963, including the Indianapolis 500 races in each season he raced. He finished in the top ten 23 times, with his best finish in 2nd position in 1953 at Phoenix.

Carter initially retired from competition in 1956 to take the Competition Director position for USAC. He returned to competition in 1959 after Henry Banks took over the position.

In his last race, at the 1963 Indy 500, he drove the innovative John Crosthwaite designed Harvey Aluminium Special 'roller skate car' with the then pioneering low profile, wide racing tyres and a stock Chevrolet engine.

He was inducted in the National Midget Auto Racing Hall of Fame in 1989 and the National Sprint Car Hall of Fame in 1991. Carter passed away 2 days after his 80th birthday on 7th May 1993 in Indianapolis, Indiana.

He contested 8 World Championship races, finishing on the podium once, scoring 6.5 points.

Eugenio Castellotti
World Championship Years Active: 1955-1957
World Championship Teams: Lancia, Ferrari

Eugenio Castellotti was born in Lodi, Northern Italy on the 10th October 1930. His family were very wealthy, which enabled Castellotti buy a Ferrari 166S sports car at the age of 20, with which he began racing.

Eugenio Castellotti participated in 14 World Championship Grands Prix, debuting on 16 January 1955. However, that year would also be one of sadness. Lancia had signed Castellotti to drive a D50 Grand Prix car alongside Alberto Ascari, but Ascari died at Monza, driving Castellotti's car and wearing Castellotti's helmet. Understandably, Eugenio had been one of the coffin bearers on Alberto's funeral at the church of San Carlo al Corso in Milan.

Castellotti won the March 1956 12 Hours of Sebring at Sebring, Florida. He followed this triumph by winning the Mille Miglia race in Brescia and the Grand Prix for sports cars in Rouen, France. Castellotti's Ferrari achieved a total race time of 2 hours 10 minutes 31.1 seconds, winning the race.

On the 14th March 1957, Castellotti was driving a new Ferrari Grand Prix car in a test session at the Modena Autodrome. He crashed against a curve of the Autodrome and his body was hurled approximately 90 meters. The car turned over several times and finished up in the members stand. No one else was injured. Doctors said Castellotti died instantly from a fractured skull.

In fourteen World Championship races, he secured one pole position, achieved 3 podiums, and scored a total of 19.5 championship points.

Eddie Cheever
World Championship Years Active: 1978-1989
World Championship Teams: Theodore, Hesketh, Osella, Tyrrell, Ligier, Renault, Alfa Romeo, Haas Lola, Arrows

Edward "Eddie" McKay Cheever, Jr. was born on the 10th January 1958 in Phoenix, Arizona. He lived in Rome as a child and was introduced to motorsports at age eight when his father took him to a sports car race in Monza, Italy. He soon began racing go karts and won both Italian and European Karting championships at age 15. He worked his way up through the levels of European Formula racing, teaming with American Danny Sullivan in Formula Three and driving for Ron Dennis in Formula Two.

It took him a couple of DNQs in Teddy Yip's Theodore before he made his proper debut in a Hesketh 308E at Kyalami early 1978. An engine problem forced him to retire after just eight laps. Two seasons later, he became a regular driver for the Osella team, but finished only once in ten races. Switching teams repeatedly as he tried to climb his way up the grid, Cheever had five points-scoring finishes for the Tyrrell team in 1981, and three podiums for Ligier the following year, including a second place at the 1982 Detroit Grand Prix in Detroit.

The 1983 season proved to be Cheever's high point in Formula One. He signed with the Renault team alongside Frenchman Alain Prost, both of whom were among the year's Championship favorites. Cheever earned four more podiums and 22 Championship points, but the team's disappointment after losing both the Drivers' and Constructors' titles late in the season brought about the replacement of both Cheever and Prost.

In six more seasons, he never drove another truly competitive F1 car. His final podium finishes in Formula One came for Arrows in the 1988 Italian Grand Prix at Monza and at the 1989 United States Grand Prix at Phoenix; at one stage in Monza, he was almost declared the winner as Ferrari had an over sized fuel tank. The podium cost him a new pair of sunglasses for the chief mechanic. At Phoenix, he was involved in a race long battle with Riccardo Patrese for 2nd place, but then had to give way at the later stages of the race when his brakes started to fade.

53

In 1990 he moved to the US to drive for Chip Ganassi Racing in the CART series. He blamed this on the ever increasing search by Formula One designers for aerodynamic efficiency. "It was becoming more and more difficult for me to compete in Formula One because the cars were getting smaller and smaller," he was quoted in the Los Angeles Times some years later. "They were shrinking, and I wasn't."

In his first attempt at the Indianapolis 500, he finished eighth and was named the race's Rookie of the Year, as well as CART's Rookie of the Year. In 1992, he qualified second for the race and finished fourth. In total, he scored four podium finishes in the series, but never won. Driving for A.J. Foyt's team, Cheever came closest to victory at Nazareth in 1995; he was leading the race on the last lap when he ran out of fuel.

In 1996 the Indy Racing League began, and Cheever moved there from CART. Cheever ran for Team Menard for the three-race series, and at the 1996 Indianapolis 500, he set the fastest race lap to date at 236.103 mph. Cheever then set up his own team and in 1998 all the pieces came together for Cheever when he took the biggest win of his career to win the 82nd Indianapolis 500. He was the first owner/driver to win the race since A.J. Foyt in 1977.

Currently, Cheever is providing television commentary on ABC for the Indianapolis 500, a position he has held since 2008.

Cheever participated in 143 World Championship Formula One races and started 132, more than any other American. He scored 70 points and stood on the podium nine times.

Louis Chiron
World Championship Years Active: 1950-1958
World Championship Teams: Maserati, Ecurie Rosier, Lancia,
Scuderia Centro Sud

One of the few pre-World War II drivers to survive the dangerous racing conditions and the horrors of war to compete in the newly formed World Championship, Louis Alexandre Chiron was a Monegasque racing driver, born on the 3rd August 1899 in Monte Carlo.

As a teenager, Louis Chiron fell in love with cars and racing. He learned to drive at a young age and joined the Grand Prix circuit after World War I where he had been requisitioned from the artillery section to serve as a chauffeur.

Competing in France, in 1926 he won his first local race, taking the Grand Prix de Comminges at Saint-Gaudens near the city of Toulouse. From there, Chiron went on to drive a Bugatti and an Alfa Romeo P3 to important wins in the Marseille Grand Prix, the Circuit of Masaryk, and the Spanish Grand Prix. In addition, he teamed up with champion marathon driver Luigi Chinetti to win the 1933 Spa 24 Hours endurance race in Belgium.

Chiron made his one and only appearance at the Indianapolis 500 in 1929, finishing in 7th place in a Delage and won the 1931 Monaco Grand Prix, making him the only Monaco-born driver to have done so. He also took multiple victories in the French and Czechoslovakian Grand Prix between 1931 and the onset of war.

When racing resumed after the War, Chiron made a comeback and drove a Talbot-Lago to victory in two French Grand Prix races. In 1949, the first Monte Carlo Rally after World War II took place and a large celebration party was given in Monaco. In what is now regarded as one of the black moments of Chiron's life, at the party, in front of numerous race organizers, race drivers, and celebrities, Chiron denounced the female driver Hellé Nice by declaring that she had been an agent of the Gestapo during the war. His unsubstantiated allegation destroyed Nice's life and she would be shunned by all, dying in abject poverty.

By the time the new Formula One championship was organized for the 1950 racing season, age was beginning to catch up with him but he still won the 1954 Monte Carlo Rally paired with Swiss race driver Ciro Basadonna.

Chiron did manage a podium finish in his fifteen World Championship races; at Monaco in 1955 in front of a hometown crowd, a few weeks before his 56th birthday he became the oldest driver to compete in a Formula One race. To the applause of Prince Rainier and his many fans he guided his Lancia D50 to a sixth place finish in the 1955 Monaco Grand Prix.

Three years later, he set another record which remains unbroken, as being the oldest driver who has ever taken part in a Formula One Grand Prix. In his last F1 race, the 1958 Monaco Grand Prix, he was 58 years old, although failed to qualify for the event.

After a remarkable 35 years in racing, Chiron still remained active as an executive with the organisation running the Monaco Grand Prix, who in turn honoured him with a statue erected along the Grand Prix circuit. On the 22nd June 1979, Louis Chiron passed away in town where he was born and had been so active in organising the Grand Prix, he was only a few weeks away from celebrating his 80th birthday.

At the end of his Formula One carrier, Louis Chiron had been entered in 19 Grand Prix, scoring 4 points and a single podium finish.

Piers Courage
World Championship Years Active: 1967-1970
World Championship Teams: Lotus, BRM, Brabham, De Tomaso

The eldest son and heir to the famous Courage brewing empire, Piers Raymond Courage was born on the 27th May 1942 in Colchester, England. Educated at Eton College, he began his racing career in his own Lotus 7. Following a brief stint touring the European F3 racing circuit in 1964 with a Lotus 22, his strong performances and good results persuaded him to pursue a full season in 1965. Whilst driving an F3 Brabham for Charles Lucas, he met Frank Williams, at that time Lucas's other driver and sometime mechanic and a person whom Courage would form a strong friendship.

Further good results, including four high-profile wins, encouraged Colin Chapman to offer Courage a seat in a Lotus 41 for the 1966 F3 season. Although the Lotus was inferior to the Brabham deisng for that season, Courage still managed to outperform them on occasion, earning him a step up to the F2 category for the 1966 German Grand Prix, where he crashed out.

Signed by the BRM works Formula 1 team for 1967, alongside Chris Irwin, his career nearly ended in ignominious failure. Courage's still-wild driving style caused him to crash out more times than was professionally healthy, and his tendency to spin at crucial moments led to the team dropping him after the 1967 Monaco Grand Prix.

He completed the remainder of the season concentrating on his drive in John Coombs's F2 McLaren M4A, finishing 4th in the unclassified driver's championship. At the end of the season he purchased the car from Coombs.

More good results in the McLaren during the winter Tasman series, including a fine win at the last race, resulted in Tim Parnell offering a drive in his works-supported Reg Parnell Racing BRM team for 1968.

In addition to a good run in F1 in 1968 - including points-scoring finishes in France and Italy - Courage also drove for old friend Frank Williams's

F2 team. When Frank Williams Racing Cars decided to make the step up to F1 in 1969, Courage was the automatic choice as driver.

In Courage's hands, Williams's dark-blue liveried Brabham BT26 was more than a match for many of the works teams. He finished second in both the Monaco Grand Prix and the US Grand Prix, at Watkins Glen.

Perhaps his finest drive of the season though was during the 1969 Italian Grand Prix at the high-speed Monza circuit. Despite an older car, and a power deficit, he managed to stay with the leading pack for the majority of the race. Only fuel starvation caused his pace to slow near the end, and he finally finished in fifth. A second fifth place, in the British Grand Prix, saw Courage finish the season on 16 points in 8th place in the drivers' championship.

Following a business arrangement with Alessandro de Tomaso, Williams switched to a newly-designed De Tomaso chassis for the 1970 Formula One season. Unfortunately the De Tomaso proved to be overweight and unreliable, and only a third place in the non-championship International Trophy alleviated a poor string of results in the early season.

The Dutch Grand Prix seemed to be going slightly better, with Courage qualifying in 9th place around the Zandvoort circuit. Running in the middle of the field, the De Tomaso's front suspension or steering broke on the bump at Tunnel Oost, causing the car to suddenly go straight on instead of finishing the bend. It then rode up an embankment and disintegrated, the engine breaking loose from the monocoque, which then burst into flames.

To lighten the De Tomaso magnesium was used in its chassis and suspension. The magnesium burned so intensely that many nearby trees and bushes were set alight. During the impact one of the front wheels broke off the car and obviously hit Courage's head, tearing away his helmet. It may safely be assumed that this impact broke Courage's neck and that he died instantly as a result, rather than suffer in the inferno.

Piers Courage participated in 29 World Championship Formula One Grand Prix. He achieved 2 podiums, and scored a total of 20 championship points.

Art Cross
World Championship Years Active: 1952-1955
World Championship Teams: Kurtis Kraft

Art Cross was born on the 24th January 24, 1918 and began racing midget cars in 1938.

During the Second World War, he received a purple heart after being wounded in Belgium when the tank he was driving was bombed just days before the Battle of the Bulge in 1944. He returned to midget cars after the war, racing in one of Pappy Hough's "Little Iron Pigs."

He was the defending AAA National Midget champion when he made his first Indianapolis start in 1952, where he won the first Indy 500 Rookie of the Year award after a fifth place finish. Cross used the money to purchase a farm near LaPorte, Indiana.

He finished second in the 1953 Indianapolis 500 behind Bill Vukovich. Despite it being one of the hottest Indy 500s on record, Vukovich and Cross completed the entire race without relief. Driver after driver entered the pit area seeking a relief pilot due to the heat, which helped Cross climb through the field. "Every time I came up to pass somebody," Cross said, "I would look over and think 'That's not Sam Hanks; that's Duane Carter,' or 'That's not Jim Rathmann; that's Eddie Johnson."

Cross led in the 1954 and 1955 Indianapolis 500 and in a rare non-Indianapolis championship start, Cross competed in the August 1955 race at Milwaukee, which was extended that year from 200 miles to 250. He was leading at 200 miles and salvaged fourth place after a late race stop for fuel.

The Milwaukee race proved to be his final start. He never announced his retirement but just stopped going to races, instead spending time with his family. For several years thereafter, the highly regarded Cross was courted by car owners seeking his services, but he never relented, not even for the legendary Novi car.

He then turned his attention to running the farm in LaPorte, Indiana, later becoming involved in a heavy equipment business and in construction.

He was inducted in the National Midget Auto Racing Hall of Fame in 1992.

On Friday 15th April 2005, Art Cross passed away on the farm that he loved, at the age of 87. He had competed in four World Championship races, scoring 8 points and finishing on the podium just once.

Jimmy Davies
World Championship Years Active: 1950-1959
World Championship Teams: Kurtis Kraft, Pawl, Ewing

Born on the 18th August 1929 in Glendale, California. Jimmy Davies was the second man to win three USAC National Midget Championships. When Davies won the 100-mile (160 km) AAA Championship race at Del Mar, California in November 1949, he became the youngest driver to win a race in a major U.S. open wheel series aged 20 years, 2 months, 29 days. This record not broken until Marco Andretti won the IRL race at Sonoma, California in 2006.

He first competed in the Indianapolis 500 in 1950, driving an Ewing finishing in 17th position. He returned a year later but only improved by one position. After a year's break he returned to finish 10th and in 1955 he achieved his only podium position with a 3rd place finish. This was the last time Davies qualified for any World Championship event.

In 1960 he won the USAC Pacific Coast Midget title as well as the National Midget Championship. He repeated as National Midget champion in 1961 and 1962.

He won 46 feature events in the midgets in his career. He travelled to Australia in 1961 and 1962, where he competed against Bob Tattersall.

Davies won the 'Night Before The 500' midget race three times, in 1960 and 1961 at Kokomo Speedway, and next year at the Indianapolis Speedrome.

Davies' midget car was stolen but was recovered a year later when a driver was killed in it at Sacramento. Davies recognized the car in the newspaper photos of the wreck.

He died on June 11, 1966 aged 36 from injuries suffered in a midget crash at Santa Fe Speedway in Chicago and was inducted into the National Midget Auto Racing Hall of Fame in 1984.

Davies was entered into eight World Championship races, finishing on the podium once, scoring 4 points.

Andrea de Cesaris
World Championship Years Active: 1980-1994
World Championship Teams: Alfa Romeo, McLaren, Ligier, Minardi, Brabham, Rial, Scuderia Italia, Jordan, Tyrrell, Sauber

Andrea De Cesaris was born in Rome on the 31st May, 1959. A multiple karting champion, he graduated to Formula 3 in Britain, winning numerous events before his tendency to make careless mistakes cost him dearly, and he finished 2nd in the championship to Chico Serra.

A wheel banging incident with Nigel Mansell broke the Briton's neck, and did little to improve Andrea's wild reputation. It was from this incident that the term "de Crasheris" started to appear. From Formula 3, he graduated to Formula 2 with future McLaren boss Ron Dennis' Project 4 team.

In 1980, de Cesaris was then picked up by Alfa Romeo for the final events of the 1980 World Championship, replacing Vittorio Brambilla who had, in turn, replaced Patrick Depailler when he was killed testing at Hockenheim.

At just 21 years old, his first race in Canada ended after eight laps because of engine failure. In his second race, at Watkins Glen in the United States, he went off at the Ninety corner on the first lap at the start and crashed into some catch fencing at the Junction corner on lap two.

However, the pair of races was the start of a 14-year Formula One career, thanks in large part to family connections with the Marlboro cigarette brand. Having ready access to what, for many years, was Formula One's most lavish paymaster helped sustain the Italian's career through some depressing troughs.

His reputation within the sport was cemented in his early years. Driving for McLaren in 1981, the paddock rumour of the time was he was causing so much damage to his cars that his mechanics refused to repair them. In the 14 races he started, he crashed or spun off eight times, a single point at Imola was not enough to convince the resurgent McLaren team to keep him on. The one race he did not start, was the Dutch Grand

Prix, after he qualified 13th his car was withdrawn because the team was worried that he would crash the car again.

Marlboro money secured 'de Crasheris' a McLaren drive in 1981

In July 1981 de Cesaris was partnerned with Henri Pescarolo in the Lancia Sportscar team and finished second to the team mates Riccardo Patrese and Michele Alboreto in a 6-hour endurance race at Watkins Glen.

Moving back to Alfa Romeo in 1982, de Cesaris showed to be more capable than his latest result would have suggested. He became the youngest man ever at that point to take pole position, at the Long Beach Grand Prix. De Cesaris was also only the second Alfa Romeo driver to capture a pole since 1952. But his immaturity was also on display. Lapping the slower car of Raul Boesel, de Cesaris waved his fist wildly, only to miss a gear and let Niki Lauda get past.

From this point onwards, de Cesaris was nearly always seen by most in the paddock as prone to occasional brilliance but more often than not, erratic behaviour.

At the 1982 Monaco Grand Prix Didier Pironi retired on the final lap with electrical trouble on his Ferrari. De Cesaris was set to inherate the lead, but ran out of fuel at the same point, allowing Riccardo Patrese to win his first Formula 1 race in 71 starts.

At the start of the Austrian Grand Prix, de Cesaris, concentrating on trying to pass the car in front of him, veered across the entire width of the track and rammed his teammate Bruno Giacomelli into the wall, taking both out. His reputation began to improve in 1983, when his Alfa Romeo now used a turbo engine. He took two second places to improve on his career-best results - at Hockenheim in the 1983 German Grand Prix.

De Cesaris came close to winning at Spa-Francorchamps, after leading for much of the race before a botched pit stop delayed him and a blown engine put him out of the race.

De Cesaris moved to Ligier in 1984, where, despite the car's promising Renault turbo engine, he did not build on his earlier success. He scored only three points during the season.

The 1985 season was worse for de Cesaris. A strong fourth place at Monaco showed early promise but the season turned into a dismal one. At the Austrian Grand Prix at the Österreichring, de Cesaris crashed heavily after 13 laps. Still stiff and sore, he' was off-form in the next race in Holland. Team boss Guy Ligier lost patience and de Cesaris was fired.

Trying to rebuild his career, de Cesaris paid to drive for Italian minnows Minardi for ther 1986 season. In an overweight car with the underpowered Motori Moderni engine, Andrea did little to improve a fast growing reputation as a blocker when being lapped. Worse still, he was more often than not outpaced by his team mate, fellow Italian and F1 rookie Alessandro Nannini. For the first time in his career, de Cesaris went an entire season without scoring a point.

Sponsorship saw him move to Brabham-BMW, but it was with the Bernie Ecclestone-owned team that Andrea began to show his raw speed. At the 1987 Belgian Grand Prix, at Spa, Belgium, de Cesaris placed third behind Alain Prost and Stefan Johansson, his first points in nearly two years.

He wouldn't finish another race that season. He usually qualified well, but the super-powerful BMW turbo would often end its races by exploding in flames, making a consistent points haul impossible.

For 1988 Brabham pulled out of Formula One and de Cesaris was again looking for a new home. He found it at the new Rial team, run by volatile German Gunter Schmidt, the former boss of the ATS outfit. The car was extremely slimline, with de Cesaris looking awfully exposed. But, with Cosworth power and brave driving, Andrea often qualified well, and took an outstanding fourth place in the Detroit Grand Prix.

For 1989, de Cesaris moved to the Marlboro-sponsored Dallara squad. Early results were again promising. A Monaco expert, Andrea was on course for a podium position in Monte Carlo, before being taken out by triple world champion Nelson Piquet at the Lowes Hairpin.

Two races later it was Andrea's turn to play the villain. After an early delay he was being lapped by Dallara team-mate Alex Caffi when he ran his fellow Italian into the wall, robbing the team of another podium. He made amends at the next race in Canada, finishing third behind Williams drivers Thierry Boutsen and Riccardo Patrese in a rain-soaked race. It would be the last time de Cesaris stood on the Formula One podium.

Dallara's promise wasn't repeated in 1990. De Cesaris was involved in a number of hairy incidents during that season, including crashing out at the start of the first lap at Interlagos, and at Imola, he forced off Alessandro Nannini during practice at Curva Villeneuve and the Italian shunted his Benetton, and was lucky to escape unhurt. Reliability was also a problem, and he again failed to score a point all season, even failing to qualify for the German Grand Prix.

It seemed after a decade of erratic endeavour that the writing was finally on the wall for Andrea de Cesaris. Dumped for JJ Lehto at Dallara, he was signed by Eddie Jordan for his team's first season in Formula One. Always a talent spotter, Jordan had run de Cesaris in Formula 3, but was typically direct in his reason for signing the Italian: experience and Marlboro money.

The Jordan 191 was one of the most striking and attractive cars seen in Formula One. Its beauty was complemented by its mechanical simplicity and speed. Sadly at the season's first race in Phoenix de Cesaris selected the wrong gear in the short pre-qualifying session, buzzed the engine and was out.

That result was no indication of what was to come. De Cesaris was again strong at Monaco, forcing his way past the Benetton of Roberto Moreno and was running in the points when the Jordan's throttle cable snapped.

In the next race in Canada he delivered finishing a strong fourth. De Cesaris then rebuffed anyone who thought this was a fluke by repeating the result next time out in Mexico. The following race in France he finished sixth. Suspension failure in Great Britain led to a massive crash but the Italian bounced back to qualify seventh and finish fifth in Germany.

He did not score again after this midseason purple patch, but his day of days came during the 1991 Belgian Grand Prix at Spa-Franchorchamps. The Belgian circuit is widely recognised as the greatest test of driver skill in modern racing. It was a place de Cesaris has always excelled. Despite the pressure of being outqualified by debutant team-mate Michael Schumacher de Cesaris was on a mission all weekend.

While Schumacher's inexperience resulted in a burned out clutch on lap one, de Cesaris moved through the field to take second position. He was in second position when his car's Ford HB V8 blew. A communication problem between Ford and the Jordan team meant the oil tank in the car was too small to service a new type of piston ring which used more lubricant.

De Cesaris finished the season 9th in the standings was his best since 1983, and it was more than anybody expected of the package. His speed had never been in doubt, but de Cesaris was now driving with his head much more than his heart, and a restraint that had been missing during much of his first ten years in Formula One. A fast and friendly car helped, but Andrea's new-found maturity behind the wheel was now in no doubt.

Despite Eddie Jordan's desire to keep de Cesaris for the 1992 season, financial realities meant it wasn't possible. Jordan had built up significant debts in his debut season. He was able to secure sponsorship from Barclay Cigarettes, but the brand was in direct conflict with Andrea's Marlboro backing. Something had to give, and the Italian left the team where he'd driven his strongest season yet.

Ken Tyrrell was quick to snap up Andrea and his sponsorship and his faith was quickly repaid when de Cesaris took a fifth in the second race of the season in Mexico. The Ilmor V-10 powered Tyrrell 020 was a handy machine, and de Cesaris was in the points three more times during the season culminating in an impressive fourth place in the Japanese Grand Prix.

1993 was very different. The Ilmor engine had been replaced with free Yamaha V10s which changed the dynamics and reliability of the car. The 020 was by then very old and was replaced mid-season by the 021. This car, featuring active suspension, was not a success. For the third time in his career, de Cesaris failed to score a point and left Tyrrell at the end of the season.

In 1994, for the first time since 1980, de Cesaris started the season without a Formula One drive. But it was an event during the Brazilian Grand Prix that revived his career. Irishman Eddie Irvine was blamed for starting a massive accident which saw Jos Verstappen barrel roll over the top of Martin Brundle. On appeal, Irvine was banned for three races. At the Pacific Grand Prix, Aguri Suzuki drove Irvine's vacated Jordan. But for the next race, the San Marino Grand Prix, Eddie Jordan brought de Cesaris back to the team where he had earned his best results back three seasons earlier.

The return didn't start well when de Cesaris wrote off a chassis during testing. He crashed again during the tragic event at Imola due to poor fitness having not driven a race distance in six months.

But, ever the Monaco specialist, he bounced back in Monte Carlo. In a mature drive, de Cesaris stayed away from trouble and away from the barriers to take a superb fourth place.

Irvine returned for the next race but Sauber had noticed the Italian's form, and signed him to replace the injured Karl Wendlinger in the Mercedes-powered machines.

Andrea's first race for Sauber was his 200th Grand Prix in Canada. Although he retired after 24 laps, he was again in the points at the next event, the French Grand Prix at Magny-Cours. However the emergency changes to technical regulations made the Sauber a handful to drive.

The career of Andrea de Cesaris then ended much as it began, when he retired with throttle problems during his last race, the 1994 European Grand Prix. After this, Sauber kept his promise to return the car to Karl Wendlinger if he was fit enough. In the end he wasn't, but de Cesaris was unreachable on holiday, so JJ Lehto replaced him for the final two Grands Prix.

Since retiring from motor-racing, de Cesaris has become a successful currency broker in Monte Carlo. It has been reported that he spends six months of the year in this occupation, the other on windsurfing around the world.

In 2005 it was announced de Cesaris would race in the new Grand Prix Masters series for retired Formula One drivers. While some drivers had spent their retirement years accumulating kilos, de Cesaris was still in top physical condition and quickly proved he had lost none of his speed, setting fastest time in the first Grand Prix Masters test at the Silverstone South circuit in England. His best race was the inaugural event at Kyalami, where he finished fourth.

Andrea de Cesaris participated in 214 grands prix achieving 5 podiums, one pole position, and scored a total of 59 championship points. He remains the driver with the most GP starts to his name without a win. He also holds records for the most consecutive non-finishes, 18 across 1985 and 1986, as well as the most successive non-finishes in a single season, 12 in 1987. Likewise, no driver has had more than his 14 DNFs in a 16-race season.

Pedro de la Rosa
World Championship Years Active: 1999-2012
World Championship Teams: Arrows, Jaguar, McLaren, Sauber, HRT

Pedro Martínez de la Rosa was born on the 24th February 1971 in Cardedeu, Catalonia, Spain. Unlike most drivers, he started his career in radio-controlled cars, specialising in 1:8 off-road. He won the European radio controlled off-road championship twice in 1983 and 1984 and was runner up in the world championship in 1986. After that he started karting in a local Spanish championship in 1988 when he was 17. He then joined the Spanish Formula Fiat Uno Championship and became champion in 1989.

In 1990, de le Rosa raced in Spanish Formula Ford 1600 and became champion. He later drove in British Formula Ford 1600 and got two podiums out of six races. In 1991, de la Rosa achieved fourth place in the Spanish Formula Renault Championship with three podium finishes.

In 1992 he was both European and British Formula Renault champion. He slipped down the order in the next two years. In 1995, he was champion of the Japanese Formula Three series and third in the Macau Grand Prix. In 1996, he finished 8th in both the Formula Nippon and All Japan GT Championship. The next year he was champion in Formula Nippon. He was also the All Japan GT Champion with Michael Krumm.

In 1998, De la Rosa was a test driver for Jordan, before joining Arrows the following season for a full-time drive, scoring one world championship point by finishing sixth in his debut race, the Australian Grand Prix. He regularly out-paced his more experienced team mate Toranosuke Takagi.

In 2000 he remained at Arrows alongside Dutchman Jos Verstappen. He scored two points, finishing sixth in the German Grand Prix and the European Grand Prix. Verstappen commented mid-season that he and de la Rosa 'work well together and we have a good partnership'. De la Rosa raced for two years with Jaguar Racing alongside Eddie Irvine, scoring 3 points in 2001 and none in 2002. At the end of the 2002 season Jaguar paid off his contract which was set to expire at the conclusion of 2003.

He then became a test driver for McLaren but raced at the 2005 Bahrain Grand Prix when Juan Pablo Montoya injured his shoulder. He finished fifth and set the fastest lap in the race. He combined his testing duties with providing race commentary for Spanish broadcaster Telecinco.

On July 11, 2006 it was announced that de la Rosa would take over the second McLaren race seat with immediate effect following Juan Pablo Montoya's departure to NASCAR. It was initially unclear whether he would remain in the seat until the end of the season, but some successful results led to him being retained.

At the Hungarian Grand Prix of 2006 de la Rosa scored his first ever podium, coming 2nd behind Jenson Button, who scored his maiden Grand Prix victory.

After a long period of speculation as to who would be Fernando Alonso's team-mate in 2007, Lewis Hamilton secured the seat. De la Rosa would carry on as the team's test driver.

Before the Australian Grand Prix of 2008, Pedro de la Rosa was elected as the new chairman of the Grand Prix Drivers' Association after a unanimous vote. De la Rosa was the preferred candidate for GPDA directors Mark Webber and Fernando Alonso. He replaced the retired Ralf Schumacher in the role.

He remained at McLaren in 2009, and as of January 2010 was the fifth most experienced test driver in history, in terms of test days. He stated that he wished to step down from the role of GPDA chairman, following the completion of his deal to drive for Sauber in 2010, and was duly replaced in the role by Nick Heidfeld at the Australian Grand Prix.

In 2010 De la Rosa drove for the newly-resurrected Sauber team. His team-mate at Sauber was Japanese driver Kamui Kobayashi who impressed at Toyota during the last two races of the 2009 Formula One season.

De la Rosa finished seven of the thirteen races he started in the 2010 season, and picked up six points from a single points-scoring finish, a seventh place finish at the Hungarian Grand Prix. De la Rosa qualified in the top ten on two occasions, at Silverstone and in Hungary as both he and team-mate Kobayashi struggled with reliability problems for the majority of the season.

He was dropped from his race seat by Sauber in favour of Nick Heidfeld after the Italian Grand Prix. De la Rosa replaced Heidfeld as test driver for Pirelli, in anticipation for their return to Formula One for the 2011 season.

After Sergio Pérez's accident in Monaco, de la Rosa replaced him for Sauber at the Canadian Grand Prix, after Pérez decided after the first free practice session on Friday, to sit out the rest of the weekend. De la Rosa managed to stay out of trouble throughout the first part of the race, affected by heavy rain, running as high as ninth before a red flag suspended the race. He eventually finished 12th after having some contact soon after the restart which required a new wing.

On 21 November 2011, it was announced that de la Rosa had signed for HRT F1 on a two-year contract, however both he and team mate Narain Karthikeyan failed to qualify for the first race of the season in Australia. At the next race weekend in Malaysia, he was able to qualify and finish 22nd in the race after receiving a drive through penalty after the race was restarted, and he was later promoted to 21st place due to Karthikeyan's 20 second penalty for an incident with Sebastian Vettel.

De la Rosa qualified ahead of Karthikeyan once again in China, and finished 21st, one lap down from the race winner. In Bahrain, he finished 20th after qualifying 22nd, although after the race he admitted that the team still needed "to gain some speed per lap" to fight their rivals on a consistent basis. Following on from this, de la Rosa finished his home race for the first time since 1999 in 19th place, the last of all classified drivers. By the end of the season the HRT team were up for sale although with no buyer de la Rosa's future in Formula One was over.

At the end of his World Championship carrer, Pedro de la Rosa had been entered in 107 Grand Prix, standing on the podium once and scoring a total of 25 points.

World Championship Years Active: 1956 – 1957
World Championship Team: Ferrari

Alfonso Antonio Vicente Eduardo Angel Blas Francisco de Borja Cabeza de Vaca y Leighton, Marquis of Portago, best known as Alfonso de Portago, was born in London, England on October 11th 1928, the 13th count of Majorada and the 17th marquis of Portago. His father was a Spanish nobleman named António and his mother a former Irish nurse. His godfather was Spanish king Alfonso XIII. He was part of an ancient family line, thus inheriting his titles.

De Portago won a $500 bet at the age of 17 when he flew his plane beneath a bridge. He participated twice in the Grand National Steeplechase at Aintree as a gentleman jockey, although he found keeping his weight down to be a struggle

He also was a bobsleigh runner, recruiting several cousins in order to form Spain's first bobsleigh team for the 1956 Winter Olympic Games in Cortina d'Ampezzo . He had had only two or three practice runs in Switzerland before buying a pair of sleds. With de Portago steering, the two-man bob finished fourth to the surprise of the traditional teams, missing out on a medal by 0.16 seconds. De Portago also won a bronze medal in the two-man event at the 1957 FIBT World Championships in St. Moritz.

De Portago began racing sports cars and won six big races, including the Tour de France automobile race, the Grand Prix of Oporto, and the Nassau Governor's Cup. He once told a reporter, I like the feeling of fear. After a while a man becomes an addict and has to have it. In Nassau during the winter of 1956, Portago trailed the car ahead of him by inches while travelling at 150 mph. De Portago used his skill to avert careening into a crowd after the driver ahead of him touched his brakes and both cars went into a 600-foot skid.

Among sports car enthusiasts de Portago was known as a two-car man, because of the many burned-out brakes, clutches, transmissions, and wrecked cars for which he was responsible. He often needed several cars to finish a race.

He participated in five World Championship Formula One Grand Prix, during 1956. His best result was a second place at the British Grand Prix, a drive which was shared with Peter Collins. Having handed over his own mount to Collins, De Portago took over Castellotti's battered car to finish 10th. De Portago received half points for Collins' subsequent drive to second place.

In January 1957, he claimed fifth in the opening race in Argentina, and was already looking forward to the Monaco GP. He would never see the day.

In the Mille Miglia, he and his co-driver Edmund Nelson were killed in a crash about forty miles from Brescia, the starting and finishing point of the 1,000 mile race and were in third place at the time.

De Portago blew a tire on his Ferrari, causing the car to go into the crowd lining the highway. His Ferrari hurtled over a canal on the left side of the road, killing five spectators, then veered back across the canal, and caused the deaths of five other onlookers on the right side of the road. Two of the dead children were hit by a concrete highway milestone that was ripped from the ground by de Portago's car and thrown into the crowd.

Alfonso de Poertago had competed in five World Championship races, standing on the podium once, scoring a total of four points.

World Championship Years Active: 1971 – 1975
World Championship Teams: Penske

Mark Neary Donohue, Jr., nicknamed "Captain Nice", was an American racing driver known for his ability to set up his own race car as well as driving it to victories.

He was born in Haddon Township, New Jersey on the 18th March 1937 and grew up in Summit, New Jersey. He graduated from Brown University in 1959 with a bachelor's degree in mechanical engineering and began racing his 1957 Corvette, winning a Belknap County hillclimb, in that car. Eventually, through networking with various SCCA drivers, he was introduced to a well-known retired race driver and as-yet unsuccessful race team owner named Roger Penske.

Donohue met another experienced race driver named Walt Hansgen while running in SCCA events around the country. Hansgen quickly realized that Donohue had unusual talent as a driver, but more importantly, had an extensive working knowledge of vehicle mechanics and dynamics, due to his engineering background.

In 1965, Hansgen invited him to co-drive a Ferrari 275 at the 12 Hours of Sebring endurance race. This would be Donohue's big break into international sports-car racing. Hansgen and Donohue combined to finish 11th in that race. Also in 1965 Mark drove a GT350 to a SCCA B Class championship and a Lotus 20 to another championship in SCCA Formula C.

Thanks to his friendship with Hansgen, word quickly spread to the Ford Motor Company about the young driver. Ford immediately signed Donohue to drive one of the GT-40 Mk II race cars campaigned at the 1966 24 Hours of Le Mans. Donohue was partnered with Australian Paul Hawkins, but the pair only completed twelve laps and finished 51st.

Donohue was invited back to Le Mans by Ford the following year. Ford had developed a new GT, the Mark IV. Donohue co-drove in the #4 yellow car with sports car driver and race car builder Bruce McLaren for Shelby American Racing. The two drivers disagreed on many aspects of

74

racing and car setup, but as a team were able to muster a fourth-place finish in the endurance classic.

The year culminated with Roger Penske contacting Donohue regarding his possible interest in driving Penske's brand new Lola T70 spyder in the United States Road Racing Championship. Donohue dominated the 1967 United States Road Racing Championship. He raced in seven of the eight races that year, winning six (at Las Vegas, Riverside, Bridgehampton, Watkins Glen, and Mid-Ohio, while finishing third at the Laguna Seca round behind Lothar Motschenbacher and Mike Goth.

In 1968, Donohue and Penske returned to defend their USRRC championship. This time he was armed with the McLaren M6A Chevrolet. Donohue did not participate in the first race of the year at Circuit Hermanos Rodriguez in Mexico City. Yet, Donohue still dominated the series, even though he suffered three DNFs (did not finishes) during the season due to mechanical problems with the M6A.

Donohue began his Trans-Am series campaign in 1967, winning three of twelve races in a Roger Penske-owned Chevrolet Camaro. In 1967 and 1968, Trans-Am schedule included two of the most prized endurance races in the world, the 24 Hours of Daytona and the 12 Hours of Sebring. Donohue finished fourth at Daytona and won the Trans-Am class at the 12 Hours of Sebring.

1968 would be a banner year for Donohue in the Trans-Am series, as he successfully defended his 12 Hours of Sebring victory by partnering with Craig Fisher and driving his Penske Chevy Camaro to victory. Donohue went on to win 10 of 13 races, a Trans-Am series record which would stand until 1997, when Tommy Kendall won the first 11 races that year in his All-Sport liveried Mustang.

Donohue was considered a leading Trans-Am driver of the late 1960s and early 1970s. His Camaros and Javelins won three Trans-Am championships (his last in 1971) while driving Camaros and AMC Javelins, all for Roger Penske Racing.

In 1969, Penske and Donohue raced in their first Indianapolis 500, where Donohue finished seventh, winning the rookie of the year award.

Donohue raced at Indianapolis each year following, finishing second in 1970 and 25th in 1971.

Donohue won the 1972 Indianapolis 500, driving as always for Roger Penske. He finished the race in his McLaren setting a record speed of 162 mph, which would stand for twelve years. The victory was the first for Penske in the Indy 500.

Donohue raced in several NASCAR Grand American races, a NASCAR pony car division from 1968 until 1971. In 1973, driving an AMC Matador for Penske Racing in NASCAR's top division, the Winston Cup Series, Donohue won the season-opening event at Riverside.

That race was Penske's first NASCAR win in a long history of NASCAR participation and remains to this day, the last non-regular driver to win a NASCAR Winston Cup road race.

Between 1972 and 1973, Penske Racing, along with Donohue as the primary test and development driver, was commissioned by Porsche to assist with development of the 917/10. Donohue extensively tested the 917-10, offering up his substantial engineering knowledge to the Porsche engineers in order to design the best possible race car to compete in the Can-Am series. During testing of the 917-10 at Road Atlanta, Donohue had recommended larger brake ducts to the Porsche engineers, in order to provide more efficient cooling, and thus less fade and degradation as a race wears on.

The Porsche engineers obliged, but in doing so, caused the new brake ducts to interfere with the bodywork closure pins, which attach the bodywork to the car. Coming out of turn seven, the rear bodywork flew off the car at approximately 150 mph, causing the car to become extremely unstable. The car lifted off the ground and tumbled multiple times down the track.

The front of the car was completely torn away, leaving Donohue, still strapped to his safety seat, with his legs dangling outside the car. Amazingly, Donohue only suffered a broken leg. George Follmer, Donohue's old Trans-Am teammate, resumed testing the 917-10 while Donohue was recuperating.

Porsche, Penske, and Donohue quickly started the development of the 917-30, complete with a reworked aerodynamic body and a 5.4-liter turbocharged Flat-12 engine whose output could be adjusted between approximately 1100 and 1500 bhp by turning a boost knob located in the cockpit.

During the development of this motor, the Porsche engineers often asked Donohue if the motor finally had enough power. His tongue-in-cheek answer was "it will never have enough power until I can spin the wheels at the end of the straightaway in high gear."

The 917-30 won every race but one of the 1973 Can-Am Championship, however, the SCCA imposed fuel limitations for all Can-Am races due to the existing Arab Oil Embargo. Because of this, Porsche and McLaren withdrew from the series. It generally is considered one of the most powerful and most dominant racing machines ever created.

Mark announced that he would retire from racing after the 1973 Can-Am season. In addition, the horrific events at the 1973 Indianapolis 500 and the subsequent death of his friend, Swede Savage, pushed him to quit.

Donohue raced in the inaugural IROC series in 1973/74, racing identical, specially-prepped Porsche RSRs. Of the four-race series, Donohue won the first and third of three races at Riverside and the final race of the year at Daytona. The only person to beat Donohue was his former Penske Trans-Am teammate, George Follmer. In winning the first IROC championship, Donohue beat the best-of-the-best racing drivers of that era from all of the major championships, such as Denny Hulme, Richard Petty, A.J. Foyt, Emerson Fittipaldi, Bobby Allison, David Pearson, Peter Revson, Bobby Unser, and Gordon Johncock.

His retirement was short-lived, however, as he was lured back to full-time competitive driving by Roger Penske when Penske formed a Formula One team, Penske Cars Ltd, to compete in the final two events of the 1974 Formula One World Championship, and to continue competing in 1975 with the new Penske PC1.

Donohue previously had debuted in Formula One on September 19, 1971 with a Penske-sponsored McLaren at the Canadian Grand Prix at

Mosport Park, finishing on the podium in third place. After being lured out of retirement by his former boss, Penske, Donohue returned to Formula One, entering into the final two races of the 1974 Formula One season. Donohue finished in 12th place at the Canadian Grand Prix, but failed to finish at the United States Grand Prix.

A full-on assault of the 1975 Formula One season was planned. The 1975 season turned out to be a difficult one for Donohue and Penske. Donohue was able to muster 5th place finishes at the Swedish Grand Prix and the British Grand Prix, but the new Penske PC1 chassis proved problematic, as evidenced by three retirements in the first six races. At the Austrian Grand Prix, Donohue's career, along with Roger Penske's Formula One aspirations, would take a tragic turn.

Midway through the 1975 F1 season, Penske abandoned the troublesome PC1 and started using the March 751. Donohue recently had arrived in Austria for the Austrian Grand Prix at the Österreichring race track following the successful closed-course speed record attempt at Talladega Superspeedway in Alabama just a few days earlier.

During a practice session for the race, Donohue lost control of his March after a tire failed, sending him careening into the catch fencing at the fastest corner on the track, Vost-Hugel. A track marshal was killed by debris from the accident, but Donohue did not appear to be injured significantly.

It is said that Donohue's head struck either a catch fencing post or the bottom of the wood frame for an advertising billboard located along side of the racetrack. A headache resulted, however, and worsened. After going to the hospital of Graz the next day, Donohue lapsed into a coma from a cerebral haemorrhage and died.

In 2003, in commemoration of Penske Racing's 50th NASCAR win, Nextel Cup driver Ryan Newman drove a Dodge Intrepid painted to resemble Donohue's 1973 AMC. Roger Penske's new Penske Racing complex in Mooresville, North Carolina is decorated with various murals of Donohue and his racing cars, most notably the AMC stock car and the various Porsche prototypes that Donohue drove through his career.

Donohue's racing tradition is carried on by his son, David Donohue, a successful road racer in his own right. He currently races a Daytona Prototype Porsche Riley for Brumos Racing in the Grand-Am racing series, who won the 2009 Rolex 24 Hours at Daytona.

Mark Donohue was entered into 16 World Championship Grand Prix, standing on the podium once, scoring 8 points.

Donohue in the Penske run March-Ford

World Championship Years Active: 1982 - 1987
World Championship Teams: Benetton, Brabham, Toleman

Teodorico Fabi was born on the 9th March, 1955 in Milan, Italy. A downhill ski racer between 1970 and 1974, Fabi studied mechanical engineering at Institute of Technology in Milan and raced motorcycles in his spare time. He started car racing when he was 21 thanks to his younger brother Corrado and Teo rose rapidly through Formula Ford 1600, winning the 1977 Italian Championship, to race a private March in the European Formula 3 series in 1978.

He scored three wins and was fourth in European Championship. As a result of his success he was recruited to the March Formula 2 factory team in 1979 and he finished 10th in the European F2 series. The following year he finished third in the series and he was expected to go into F1 with RAM March in 1981. The drive eventually went to Derek Daly and so Fabi was forced to go to America where he raced in CanAm for Paul Newman.

He won four races but just missed the title. He was very fortunate to emerge unhurt from a crash which put his car into the trees at Elkhart Lake. In 1982 he was offered a Toleman Formula 1 drive alongside Derek Warwick. He also raced for the Lancia factory team in sportscars, winning the Nurburgring 1000 with Formula One drivers Riccardo Patrese and Michele Alboreto.

His Formula One results were not spectacular and in 1983 he was offered the chance to race for the Skoal Bandit Forsythe Racing team in Indycar, using the new March 83C.

He won four races and was named Rookie of the Year, just failing to win the CART title and playing an important role in establishing March in the United States of America. He had re-signed for Forsythe when he received an offer from Bernie Ecclestone to drive for the Brabham-BMW F1 team.

In the end he organized a deal to run in both CART and F1 with his brother Corrado standing in for him at Brabham. In the midseason, however, he decided to concentrate on F1 and left his CART drive to Kevin Cogan. Teo finished third at Detroit in his Brabham.

That autumn Teo's father died and for six months he retired from racing to run the family's talcum powder mine. He was then approached by the new Benetton team and asked to drive for them and he stayed with Benetton until the end of 1987, scoring three pole positions but only one third position.

Fabi at the season opening Brazilian Grand Prix, in 1987

In 1988 he went back to Indycar racing to be the driver of the Quaker State March-Porsche. The team was not a great success but in 1989 he won at Mid-Ohio. Fabi stayed with Porsche in 1990 until the company stopped its CART program and then he joined Tom Walkinshaw Racing's Jaguar World Sportscar team.

In 1991 he took the Jaguar XJR-14 to victory in the World Sportscar Championship. He was signed by Toyota Team TOM'S in 1992 but failed to win any races and when the World Sportscar Championship was cancelled at the end of the year Teo went back to CART, driving for the Hall/VDS team. He stayed with Hall in 1994 but then decided to retire from racing having reached the age of 40.

During his Formula One career, Teo Fabi competed in 71 Grand Prix, scoring two podiums and 23 points.

Rudi Fischer
World Championship Years Active: 1951–1952
World Championship Teams: Espadon

Rudolf "Rudi" Fischer was born on the 19th April 1912 in Stuttgart, Germany. Fischer participated in eight World Championship Grand Prix, achieving two podium finishes, and scored a total of 10 championship points. He also participated in numerous non-Championship Formula One and Formula Two races.

Fischer finished third in a race which marked the reopening of the AVUS, a German motor racing circuit. It had been closed for a 14 year period and was damaged during World War II.

A crowd of 350,000 watched Paul Greifzu of Suhl, Thuringia, win in a car he built himself. Fischer drove a Ferrari to third place. In the 1952 Swiss Grand Prix, in Bern, Fischer finished second to Piero Taruffi; both drivers were in Ferraris.

Fischer was the leader of the "Écurie Espadon" team, which was the entrant name for most of his racing career.

Écurie Espadon was composed of a group of Swiss amateur gentleman racers. The word "Écurie" was used at the beginning as most of the team's cars were French, generally Gordinis. Later the team's equipment changed to Ferraris and other Italian vehicles, thus the name of the team changed to use the equivalent Italian word "Scuderia".

At the end of 1952 he gave up on Formula One and returned to his restaurant business. Fischer passed away in Lucerne, Switzerland on the 30th December 1976 – he was aged 64.

Ron Flockhart
World Championship Years Active: 1954 – 1960
World Championship Teams: Maserati, BRM, Connaught, Cooper, Lotus

Born in Edinburgh, Scotland on the 16th June 1923, Ron Flockhart was an Army Captain, and held a Bachelor of Science degree – which provided his engineering training and background.

He started competing in unofficial events whilst serving in Italy and Egypt during the late 1940's and by 1951 was racing in a Joe Potts Formula 3 car.

Flockhart purchased the famous ERA R4D from Raymond Mays and in 1953 had a very successful season, beating one of the works BRMs at Goodwood. With podium finishes at Goodwood, Charterhall, Snetterton and Crystal Palace, as well as several hill climb successes, his rise to prominence had begun.

He was third in the 1956 Italian Grand Prix driving a Connaught which brought him to the attention of BRM for whom he drove for three intermittent and largely unproductive seasons until the end of 1959. He drove a works Lotus 18 to sixth place in the 1960 French Grand Prix and had his last Formula 1 outing in a works Cooper in the US Grand Prix at Riverside later that same year

Ron was a double Le Mans winner. In 1956, driving an ex-works Jaguar D-type for the small Scottish team Ecurie Ecosse, he won the Le Mans 24 hours endurance race with co-driver Ninian Sanderson. The following year he won again for the same team, this time with Ivor Bueb, setting a distance record of 2,732.8 miles.

Flockhart died in 1962, crashing his Mustang aircraft into the Dandenong Hills while preparing a second attempt to break the flying record from Australia to England.

He participated in 14 World Championship Formula One Grand Prix, achieving 1 podium, and scored a total of 5 championship points.

George Follmer
World Championship Years Active: 1973
World Championship Teams: Shadow

George Follmer was born in Phoenix, Arizona on 27th January, 1934, and to date is the only professional racing driver from the United States who has competed in Indy Cars, NASCAR, Formula 1, the World Endurance Championship, Can-Am, Trans-Am and IMSA.

His first racing season, 1960, saw California Sports Car Club "Rookie of the Year" honours, followed by "Driver of the Year" and the SCCA U.S. Road Racing Championship title in 1965.

George Follmer's impressive career start was followed by milestone after milestone, comprising a driving history equalled by few and surpassed by none. Driving racing machines now considered classics of the sport, some of Follmer's professional highlights follow.

Follmer won the 1965 USRRC Championship with an amazing performance driving an under-two-litre Lotus 23 powered by a Porsche 904 engine against such big-block performers as Jim Hall and Hap Sharpe in the classic Chaparral.

Co-driving with Peter Gregg in a Porsche 904. Follmer took a class victory in the tortuous 1966 Sebring 12 Hour endurance classic. As a teammate to Mark Donohue in 1967 and '68, George was the 1968 SCCA Trans-Am series runner-up to Donohue.

Between 1966 and 1971 he drove a number of cars in the USAC Championship including a Mecom Lola, a Sunoco Lola, a Lola-Ford 67B, an AVS Shadow and a McLaren M8B, Follmer set nine Can-Am track records, failing to finish only once. He had 25 career starts, including the 1969-1971 Indianapolis 500 races. He finished in the top ten 11 times, with his one victory in 1969 at Phoenix International Raceway - the only Stock Block powered car ever to win a race in United States Auto Club Indy Car history.

In 1972, George Follmer became the first and only driver ever to win both the Trans-Am and Can-Am championships, winning nine of fourteen races run. His first Can-Am race that year came about when Mark Donohue was injured and Roger Penske called upon Follmer as a temporary replacement. Never having seen the car or practiced in it. George drove the legendary Porsche 917 10K 'Turbo Panzer" to victory. His performance in the car convinced Penske to keep Follmer and ran a two-car team when Donohue recovered. George won five Can-Am races, with three pole positions and five fastest race lap records.

For 1973, Follmer moved to Formula One.   His first Formula 1 Grand Prix in 1973 resulted in a sixth place finish at the South African GP, garnering championship points; a significant accomplishment for any professional driver. In his second Grand Prix, George finished third in Spain behind Emerson Fittipaldi and Francois Cevert. Follmer ran the full season for the American UOP Shadow effort teamed with Jackie Oliver and the late Peter Revson.

Follmer's Shadow-Ford at Montjunc Park in 1973

1974 represented another phenomenal season for George, with eleven top-ten finishes in NASCAR stockers driving the Bud Moore RC Cola Ford Torino along with another second place in the Can-Am Championship.

Follmer was the SCCA Trans-Am Champion in 1976, driving a Porsche 934 Turbo to victory on five occasions. Racing a Porsche in selected IMSA events only throughout 1977, George finished second in the Watkins Glen 6-Hour endurance race teamed with Jackie Ickx, and second at Mid-Ohio with Al Holbert.

Competing again in IMSA, George took first place at Laguna Seca in a Porsche 935 in 1978, and placed third at Riverside teamed with Derek Bell. Also running Can-Am that year, Follmer won he San Jovite race.

An accident at Laguna Seca put him out of action for the reast of 1978 and 1979. In 1980 he ran only selected IMSA and Can-Am events, capping his "comeback" with one Trans-Am win at Charlotte and another most gratifying victory at Laguna Seca.

Though long-retired from professional motorsports competition, Follmer still competes in vintage races, often driving the very same cars in which he competed during his heyday.

He was inducted in the Motorsports Hall of Fame of America in 1999 in the sports car category.

At the end of his Grand Prix carrer, Georg Follmer had been entered in 13 races, scoring five points and finishing on the podium once.

Don Freeland
World Championship Years Active: 1953–1960
World Championship Teams: Phillips, Kurtis Kraft, Watson

Born in Los Angeles, California, on the 25th March 1925, Don Freeland served in the Navy as a mechanic during World War II. After the war, he began racing,starting with roadsters in Southern California before moving into AAA and USAC Championship Car series from 1952 to 1962, with 76 career starts. He finished in the top ten 41 times, with a best finish of second place occurring 3 times.

Freeland competed in the Indy 500 each year from 1953 to 1960. He appeared headed for a second place finish in 1955 before a transmission failure ended his day 22 laps prior to the end of the race. He came back with a best Indy finish of third the next year. He also finished in the top ten in 1954 and 1958.

He died aged 82 in San Diego after a period of declining health, Indianapolis Motor Speedway said Tuesday.

Don Freeland participated in 8 World Championship races.and finished on the podium once, scoring a total of 4 championship points.

Paul Frère
World Championship Years Active: 1952–1956
World Championship Teams: HWM, Gordini, Ferrari

Some times a person comes along whose gift and talent in one discipline can transcend into another. Paul Frere was once such individual. Born in Le Havre, France on the 30th Janauary 1917, he started racing motor cycles in Belgium in 1946. At the same time he was also a successful rower winning three Belgian championships. In 1946 and 1947 he won the national title in a coxless four. In 1946 he also won it with the coxed four.

In 1948 he switched to cars but did not really make his mark until 1952 when he made his F1 debut in Belgium with an Ecurie Belge HWM. Frere competed in 11 Grands Prix after winning the non-championship Grand Prix des Frontieres at Chimay in 1952. He was taken on by Ferrari and in 1956 finished second to Peter Collins in a Lancia-Ferrari at the Belgian Grand Prix.

His successes in sports car racing included class wins at Le Mans and on the Mille Miglia in 1953. He also won the Spa 1000 and was on the pdoium twice at Le Mans before his victory at the 1960 24 Hours of Le Mans, driving for Ferrari with fellow Belgian teammate Olivier Gendebien.

After retiring from active racing in 1960, he worked as an automotive journalist based in Europe. Frère, along with Piero Taruffi and Denis Jenkinson, was one of the first writers to treat motor racing as a skill that could be analyzed, explained, and taught. His 1963 book, Sports Car and Competition Driving is still a standard reference in the field.

Frère was also an expert on Porsche cars, in particular the Porsche 911, writing the definitive book on this series, The Porsche 911 Story.

Only weeks before his 90th birthday in January 2007, he was badly injured in an accident near the Nürburgring. Driving a VW Golf, Frere, suffered a shattered pelvis, several broken ribs and punctures to both lungs. He was hospitalised for 14 days in intensive care.

Paul Frère died on 23rd February 2008 in Saint-Paul-de-Vence (France). Turn 15 at the Circuit de Spa-Francorchamps, formerly the first part of the Stavelot corner, has been renamed in his honour.

During his World Championship carrer Frere competed in 11 races, scoring 11 points and finishing on the podium once.

Olivier Gendebien
World Championship Years Active: 1956 - 1961
World Championship Teams: Ferrari, Reg Parnell Racing, Emeryson

Hailed as one of the greatest sportscar races of all time, Olivier Gendebien was born on the 12th January 1924 in Brussels, Belgium. An heir to the industrial holdings of the Solvay family, Gendebien studied engineering at university.

When World War II erupted and the Nazis occupied Belgium, he joined the Belgian resistance movement. Fluent in the English language, he served as the liaison with the British agents being parachuted into Belgium. Later in the War he went to England, serving with the British army as part of a Belgian paratrooper unit. When the war ended Gendebien switched to the study of agriculture, spending several years working in forestry in the Belgian Congo where he met a rally driver named Charles Fraikin.

On his return to Belgium, Gendebien entered a Veritas sports car in the 1955 Grand Prix des Frontières at Chimay. However, following this race he switched his focus, and teamed up with Fraikin to compete in rally racing in a Jaguar. Together with Pierre Stasse, Gendebien won the sixth running of the Tulip Rally in Zandvoort in April 1954, this time using an Alfa Romeo 1900 TI.

The Gendebien and Fraiken partnership gained the nickname "the eternal bridesmaids", owing to their number of second-place finishes, but after two previous attempts they triumphed in the Liège-Rome-Liège Rally and the Coppa d'Oro delle Dolomiti in 1955, driving a Mercedes-Benz 300SL.

Gendebien's success in rally competitions brought him to the attention of Enzo Ferrari, who offered him a contract to drive a Ferrari in sports car events and selected Grands Prix. Much respected as a true gentleman by everyone who knew him, he remained a member of the Ferrari team until he retired from racing.

Enzo Ferrari summed him up as "a gentleman who never forgets that noblesse obliges and, when he is at the wheel, he translates this code of behaviour into an elegant and discerning forcefulness."

He made his World Championship début at the 1956 Argentine Grand Prix, with the Ferrari team, but it was during a stint driving for the British Racing Partnership's Yeoman Credit Racing team in 1960 that Gendebien scored his best finishes; he took second in the 1960 French Grand Prix and third in front of a home crowd at the 1960 Belgian Grand Prix.

The second of these was a somewhat bitter-sweet success, as Gendebien's team-mate at the time, Chris Bristow, was killed in an accident during the race. Gendebien himself walked away with slight injuries in October 1961 after his Lotus-Climax failed to negotiate a turn during practice for the 1961 United States Grand Prix at Watkins Glen, New York. The car flipped over and Gendebien's shoes were torn off by the impact.

It was in sports car racing, particularly the long distance and endurance events, where Gendebien excelled. Piloting a 2.5-liter Ferrari, Gendebien teamed up with Maurice Trintignant to place third in the 1956 24 Hours of Le Mans. They were seven laps behind the winners, privateer Ecurie Ecosse Jaguar drivers Ron Flockhart and Ninian Sanderson.

The 1958 Grand Prix of Buenos Aires was a 1,000 kilometer event in which Gendebien paired with Wolfgang von Trips. They finished second to a fellow Ferrari pairing Phil Hill and Peter Collins. The same year he partnered with Hill and won the prestigious 24 Hours of Le Mans. Their victory came in a 3-liter Ferrari and secured the World Sportscar Championship for the Ferrari factory. Hill became the first American to win the event and their Ferrari was the sole factory-sponsored car running at the end.

Ferrari drivers took the first three positions at the conclusion of the 1961 24 Hours of Le Mans and, as they were to be again the following year, Hill and Gendebien were first. The duo were a natural fit and together they won the Le Mans race three times in total, with Gendebien winning it a fourth time, partnered by fellow Belgian Paul Frère in 1960.

Gendebien's record number of Le Mans victories was not exceeded until 1981, when fellow-Belgian Jacky Ickx won for the fifth time.

Away from Circuit de la Sarthe, Gendebien also triumphed in the Targa Florio, the 12 Hours of Sebring, the 12 Hours of Reims and the 1000 km Nürburgring.

When asked about the key to winning as a race car driver, Gendebien responded: "It is a matter of taking the corners a little faster than one would want." In honour of Gendebien's three wins at the 12 Hours of Sebring, the turn onto the Ullman straight is named after him.

Married with three children, Gendebien's wife pressured him to get out of the dangerous sport of automobile racing where more than two dozen of his competitors had died at the wheel. At 38 years of age, in 1962 Olivier Gendebien retired following his fourth victory at Le Mans.

Independently wealthy, and an avid skier, tennis player, and equestrian rider, he devoted the rest of his life to running a variety of businesses. In 1998 King Albert II awarded him the Belgian Order of the Crown.

Olivier Gendebien died in 1998 at his home in Les Baux de Provence in southern France. He was entered into 15 races, finishing on the podium twice, socring a total of 18 points.

Bruno Giacomelli
World Championship Years Active: 1977–1990
World Championship Teams: McLaren, Alfa Romeo, Toleman, Life

Bruno Giacomelli born on the 10th September 1952 in Poncarale, Brescia. His early racing carrer was In Formula Three, where he led from start to finish the 1976 Monaco Grand Prix Formula Three support race. Giacomelli retired from the Formula Two Pau Grand Prix in May 1977, after his car made contact with one driven by Jacques Laffite. However he managed to score three F2 wins in 1977, at Vallelunga, Mugello and Donington Park and finished fifth in the championship.

Giacomelli dominated the following season, winning eight of the 12 races on his way to the title and beating runner up Marc Surer by 29 points.

Giacomelli made his first foray into F1 driving a handful of races for the McLaren team in 1977 and 1978, with a best finish of seventh in the 1978 British Grand Prix. After winning the European F2 title, he switched to Alfa Romeo for their return to building F1 cars in 1979.

Giacomelli in the McLaren-Ford at Monza, 1977

Alfa Romeo only entered their 177 and 179 cars in a handful of events that year, and Giacomelli could only achieve a best of 17th place in the 1979 French Grand Prix. However the following year the team looked more promising. Giacomelli earned a surprise 6th qualifying position for Alfa Romeo at Brands Hatch for the 1980 British Grand Prix.

Giacomelli posted a third place qualifying time for the 1980 Italian Grand Prix at Imola. Three of his six mechanics sustained injuries on the Friday before the race, when their helicopter crashed en route to the track. He took pole position for the 1980 United States Grand Prix at Watkins Glen, improving on his opening day time by 1.25 seconds. However despite these flashes of speed the car was severely unreliable - Giacomelli only managed to finish three of the season's fourteen races, although two of his finishes were fifth places at the season-opening 1980 Argentine Grand Prix and the 1980 German Grand Prix, thus netting him four points and placing him 16th in the drivers' championship.

In 1981 the car was somewhat more reliable, with Giacomelli being a classified finisher in eight of the season's 15 races - however he struggled to achieve good results until the end of the year, with a fourth and a third in the season-ending Canadian and Caesars Palace Grands Prix respectively - the latter was Giacomelli's only podium finish in F1, and he achieved his best ever championship finish by ending up 15th in the drivers' standings.

For 1982 Alfa Romeo introduced their new 182 chassis to replace the ageing 179; however the new chassis proved to be unreliable in the first half of the season. In the second half it was reliable enough to allow Giacomelli to finish all but two of the races, however the year only yielded one points finish for him with a fifth in Germany.Giacomelli was eliminated at the start of the 1982 Belgian Grand Prix at Zolder when his Alfa Romeo collided with the two ATS cars of Eliseo Salazar and Manfred Winkelhock.

Alfa Romeo recruited Mauro Baldi to partner Andrea de Cesaris for the 1983 Formula One season and Giacomelli joined Toleman. Giacomelli was outperformed by his team-mate Derek Warwick, though he did manage to pick up a final F1 point at the 1983 European Grand Prix at Brands Hatch.

He made 11 starts in CART in 1984 and 1985, 10 of which were for Patrick Racing. His best finish was a 5th place on the Meadowlands street course in 1985. He attempted but failed to qualify for the 1984 Indianapolis 500.

In 1990, Giacomelli returned to F1 with the Life outfit, taking over from Gary Brabham who left the team two races into the season. The car, saddled with an ineffectual and fragile W12 engine, struggled to get within 20 seconds of the pole time at many circuits and Giacomelli failed to even get out of pre-qualifying at any of the 12 Grands Prix he contested with the team.

At the Italian Grand Prix the team reverted to a more conventional Judd V8 engine, but the car had not been adapted for the new engine and the team were unable to properly fit the engine coverleading to them pulling out of the event without completing a single lap. When Giacomelli was able to drive the Judd-powered car in Spain he found himself 18 seconds off the pace despite the new engine. With money in short supply and few hopes of improving their desperately uncompetitive package the team folded before the final two races of the season, ending Giacomelli's F1 career.

In 82 Grand Prix entries, Bruno Giacomelli scored 14 World Championship points, one pole position and finished on the podium once.

Timo Glock
World Championship Years Active: 2004 – 2012
World Championship Teams: Jordan, Toyota, Virgin, Marussia

Born in Lindenfels, West Germany on the 18th March 1982, Timo Glock began his motorsport career in 1998 at the age of 15. He won several karting championships as well as the BMW ADAC Formula Junior Cup in 2000 and the Formula BMW ADAC Championship in 2001.

In his first German Formula Three Championship season in 2002, he finished third in the standings en route to rookie of the year honours. In 2003, he competed in the Formula Three Euroseries, winning three races and scoring three other podium finishes, which were enough to place him in fifth position in the Championship.

Glock was signed as Jordan Grand Prix's test driver for the 2004 Formula One season and made his Formula One debut at the Canadian Grand Prix replacing Giorgio Pantano for one race. He finished 11th, but inherited 7th following the disqualification of the Williams and Toyota cars and thus scored two points on his debut.

He finished the season with Jordan, taking over from Pantano for the last three races. Glock's sponsorship with Deutsche Post helped bring back the colours of DHL to Jordan.

For the following season Glock shifted his career to the United States, racing in the Champ Car World Series with Paul Gentilozzi's Rocketsports team. His best finish was second place at the Circuit Gilles Villeneuve at the Molson Indy Montreal in Canada, where he was defeated by Oriol Servia. In the closing laps of the race Glock twice retained the lead over Servia by missing the track's final chicane. As the rules require drivers who gain or retain a position by driving off the racing surface to give way, Glock was asked to move over by Champ Car officials, and let Servia take the lead. Glock obliged midway through the final lap, giving him enough time to try and take the lead back, but to no avail. Glock finished 8th in the final season points standings and won the Champ Car World Series' Rookie of the Year award.

In 2006, Glock raced in Europe in the GP2 Series, the recognised feeder series for Formula One. He started with the midfield BCN Competicion team, gaining average results. In mid-season, however, he moved to the front-running iSport team and after a string of improved results finished fourth in the drivers' standings. In 2006 he tested an F1 car again for BMW Sauber, which led to him being signed in December as the team's second test driver for 2007.

Glock was also re-signed for 2007 by iSport and won one feature race and four sprint races on his way to the championship. Following the serious crash of regular Formula One BMW driver Robert Kubica in Canada, it was speculated that Glock might take over the drive. However, the team instead chose its lead test driver Sebastian Vettel. Vettel's drive as a fill-in helped him get a full-time racing seat with the Toro Rosso team later in the season, starting at the Hungarian Grand Prix, and Glock was then promoted to the main test and reserve driver for BMW.

After winning the GP2 Series in 2007, Glock was connected to several F1 teams. He signed a contract with Toyota F1, though still under a test driver contract with BMW, which led to the dispute being brought before the Contract Recognition Board. In November, the CRB ruled that Glock was free to race for Toyota in 2008 and shortly afterwards Glock signed a three-year contract to replace Ralf Schumacher at Toyota.

He scored his first points of 2008 in the Canadian Grand Prix, finishing 4th ahead of Felipe Massa's Ferrari. Glock qualified a career-best fifth at the Hungarian Grand Prix, and finished the race in second place ahead of reigning world champion Kimi Räikkönen. At the Singapore Grand Prix, Glock finished 4th, one of his best of the season.

In the final race of the 2008 season, the Brazilian Grand Prix, Glock was seventh with a few laps to go and opted to remain on the track with dry-weather tyres, while most of the other drivers opted for wet tyres because to rain falling during the final laps of the race. Starting the final lap, Glock was fourth, but he was passed by Toro Rosso's Sebastian Vettel and McLaren's Lewis Hamilton in the final corners. Hamilton's pass on Glock was enough for him to win the 2008 Drivers' Championship.

Glock finished the race in sixth and the championship in tenth position, with 25 points, behind teammate Jarno Trulli.

2009 started well enough for Glock. After being in the top 10 in all 3 practice sessions in Australia, he qualified 6th on the grid. However, the rear wing of both Toyota's was deemed to be too flexible and thus illegal. This meant his time was cleared and he started 19th. During the race, he worked his way through the pack, pulling off forceful manoeuvres, including one on Fernando Alonso and one on Sébastien Buemi to finish in 5th place. However, after the race, Lewis Hamilton was disqualified and stripped of his 4th place finish, and Glock was promoted to 4th. A week later in Malaysia, he qualified 5th, but started 3rd after penalties to both Sebastian Vettel and Rubens Barrichello. At the start of the race, Glock slipped to 8th, but an inspired tyre choice as the rain started, coupled with precise driving, saw Glock finish in 3rd when the race was ended early on lap 32.

Consecutive seventh places for Glock in the rain in China, and in the dry in Bahrain had given him a total of 12 points for the season. Glock earned his second podium of the season when he finished 2nd behind Lewis Hamilton at the Singapore Grand Prix after qualifying in 6th. The race began well when Glock passed Alonso and was given a place by Mark Webber who was forced to let Alonso overtake. Late in the race Glock seemed set for 3rd place until Nico Rosberg crossed the white line exiting the pits, earning him a drive through penalty and allowing Glock to easily take 2nd place.

In qualifying for the 2009 Japanese Grand Prix, Glock crashed heavily at the last corner and was airlifted to hospital with a leg injury. As he was not fit to race, Jarno Trulli was the only driver representing Toyota.

On 11 October 2009, Toyota confirmed that its test driver Kamui Kobayashi would make his race debut in the Brazilian Grand Prix, as Glock had suffered further complications from his accident, resulting in a cracked vertebra and he would not be guaranteed to be fit in time to race in Brazil and Abu Dhabi. Toyota pulled out of F1 at the end of 2009, leaving an uncertain future for Glock.

Glock's future for a time appeared uncertain, but on 17 November new team Manor Grand Prix announced that he had signed for them and would be their lead driver for the 2010 and 2011 seasons. Manor became Virgin Racing in November 2009 and with that Glock's former GP2 rival Lucas di Grassi would become his team mate. Glock started the 2010 season with three successive retirements in Bahrain, Australia and Malaysia. In addition, he failed to start the Chinese Grand Prix due to engine failure; This was despite good qualifying performances which saw him out-qualify all of the new teams' drivers in Bahrain and regularly start higher than his team mate Di Grassi. The Spanish Grand Prix was where he recorded his first finish for the team, and his first finish of the season with 18th place. Glock's best result of the season saw him finish in 14th in Japan, the team's best result of the year.

On 24 July 2011, it was announced that Glock had signed a 3-year extension to his current contract, committing him to Virgin until 2014.

The Virgin team was renamed as Marussia F1 for the 2012 season and he would partner his third teammate in his three years at the team, French rookie Charles Pic. Marussia were forced to pull out of pre-season testing after failing a crash test for rear impact but eventually they passed allowing Glock to compete in the opening race.

Glock started the 2012 season strongly by finishing 14th in Australia which equaled his highest ever finish with the Virgin/Marussia team, before he achieved 14th again in Monaco, and retired from the Canadian Grand Prix race with a brake malfunction. It was reported at the Hungarian Grand Prix that a feud was brewing between Glock and his teammate after Pic blocked him during qualifying. Glock finished the race 21st after battling with Michael Schumacher and Pedro de la Rosa.

At Singapore, he produced his best result for Marussia, finishing in 12th place after a faultless performance. This crucially pushed Marussia into 10th place in the Constructors' Championship, due to a better non-points finishing record. He encountered Schumacher again in Abu Dhabi and let him pass to overtake Heikki Kovalainen who was in the crucial 12th place needed to demote Marussia to 11th in the Constructors' Championship. In São Paulo, he was running strongly and ahead of the

Caterhams until he was hit by Jean-Éric Vergne. He claimed this 'destroyed his race' with Petrov ultimately passing Charles Pic to take 10th spot for Caterham in the championship.

For the 2013 season he was due to remain with Marussia, however on 21 January 2013 it was confirmed that Timo had left Marussia by mutual consent. He then signed to race for BMW in the DTM Championship.

During his World Championship carrer, Timo Glock competed in 95 Grand Prix, scoring 51 points and finishing on the podium three times.

Paul Goldsmith
World Championship Years Active: 1958-1960
World Championship Teams: Epperly, Kurtis Kraft

Paul Goldsmith was born on the 2nd October, 1927 in Parkersburg, West Virginia and was a famous A.M.A. Grand National Championship motorcycle racer during the late 1940s through the mid-1950s.

His first victory came in 1952 aboard a Harley Davidson at the Milwaukee Mile. His most famous victory was at the 1953 Daytona 200. Later in 1953, he won a 100-mile event at the grueling Langhorne cinder track. He was awarded the Most Popular Rider of the Year Award for his efforts.

In 1954, Goldsmith had one victory at Charity Newsies at Columbus, Ohio, and four podium finishes. He finished second in the first year of the Grand National Series behind his former pupil Joe Leonard. In 1955 he won his final AMA event at Schererville, Indiana, but was frequently running stock cars.

He was the winner of the final race at the famous Daytona Beach Road Course in 1958. He was also the only driver to win the Daytona Beach Road course both in a stock car and on a motorcycle. Goldsmith competed in 8 races in the USAC Championship Car series, between 1958 and 1963 with 6 of those starts in the Indianapolis 500.

He finished in the top five twice at Indy, following up a 5th place finish in 1959 with a 3rd in 1960. His placing in the 1960 event would be his only World Championship podium place. Goldsmith was the 1961 USAC Stock Car champion, with 7 poles, 10 wins, 16 top-five finishes in 19 races. Goldsmith won his second consecutive USAC championship in 1962 with 6 poles, 8 wins, and 15 top-five finishes in 20 races.

Later in life Goldsmith became a pilot. Flying a Cessna 421, he transported engines and parts to and from races.

During his World Championship carrer Paul Goldsmith competed in three Grand Prix, finishing on the podium once, scoring a total of six points.

101

Masten Gregory
World Championship Years Active: 1957 – 1965
World Championship Teams: Maserati, Cooper, Behra-Porsche, Lotus, Lola, BRM

Known as the "Kansas City Flash", Masten Gregory was born in Kansas City, Missouri on the 29th February, 1932. The youngest of three children and heir to an insurance company fortune, Gregory was well known for his youngish looks and thick eyeglasses, one of the rare drivers to wear eyeglasses during that time, a practice still very uncommon even today.

His father died when he was three years old, and Gregory used his inheritance to buy a Mercury-powered Allard, which he drove in his first race, the 50-mile SCCA race in Caddo Mills, Texas in November 1952. He retired from that race due to head gasket failure, but installed a new engine in his car to race at Sebring in 1953, where he again retired, this time due to a rear suspension failure.

Gregory's first win came in just his third race, in Stillwater, Oklahoma. Changing to a Jaguar, Gregory won several races in America, including the Guardsmans Trophy in Golden Gate Park, San Francisco and a race at Offutt Air Force Base in Omaha, Nebraska – a race that was run in front of 50,000 spectators, supposedly was the highest attendance for an SCCA event at that time. After being black-flagged in a race at Chanute Air Force Base, Masten displayed his characteristic sense of humor by showing up at his next race with black-flags painted on his car, which were used as a background for his car number 58.

At the end of 1953, Gregory was invited to his first international sports car race - the 1000 km Buenos Aires in Argentina, which he finished in 14th due to water pump problems.

Throughout 1954 and 1955, Gregory competed in European races, including the Tourist Trophy at Dundrod and the 24 Hours of Le Mans. Moving back to America in 1956, Gregory entered several SCCA races, often winning. In 1957, he had another attempt at the Argentine 1000 km race, this time winning.

On the back of this performance, Gregory was offered a drive with Mimo Dei's Scuderia Centro Sud, a privateer Formula One team using the Maserati 250F. His first race was the 1957 Monaco Grand Prix, where he scored an impressive 3rd place finish, the first podium for an American in a World Championship Grand Prix. He followed this with a string of good results, coming 8th in the German Grand Prix and 4th in both the Pescara and Italian Grands Prix. Despite only competing in half of the races, Gregory ended the 1957 season in 6th place in the championship.

Gregory only competed in four Grands Prix in the 1958 season, due to injuries sustained through one of his trademark bailouts when his car was set to crash, this time in a sports car race at Silverstone in England. Afterwards Masten stated that he lost control of his car when he got into the grass going into a corner as an evasive maneuver when a "little Porsche" moved over unexpectedly in front of him. When asked why he jumped out of the car Masten replied, "You should have seen what I was going to hit! A huge earth embankment!"

He did manage a 4th place at the Italian Grand Prix, and a 6th in the last race of the year, this Moroccan Grand Prix. Moving to Cooper-Climax for the 1959 season alongside Jack Brabham and Bruce McLaren, he scored two podium finishes - a 3rd place at the Dutch Grand Prix, and a career-best 2nd at the Portuguese Grand Prix. However, he missed the final two races of the season, again due to injuries sustained jumping from a car moments before it crashed.

He finished 8th in the Championship, and with teammate Brabham winning the World Championship, Cooper won their first Constructor's Championship. Gregory scored a pole position and set a course record at the non-Championship race at Aintree, but his contract with Cooper was not renewed for the following year.

Gregory continued in Formula One until 1965, but mainly with uncompetitive independent teams. He was unable to reproduce the results he obtained early in his career, his best being a 6th at the 1962 United States Grand Prix at Watkins Glen with the UDT Laystall team, in a Lotus 24. Running 4th, just behind eventual winner Dan Gurney at the

French Grand Prix, Gregory retired with ignition problems, losing possibly his best chance at a maiden Grand Prix victory.

After his release from Cooper, Gregory also went back to competing in sports car races, setting the overall fastest lap at the 1960 24 Hours of Le Mans. He won the 1961 1000 km Nürburgring, driving alongside Lloyd "Lucky" Casner in a Maserati Tipo 61 for the America Camoradi Racing Team. In the same year, Gregory finished 5th in the 24 Hours of Le Mans in a Porsche RS61 Spyder. 1962 saw Gregory win the Canadian Grand Prix sports car race at Mosport Park in a Lotus 19-Climax.

In 1964, Gregory again competed in the 24 Hours of Le Mans, this time in a Ford GT40. He retired from the race in the 5th hour due to gearbox difficulties. The following year, Gregory teamed up with Austrian Jochen Rindt, and the pair won the race in a North American Racing Team Ferrari 250 LM. It was the first time that an American entry had ever won the prestigious race. This was easily the biggest win of Masten's career. It also happened to be a big win for Goodyear since this was the first time a car fitted with Goodyear tires finished first overall in an international race. Interesting to note, to this date the 1965 win was the last time a Ferrari has won Le Mans outright. This was also the year in which Gregory raced in the Indianapolis 500, starting from the back of the grid and working his way up to 5th before being forced to retire due to an engine problem.

Gregory then began to wind down his motor racing career, continuing to compete in international sports car races with some good results including a second-place finish at the 1966 1000 km race at Monza alongside John Whitmore.

Following his good friend Jo Bonnier's death at the 1972 Le Mans race, Gregory stopped racing, and retired to Amsterdam, where he worked as a diamond merchant before operating a glassware business.

On November 8, 1985, Gregory died in his sleep of a heart attack at his winter home in Porto Ercole, Italy. During his World Championship carrer, Masten Gregory was entered into 46 Grand Prix, finishing on the podium three times, scoring 21 points.

Romain Grosjean
World Championship Years Active: 2009 – to date
World Championship Teams: Renault, Lotus

Romain Grosjean born was born on the 17th April 1986 in Geneva, Switzerland. He won all ten rounds of the 2003 Swiss Formula Renault 1.6 championship and moved to the French Formula Renault championship for 2004.

He was seventh in that first season with one win and champion in 2005 with ten victories. Grosjean also appeared in the Formula Renault Eurocup and finished on the podium twice in Valencia.

With his results and potential in the Formula Renault series, Romain joined the Renault Driver Development programme for the continuation of his career.

Grosjean made his F3 debut at the demanding Macau Guia Circuit, standing in for Loïc Duval at Signature-Plus. He qualified 19th and raced to ninth, beating team-mates Fabio Carbone and Guillaume Moreau.

He did a full season in the Formula Three Euroseries in 2006 but had a tough year, taking only one podium finish and ending the year 13th. But in a one-off appearance in the British Formula Three Championship he started on pole position for both races at Pau, won both and set fastest lap in each.

He stayed in the F3 Euroseries for 2007 but stepped up to ASM Formule 3, for which Jamie Green, Lewis Hamilton, and Paul di Resta won the previous three titles. Sébastien Buemi led the championship in the early stages but Grosjean moved ahead with a victory in the ninth race of the season at Mugello. He maintained a lead in the standings from that point onwards and won the title at the final round of the year with one race in hand.

Grosjean took pole position for the prestigious Masters of F3 race at Zolder but finished 14th after stalling at the start.

Grosjean drove for ART in the inaugural GP2 Asia Series season alongside Stephen Jelley, winning both races of the first round of the championship. He went on to win the championship with four race victories and sixty-one points overall. He stayed with ART Grand Prix team for the 2008 GP2 Series season. His team-mates were Luca Filippi and Sakon Yamamoto.

In the first round at the Circuit de Catalunya Grosjean started 11th after engine problems in qualifying. He rose through the field to finish fifth in the feature race, giving him fourth on the grid for the shorter sprint race. After a good start Grosjean was up to second and then passed Kobayashi for the lead. But Grosjean made a mistake on a late rolling restart and Kobayashi tried to pass him again for the lead. Grosjean moved across on Kobayashi to keep the position but the stewards decided his defensive move was illegal and gave him a drive-through penalty dropping him to 13th at the end of the race. Victory in the sprint race at Istanbul, the fourth round of the season, moved Grosjean into second place in the championship. Despite dropping back from this position, he finished the season fourth and achieved the distinction of being the highest-placed rookie in the championship.

2008 Formula Three Euroseries season champion Nico Hülkenberg joined Pastor Maldonado at ART for 2009, forcing Grosjean out of the team. Nonetheless, Renault placed him at 2008 team champions Campos Grand Prix for 2009, now known as Barwa Addax. Despite missing the last four rounds, Grosjean finished fourth in the championship standings.

He was confirmed as Renault's test driver for 2008, replacing Nelson Piquet, Jr., who graduated to a race seat., driving a Formula One car for the first time at the UK round of the 2008 World Series by Renault weekend at Silverstone on 7 and 8 June 2008, where he gave a number of demonstrations of the previous year's R27 car.

He initially continued in the test driver role at Renault for 2009, but took over Piquet's seat in the wake of the Crashgate controversy from the European Grand Prix onwards.

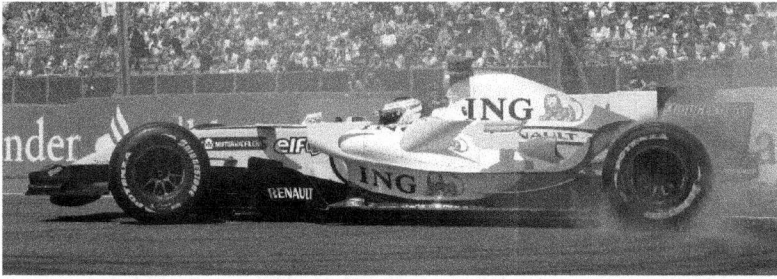

Romain Grosjean as a Renult Development Driver entertaining the crowds

Grosjean qualified 14th on his Formula One debut. He was knocked out of Q2 0.323 seconds off the pace of team mate Fernando Alonso. He finished 15th in the race after a first lap collision with Luca Badoer necessitated a stop for a new front wing.

At the season ending Abu Dhabi Grand Prix, Grosjean qualified 19th, and finished 18th and last, complaining of brake problems during the race. He said afterwards that he had "learnt an enormous amount this year, especially being team mate to Fernando". After the end of the season news reports had doubts that Grosjean would keep his seat into 2010, On 31 January 2010 Renault confirmed that Grosjean's former GP2 team mate at the Addax Team, Vitaly Petrov would be the team's second driver alongside Robert Kubica for the 2010 season leaving Grosjean without a Formula One drive for 2010.

However, it was confirmed by tyre manufacturer Pirelli that Grosjean would complete a test for the company in anticipation for their return to supplying tyres to the F1 grid in 2011. Grosjean replaced Nick Heidfeld, who left his testing duties to take up a race seat at Sauber.

After leaving Formula One, Grosjean became involved in sportscar racing. In March 2010, Grosjean secured a drive in the inaugural FIA GT1 World Championship, driving a Ford GT1 for the Matech Competition team alongside German driver Thomas Mutsch. The drivers won the opening Championship Race of the season in Abu Dhabi and added a second victory at Brno in May to lead the standings after the first three rounds of the season.

In June, Grosjean made his debut at the Le Mans 24 Hours endurance race, sharing the Ford GT1 with regaulr partner Mutsch and Jonathan Hirschi. After qualifying third in the LMGT1 class, they were forced to retire from the race after 171 laps.

Later that month, Grosjean made a return to single-seaters, racing for the DAMS team in the third round of the Auto GP season at Spa-Francorchamps. After dominating practice and taking pole position, he won the feature race before finishing second to Carlos Iaconelli in the sprint event. Over the course of the weekend, Grosjean accumulated 18 points out of a possible 19 on offer and took away €80,000 prize money as the event's top points scorer. He went on to win three more races to take the title at Monza 16 points ahead of second place man Edoardo Piscopo.

On 20 July 2010, Grosjean announced that he would return to GP2 with the DAMS team. He replaced the then Renault test driver Jérôme d'Ambrosio for the German round of the championship. He later substituted for D'Ambrosio's injured team-mate, Ho-Pin Tung, from the Belgian round onwards, finishing 3rd in Belgium and Abu Dhabi to take fourteenth place in the drivers' standings, only two positions behind D'Ambrosio.

Grosjean won the 2011 GP2 Asia Series and GP2 Series championships on his full-time return to the category. He took two pole positions and one race victory to win the Asia Series by six points from Jules Bianchi, and also won the first race of the main series to lead that championship as well. He lost the championship lead to Giedo van der Garde, after the second round of the series, after an event which was hampered by a disqualification due to a technical infringement, but regained it again the following week at Monaco, scoring points in both races despite starting from last place on the grid. After scoring four further wins as part of a mid-season run that included six consecutive podium finishes, he pulled clear of his pursuers and clinched the championship at the penultimate round at Spa-Francorchamps.

At the start of 2011, Grosjean returned to the newly branded Lotus Renault GP team as one of five test drivers along with Bruno Senna, Ho-

Pin Tung, Jan Charouz and Fairuz Fauzy. Lotus Renault had planned to run Robert Kubica and Vitaly Petrov throughout 2011 but Kubica had a horrific rally accident and was unable to drive during 2011. Former BMW Sauber team mate Nick Heidfeld replaced Kubica for the first 11 races before himself being replaced by Senna from the Belgian Grand Prix onwards. In late October 2011, Lotus Renault announced that Grosjean would drive in the Friday practice session in the Abu Dhabi Grand Prix (replacing Senna) and the Brazilian Grand Prix (replacing Petrov).

On 9 December 2011, it was announced that Grosjean would make his comeback to Formula One in 2012, taking the second seat at the newly renamed Lotus F1 Team (formerly Renault, the team that Grosjean raced with in 2009) alongside 2007 World Champion Kimi Räikkönen.

At the Australian Grand Prix, Grosjean set the second fastest time in the final free practice session, while team-mate Räikkönen was eliminated in the first part of qualifying. Grosjean made it into the top ten – for the first time, as his previous best was twelfth place, ultimately qualifing in third position.

At the following race in Bahrain he finished third, collecting his first Formula One podium and the first for a French driver since Jean Alesi at the 1998 Belgian Grand Prix. In Spain Grosjean started third, finished fourth and set his first fastest lap in Formula One; the first for a French driver since Jean Alesi at the 1996 Monaco Grand Prix. At the 2012 Canadian Grand Prix, he collected his second F1 podium with a career best finish of second, behind Lewis Hamilton.

At Valencia, Grosjean was running second when the car's electronics malfunctioned forcing the Frenchman's first mechanical-related retirement of the season. At the British Grand Prix, Grosjean topped the timesheets during Practice 1 on Friday, but qualifying did not go as well. Right at the end of Q2 he spun into the gravel at the final corner after managing to get into Q3, this meant he could not take any further part in qualifying and started from tenth, although he was promoted to ninth after Nico Hülkenberg took a grid penalty.

At the start of the race he was involved in an incident with Paul di Resta as the Force India driver clipped Grosjean's front wing meaning he had to pit for a new one. However Grosjean fought back through the field to finish in sixth just behind his team mate. At the Hungarian Grand Prix, Grosjean qualified second, the first time a French Formula One driver had started on the front row of the grid since Jean Alesi at the 1999 French Grand Prix; Grosjean finished third in the race behind Hamilton and teammate Räikkönen.

Grosjean has been involved in a number of first-lap accidents in his first full season of F1, including this collision with Mark Webber at the first corner of the 2012 Japanese Grand Prix.At Spa Grosjean caused a multicar pile-up at the start of the race, with Lewis Hamilton, Fernando Alonso and Sergio Pérez all eliminated from the race as well as Grosjean; the incident was started when Grosjean drove into Hamilton on the approach to the La Source corner.

Grosjean was given a one race ban post-race, as well as a fine of €50,000, with the FIA saying in a statement "The stewards regard this incident as an extremely serious breach of the regulations, which had the potential to cause injury to others. It eliminated leading championship contenders from the race. The stewards note that the team conceded the action was an extremely serious mistake and an error of judgement. Neither the team nor the driver made any submission in mitigation of penalty."

He was replaced for the 2012 Italian Grand Prix by Lotus test and reserve driver Jérôme d'Ambrosio. His team boss, Éric Boullier said that Grosjean learned an important lesson following his ban, however just one Grand Prix later Grosjean crashed into Mark Webber at the first corner with the Australian branding him a "First Lap Nutcase". Grosjean's actions have been condemned by many drivers in the paddock. At Abu Dhabi Grosjean was involved in another first lap incident, then in São Paulo Grosjean hit the back of Pedro de la Rosa's HRT in qualifying.

On December 14–16 Grosjean won the Race of Champions after a Grand Final victory over Le Mans legend Tom Kristensen at the Rajamangala Stadium in Bangkok. The day before Grosjean got the second place in

Nations' Cup event along with his teammate Sébastien Ogier in the French team. The winners were Sebastian Vettel and Michael Schumacher from the German team.

On 17 December 2012, it was confirmed to Grosjean would stay at Lotus for the 2013 season.

He had three points-scoring finishes at the three opening races before receiving a new chassis to help his chances at Bahrain; he qualified 11th and climbed to third. At the next race in Spain, his suspension failed on lap 9. He qualified 13th at Monaco, but his race ended when he crashed into the back of Daniel Ricciardo, earning him a 10-place grid penalty for the next race.

At the Canadian Grand Prix he started last on the grid as a consequence of the 10-place grid penalty earned previously. He came back in 8th position in race but finished the race in 13th position as he had to pit stop a third time due to heavy tyre wear. On the first lap of the British Grand Prix Grosjean was squeezed in between two cars and crashed into Webber, damaging the front wing of Webber's car. Grosjean later retired on the last lap as he was in 8th position due to serious front wing damage. At the German Grand Prix after qualifying 5th he led the race for a while and seemed to be on a faster pace than Sebastian Vettel but the intervention of the security car changed the race. He was forced to let his team mate Kimi Räikkönen pass towards the end of the race as Räikkönen had faster tyres. Grosjean resisted to Fernando Alonso to earn his second podium of the season as Vettel went to win the race and Räikkönen came second.

Towards the end of the season was able to consistently deliver outstanding performances, including the Japanese Grand Prix at Suzuka which he led before loosing out in the pit stops to the Red Bulls, although he did score a further podium finish.

At the end of the 2013 World Championship, Romain Grosjean has made 45 Grand Prix starts, finishing o nthe podium nine times with a current carrer score of 228 points.

Mauricio Gugelmin
World Championship Years Active: 1988 - 1992
World Championship Teams: March, Leyton House, Jordan

Maurício Gugelmin was born in Joinville, Brazil on April 20, 1963 into a wealthy family. His father is a timber merchant and a collector of antique cars. Gugelmin started racing go-karts as a child in Brazil in 1971, winning his local championship nine years in a row from 1971 to 1979. He progressed to the Brazilian national championship in 1980, which he also won. He progressed to single-seater racing cars in 1981, when he won the Brazilian Formula Fiat Championship.

In 1982 he took a step familiar to many Brazilian drivers at the time and moved to the United Kingdom to further his racing career. He was a longtime friend of future Formula One world champion Ayrton Senna, who was already racing in the UK, and the two shared a house in Surrey from 1982 to 1987.

Senna, having previously been a Formula Ford driver with the Van Diemen team, used his influence within the organisation to secure Gugelmin a race seat with them for 1982. By the end of the year, Gugelmin was British Formula Ford 1600 cc champion. He followed this up by finishing as runner-up in the British Formula Ford 2000 cc series the following year. He moved to the European Formula Ford series in 1984, and won the title at his first attempt.

A step up to Formula Three followed in 1985 with West Surrey Racing, winning the British championship and the prestigious Macau Grand Prix. Gugelmin then spent two years in Formula 3000, the final step before Formula One. Gugelmin took one victory in Formula 3000, at Silverstone in 1986 while driving for the Ralt factory team.

An attempt was then made to put Gugelmin into the Team Lotus Formula One suqad alongside Senna but that did not work out and he was overlooked in favour of Johnny Dumfries. Thus, Gugelmin entered Formula One with the March team in 1988, as team-mate to Ivan Capelli. The season started badly as Gugelmin suffered five retirements from the first six races due to mechanical failure, but soon afterwards he took his first points scoring finish with fourth place at the British Grand Prix. Gugelmin scored points in one other race with fifth place at the Hungarian Grand Prix. He finished the season as the highest-scoring newcomer in the Formula One World Championship, ending the year in 13th position overall.

1989 was barren for the March team, and Gugelmin took their only points scoring finish of the year at the Brazilian Grand Prix. He finished in third position; an excellent result given that March were financially troubled. At the French Grand Prix, Gugelmin was involved in a large accident at the start of the race which resulted in a spectacular barrel roll. A photograph of the accident was later selected for a London Exhibition as one of Formula One's most striking photographs. The race was stopped as a result; Gugelmin took the restart from the pit lane and set the race's fastest lap, the only one of his F1 career.

In 1990 the March team was sold, and became known as Leyton House. Gugelmin was once again partnered by Capelli, but the team's CG901 chassis proved troublesome and between them they failed to qualify six times, including at the Mexican Grand Prix. However, at the next race, the French Grand Prix, modifications had been made to the car which improved the performance. Running the whole race without changing their tyres, Capelli and Gugelmin ran first and second during the race. Gugelmin retired mid-race with engine problems and Capelli was passed by Alain Prost for the lead late in the race. Gugelmin also scored a point for finishing sixth in Belgium.

1991 saw internal turmoil at the team with several key staff leaving. The car lacked pace and both Gugelmin and Capelli struggled; the team scored just one point all season. Gugelmin's best result amounted to three seventh place finishes, although he retired from eight of the season's sixteen races.

In September, the team's principal, Akira Akagi, was arrested on suspicion of fraud. Funds were in short supply and Gugelmin made the decision to leave the team at the end of the year. A switch to the Jordan team for 1992 did not improve Gugelmin's fortunes. The team struggled with financial difficulties and scored only one point all year. The

Yamaha engine suffered from a lack of power and the car was unreliable. Gugelmin failed to finish eleven out of the sixteen races, and scored no points. With no reasonable Formula One drive available for the following year, Gugelmin decided to look else where.

Gugelmin signed with Dick Simon Racing to take part in the North American Champ Car racing series for the last three races of 1993. Although races at Mid Ohio and Nazareth resulted in non-finishes, Gugelmin finished 13th at Laguna Seca although this was not high enough to receive any points. Despite this, Gugelmin demonstrated promise.

In 1994, Gugelmin signed with Chip Ganassi Racing to partner Michael Andretti who returned to the series after a season in Formula One. Andretti was more successful than Gugelmin, and took two wins, including Reynard's first win in Champ Car at Surfers Paradise. Gugelmin was hindered by a lack of cooperation between his and Andretti's crews, and his first full-time year in the Champ Car World Series resulted in seven points finishes and 16th in the points standings.

1995 started promisingly as Gugelmin finished as runner-up to Jacques Villeneuve in the opening round at Miami. He had a strong race at the Indianapolis 500, finishing in sixth place after leading the most laps of all the drivers. Eight additional points finishes, including a third place at the final round at Laguna Seca, meant he finished tenth in the final points standings, nine places ahead of experienced team mate and former series champion Danny Sullivan.

For 1996, Gugelmin was partnered at PacWest by the British driver, Mark Blundell. He established a reputation for being quick at superspeedway tracks after taking a second and a third place at the two events at Michigan International Speedway. On top of this he took four other points finishes, finishing mid-table in 14th place.

For 1997, the PacWest team switched to using Firestone tyres and Mercedes-Benz engines. The package was competitive throughout the year and Gugelmin and Blundell finished fourth and sixth in the championship respectively. Gugelmin's notable races of the year include the Detroit Indy Grand Prix, where Gugelmin was leading the race on the last lap when he ran out of fuel, and the Molson Indy Vancouver, where Gugelmin won his first Champ Car race. In qualifying for the final race of the season at the California Speedway, Gugelmin set a world record for the fastest ever lap of a closed race track at 240.942 mph.

1998 proved not to be as successful. Setbacks plagued the team and they struggled to get to grips with the new chassis. Gugelmin showed determination, and scored nine points-scoring finishes. A highlight was Gugelmin leading 40 laps during the final event at California Speedway, en route to fifth place. Gugelmin was unable to reproduce his race-winning form, and finished no higher than 15th position in the final standings over the next three years.

In 2000, Gugelmin was named as the chairman of the Championship Drivers Association, the organisation set up to represent the interests of the drivers in the Champ Car World Series.

2001 proved to be a difficult year for Gugelmin. During the practice session for the race at Texas Motor Speedway, he crashed after he lost control in the second turn and hit the wall with a force of 66.2 g, before a second impact with the wall which exerted a force of 113.1 g. The event was eventually called off after drivers complained of dizziness, nausea and blurred vision, which were caused by the high g-forces experienced when driving at speed on the track.

During the week before the race at Nazareth Speedway, Gugelmin's son, Giuliano, died from respiratory complications. Giuliano was quadriplegic and a lifelong sufferer from cerebral palsy owing to complications at birth. The PacWest team announced that Gugelmin would not be taking part in the race. Gugelmin's team mate at PacWest, Scott Dixon, won the race beating Kenny Bräck into second place.

At the end of 2001, Gugelmin decided to retire from the sport, stating "I definitely want to spend more time with my family. After those two big accidents, and Alex [Zanardi]'s deal in Germany, I said, 'That's it. Forget it.' "Zanardi lost both legs in a crash during a Champ Car race at the Lausitzring in Germany in September 2001.

In 2003 Gugelmin was announced as a competitor by the organizers of the new Renault Megane Super Cup in his native Brazil. However, the series didn't launch and since then Gugelmin has made no competitive appearances in motorsport.

Following his retirement, Gugelmin put his Florida mansion up for sale and moved back to live in Brazi. He runs the family business along with his brother, Alceu, and has also done consultancy work for Mercedes-Benz subsidiary AMG.

During his World Championship carrer, Maurício Gugelmin was entered into eighty races, finishing on the podium once. He scored 10 points.

Mike Hailwood

World Championship Years Active: 1963 - 1974
World Championship Teams: Lotus, Lola, Surtees, McLaren

Stanley Michael Bailey Hailwood, was born on the 2nd April 1940 at Langsmeade House, Great Milton in Oxfordshire, His father was a successful motorcycle dealer and racer and as such, Hailwood had a comfortable upbringing. He learned to ride at a young age on a minibike as a small boy in a field near his home. He was educated at Pangbourne College, but left early and worked for a short time in the family business before his father sent him to work at Triumph motorcycles.

His first bike race was in 1957, at Oulton Park. In 1958, he teamed with Dan Shorey to win the Thruxton 500 endurance race. By 1961, Hailwood was racing for an up and coming Japanese factory named Honda. In June 1961, he became the first man in the history of the Isle of Man TT to win three races in one week when he won in the 125 cc, 250 cc and 500 cc categories. He lost the chance at winning a fourth race when his 350 AJS broke down with a broken gudgeon pin whilst leading. Riding a four-stroke, four-cylinder 250 cc Honda, Hailwood won the 1961 250cc world championship.

In 1962, Hailwood signed with MV Agusta and went on to become the first rider to win four consecutive 500cc World Championships. After his success with MV Agusta, Hailwood went back to Honda and won four more world titles in 1966 and 1967 in the 250 cc and 350 cc categories.

Hailwood is remembered for his accomplishments at the famed Isle of Man TT. By 1967, he had won 12 times on the island mountain course. He won what many historians consider to be the most dramatic Isle of Man race of all time, the 1967 Senior TT against his great rival, Giacomo Agostini. In that race he set a lap record of 108.77 mph on the Honda 500-4 – a record that would stand for 8 years.

In 1968, Honda pulled out of Grand Prix racing, but paid Hailwood £50,000 not to ride for another team, in expectation of keeping him as its rider upon return to competition. With no other factory racing teams available to compete against MV Agusta, Hailwood decided to follow another motorcycle great John Surtees and tried racing cars.

During his auto racing career, Hailwood never achieved the same level of success that he had on motorcycles. He won the 1972 Formula Two European title and earned a podium finish at the 1969 24 Hours of Le Mans.

Hailwood was in contention for a victory at his first Formula One race in 6 years, the 1971 Italian Grand Prix. He and 3 other drivers finished 1-2-3-4 over two-tenths of a second, Hailwood finishing fourth.

He was recognised for his bravery when in the 1973 South African Grand Prix he went to pull Clay Regazzoni from his burning car after the two collided on the second lap of the race. Hailwood's driving suit caught fire, but after being extinguished by a fire marshall he returned to help rescue Regazzoni, an act for which he was awarded the George Medal, the 2nd highest gallantry award that a British civilian can be awarded. Mike left Formula One after being injured badly at the 1974 German Grand Prix at the Nürburgring.

In 1978 after an 11 year hiatus from motorcycling, Hailwood performed a now legendary comeback at the Isle of Man TT. Few observers believed the 38-year-old would be competitive after such a long absence. Riding a Ducati 900SS, he was not only competitive, but managed a hugely popular win. He raced the following year at the Isle of Man TT before retiring for good at the age of 39. In that final Isle of Man appearance, Hailwood rode a two-stroke Suzuki RG 500 to victory in the Senior TT. He then opted to use that same 500cc bike in the Unlimited Classic and diced for the lead with Alex George for all 6 laps in yet another TT epic. A minute or two apart on the road, they were rarely a few seconds apart on time each lap, Hailwood losing by just 2 seconds.

On Saturday, 21st March 1981, Mike Hailwood set off in his Rover SD1 with his children Michelle and David to collect some fish and chips. As they returned along the A435 Alcester Road through Portway Warwickshire near their home in Tanworth-in-Arden, a truck made an illegal turn through the barriers into the central reservation, and their car hit it.

Michelle, aged nine, was killed instantly; Mike and David were taken to hospital, where Mike died two days later due to severe internal injuries, he was 40 years old. David survived. The truck driver was fined £100.

Hailwood claimed to have been told by a fortune teller in South Africa that he wouldn't live to 40 and would be killed by a truck. Later that year part of the TT course was named Hailwood's Height in his honour.

Mike Hailwood participated in 50 Formula One Grands Prix. He achieved two podium finishes, and scored a total of 29 championship points.

Nick Heidfeld
World Championship Years Active: 2000 – 2012
World Championship Teams: Prost, Sauber, Jordan, Williams, BMW, Lotus

Nick Lars Heidfeld was born on the 10th May 1977 in Mönchengladbach, in what was then West Germany. He started racing karts at the age of 11 in 1988. In 1994 he moved into the German Formula Ford series, gaining widespread attention by winning 8 of the 9 races to take the title that season.

In 1995 he won the German International Formula Ford 1800 Championship, and came second in the Zetec Cup. This led to a drive in the German Formula Three Championship championship for 1996, where he finished third overall, after taking 3 wins. He entered the end of the season Macau Grand Prix and won the first heat of the race, attracting the attention of compatriot Norbert Haug, who later signed him up for the West Competition team.

In 1997 Heidfeld won the German F3 Championship for Bertram Schäfer Racing, with support from McLaren/West, including a win at the Monaco Grand Prix Formula Three support race. The following year he won three races and was runner-up in the International Formula 3000 championship, with the West Competition team. At the final race of the season he was demoted to the back of the grid from pole position, after his team used non-compliant fuel. He finished the race ninth and out of the points, losing the championship by seven points to Juan Pablo Montoya.

During 1998, he was also the official test driver for the McLaren-Mercedes Formula One team. In 1999, he won the International Formula 3000 Championship, and was a member of the Mercedes squad that raced at the 1999 24 Hours of Le Mans, but the team withdrew after the Mercedes-Benz CLR back-flipped on the Mulsanne straight while Peter Dumbreck were driving.

Heidfeld was signed as a race driver for the Prost Grand Prix F1 team for the 2000 season, alongside Formula One veteran Jean Alesi. Heidfeld struggled with his new car and suffered a string of retirements, as well as colliding with his team mate on more than one occasion.

He departed Prost at the end of that season, before signing a three-year contract with Sauber for 2001. He was partnered with then rookie driver Kimi Räikkönen. After the announcement of Mika Häkkinen's retirement, many thought that Heidfeld would replace him in the McLaren team, as he had outperformed Räikkönen over the year, including a podium position in the Brazilian Grand Prix and his long term links with McLaren engine supplier Mercedes-Benz. However, the McLaren seat went to Räikkönen, and Heidfeld stayed with Sauber for 2002 and 2003, where he raked up a small number of points finishes. In 2002 he outperformed another rookie team mate, Felipe Massa, but was then beaten by his more experienced fellow countryman, Heinz-Harald Frentzen, in 2003.

At the end of the 2003 season, Heidfeld was replaced at the Sauber team by Jordan's Giancarlo Fisichella and looked to be without a race seat for the 2004 season. However, after a number of moderately successful tests, it was announced that Heidfeld would race with the Jordan team, alongside rookie Giorgio Pantano. Heidfeld had a poor season because of the slow and unreliable EJ14. He finished seventh at the Monaco Grand Prix and eighth at the Canadian Grand Prix and finished the season with three points.

During the winter of 2004–2005, Heidfeld tested with the Williams team, in a 'shootout' against Antônio Pizzonia for the second race seat alongside Mark Webber. At the Williams launch in January 2005, it was announced that Heidfeld would be the race driver for the team that year. At the seventh race of the 2005 season at the Nürburgring circuit, his home Grand Prix, Heidfeld took his first ever pole position. He also achieved his best race position to-date in Monaco where he finished second, which he equalled at the Nürburgring.

Heidfeld gained a contract with his then Williams' engine supplier, BMW, when they bought the Sauber team and entered Formula One as BMW Sauber for the 2006 season.

During his first seaon with the team, Heidfeld scored points several times. At Melbourne he ran as high as second until the safety car came out. He eventually finished fourth. The Hungarian Grand Prix saw Heidfeld give BMW Sauber their first podium finish and best result of the year, when he finished third, even though he had only qualified tenth on the grid.

Heidfeld started the 2007 season strongly. In Bahrain, he chased down and overtook reigning world champion Fernando Alonso around the outside, finishing half a minute ahead of his BMW teammate Kubica. He scored three fourth places in the opening three races, a sixth in Monaco, and a second place at the Canadian Grand Prix, where he also out-qualified both Ferraris, equalling his best ever Grand Prix finish. After retiring from fifth place at Indianapolis, he was outscored by team-mate Kubica at both Magny-Cours and Silverstone. At an eventful European Grand Prix at the Nürburgring, Heidfeld's home circuit, where he collided with Kubica on the opening lap, he recovered and overtook Kubica on the final lap to finish sixth, despite making six pitstops during the race. Heidfeld returned to form in Hungary, qualifying second and finishing third to score his and BMW's second podium of the season. He finished fourth at the Turkish and Italian Grand Prix, and fifth in the Belgian Grand Prix. He eventually finished a career-best fifth in the championship with 61 points, outpointing Kubica by 22.

After several months of negotiations, BMW confirmed that Heidfeld would stay with the team for 2008. He started the season strongly, finishing second in Australia after qualifying fifth. In Malaysia, he qualified fifth but dropped down to tenth at the first corner after being pushed wide by Jarno Trulli. He got back up to sixth, also setting his first ever fastest lap in the process. In Bahrain he started from sixth place but he did not gain a place at the start, but passed Trulli and Heikki Kovalainen to climb up to fourth. He finished there and this fourth gave him second in the championship.

Kubica and Heidfeld made BMW Sauber history by securing the third-year team's first victory, and first one-two finish respectively in Canada. Heidfeld had a disappointing race in France, failing to score any points. He came back strongly at the British Grand Prix, starting fifth and finishing second in the wet conditions. Another strong performance, where he set the fastest lap of the race for the second time this season, was his home grand prix at the Hockenheimring showed that, for the time being, he had reversed the performance deficit to his team mate. Another second place finish at the Belgian Grand Prix, followed by 5th and 6th place finishes in Italy and Singapore respectively put him just one point behind current World Champion Kimi Räikkönen with just three races remaining.

In the last three races Heidfeld scored four points, ending in sixth place in the standings after being passed by Fernando Alonso at the last round of the season. However, Heidfeld became only the second driver to finish 18 races in a single season, after Tiago Monteiro completed the same feat with Jordan in 2005. Heidfeld also became the first driver to finish every single race in a season since Michael Schumacher in 2002.

Heidfeld tied Stefan Johansson's record for most podium finishes without a win by finishing second at the 2009 Malaysian Grand Prix. He scored a further 2 points at the Spanish Grand Prix, and finished 5th at Spa to score another 4 points. A seventh place finish at Monza added a further 2 points to his 2009 tally. Nevertheless, four points-scoring finishes in the final six races secured him thirteenth position in the Drivers' Championship, two points ahead of team mate Kubica. In Singapore, Heidfeld's run of 41 consecutive classified finishes was brought to an end due to a collision with Force India's Adrian Sutil.

With BMW's decision to withdraw from the sport at the end of the 2009 season, Heidfeld's future in Formula One was uncertain. It was mentioned that he was considered to drive for Mercedes GP alongside fellow German Nico Rosberg but the team signed fellow German Michael Schumacher instead.

Heidfeld was then tipped for a seat at Sauber alongside Kamui Kobayashi but they decided to go with Pedro de la Rosa. Heidfeld was then confirmed as the test and reserve driver for Mercedes.

In August 2010, with Heidfeld not yet having driven the Mercedes MGP W01 car, the team released him from his contract so that he could become the Pirelli tyre company's test driver. Heidfeld tested a Toyota TF109 car fitted with Pirelli tyres on a number of occasions in 2010, ahead of the firm's replacement of Bridgestone as the sport's sole tyre supplier in 2011.

Heidfeld completed three tests for Pirelli in Mugello, Paul Ricard and Jerez before being released from his duties to join Sauber, with his place being taken by Romain Grosjean

Heidfeld returned to the Formula One grid, replacing Pedro de la Rosa at the Sauber team for the remainder of the 2010 season. This marked his third spell with them.

On 9 February, Lotus Renault GP confirmed that Heidfeld would be sharing testing duties with Bruno Senna on the Saturday and Sunday of the four-day test at Jerez, to evaluate the drivers in preparation of replacing the injured Robert Kubica, who had suffered a crash whilst rallying in Italy, for the 2011 season. Heidfeld was confirmed as Kubica's replacement on 16 February 2011.

In Australia, the first race of the season following the cancellation of the Bahrain Grand Prix, Heidfeld qualified 18th and ended 12th. Heidfeld finished third, after starting sixth, in the Malaysian Grand Prix at Sepang, breaking Stefan Johansson's record of 12 podiums without a win. He added another 12th place in China, before a seventh place finish in Turkey after a close battle with team-mate Petrov. Two eighth places in Spain and Monaco were followed by a retirement at the Canadian Grand Prix, after running into the back of Kamui Kobayashi and causing damage to his front wing, which broke under acceleration and collapsed under the car. He was forced to retire after his car caught fire after exiting the pit lane on lap 25 in the Hungarian Grand Prix. Heidfeld was replaced by Bruno Senna ahead of the Belgian Grand Prix, before officially parting company with the team on 2 September 2011.

In February 2012, it was confirmed that Heidfeld would join the Rebellion Racing team to contest both the Le Mans 24 Hours and selected races of the FIA World Endurance Championship. In addition to

Le Mans, he also raced at the Sebring 12 Hours and Spa 6 Hours, sharing a Lola-Toyota LMP1 car with team-mates Neel Jani and Nicolas Prost. The car finished 32nd overall and seventh in class at Sebring after encountering problems, before leading home a Rebellion one-two in the unofficial privateer class at Spa, finishing fifth overall behind the four works Audis. At Le Mans, Heidfeld and his team-mates went one better by finishing fourth, splitting the Audis after a fast and problem-free run.

Despite scoring regular podium finishes in 2005 with Williams, and in 2007 and 2008 with BMW Sauber, Heidfeld has yet to win a race since entering Formula One in 2000. Heidfeld also currently holds three other records; he is the driver who has scored the highest number of world championship points without a Grand Prix win, holds the record for the most podium finishes without a Grand Prix win and has the most second place finishes without a win, with 8. He also holds the record for the most consecutive race classifications with a tally of 41, and shares the record for most finishes in a season with Tiago Monteiro and Felipe Massa after finishing all 18 races in the 2008 season.

At the end of his Formuka One carrer, Nick Heidfeld and been entered into 185 Grand Prix, achieveing 13 podium finishes and scoring 259 points.

Hans Herrmann
World Championship Years Active: 1953-1969
World Championship Teams: Veritas, Mercedes, Maserati, Cooper, BRM, Porsche

Hans Herrmann was born on the 23rd February, 1928 and is a baker by trade. He became a sport-car legend, taking part in now legendary road races like Mille Miglia, Targa Florio and Carrera Panamericana and is one of the few remaining witnesses of this era.

His career began appropriately: in 1952, in a private Porsche 356, he took part in hill climbs, rallies and reliability runs. The very next year, he came fifth in the Lyon-Charbonnières Rally, together with Richard von Frankenberg in a Porsche 356.

Thereupon Porsche's racing manager at that time, Huschke von Hanstein, brought him into Porsche works team. In 1953, Herrmann went to the start for the first time in the 24 Hours of Le Mans where, together with co-pilot Helm Glöckler in a Porsche 550 Coupé, he gained a best of class victory in the category up to 1.5 liters capacity at his very first try.

After Herrmann had also secured the title of German Sports Car Champion in the same year, he attracted the attention of Mercedes-Benz head of racing Alfred Neubauer, who integrated the 26-year-old into his works team along with Juan Manuel Fangio, Stirling Moss and Karl Kling

From 1954 to 1955, he was part of the Mercedes-Benz factory team, as a junior driver behind Juan Manuel Fangio, Karl Kling, Hermann Lang and later Stirling Moss. When the Silver Arrows came back for the 1954 French Grand Prix to score a 1–2 win, Herrmann drove the fastest lap but had to retire. A podium finish at the 1954 Swiss Grand Prix was his best result in his Grand Prix carrer.

Herrmann had a remarkable Mille Miglia race in 1954, when the gates of a railroad crossing were lowered in the last moment before the fast train to Rome passed. Driving a very low Porsche 550 Spyder, Herrmann decided it was too late for a brake attempt anyway, knocked on the back of the helmet of his navigator Herbert Linge to make him duck, and they barely passed below the gates and before the train, to the surprise of the spectators.

In the 1955 Argentine Grand Prix his Mercedes-Benz team mates Kling and Moss had to abandon early due to the extremely hot conditions on the southern hemisphere in January. Herrmann was called in to share his car with them for a 4th place finish, giving one point each. Fangio won with two laps more. Hans was quick in the 1955 Mille Miglia with the Mercedes-Benz 300 SLR, comparably or even faster than Moss, but was less lucky than in 1954, as he had to abandon the race.

A crash in practise for the 1955 Monaco Grand Prix put Herrmann out for the ill-fated 1955 season, even though a comeback in the Targa Florio was intended.

The next years saw Herrmann racing for many marques, in F1 for Cooper, Maserati and BRM. In Berlin's AVUS during the 1959 German Grand Prix the brakes of his BRM failed, he crashed in a spectacular way, being thrown out of the car and sliding along the track with the car somersaulting in the air.

With different versions of the Porsche 718 being used as a sportscar and as Formula Two, Herrmann scored some wins for Porsche, mainly both the 1960 12 Hours of Sebring and Targa Florio. When it was turned into a Formula One in 1961 due to the rule changes, the results in F1 were disappointing. Herrmann finished 15th and last in the 1961 Dutch Grand Prix, which was one of only two races in F1 history to have no retirements.

He left Porsche at the beginning of the following year, feeling that he as a local from Stuttgart was not being looked after, compared to Californian Dan Gurney and 1959 GP-winner Jo Bonnier from Sweden.

With the small cars of the Italian Abarth marque Herrmann spent 1962 to 1965 driving in minor races and hillclimbing events. He only took outright wins in lesser sports car racing events, such as at AVUS or the 500 km Nürburgring. The Abarths were hard to beat in their classes from 850cc to 1600cc, though. Being the only pro in a small team Hermann learned a lot about testing and developing, which helped him later.

127

However, being dissatisfied with the preparation of his car for the 1965 Schauinsland practice, Hans went home to witness the birth of his son, Dino. At the end of the year he left Abarth for good to return to the manufacturer closer to his home.

In 1966 he returned to Porsche for a comeback in the World Sportscar Championship, as Porsche started a serious effort there. Following several podium finishes with the still underpowered two liter Porsche 906 and later models, he won the 1968 24 Hours of Daytona in a 907 as well as the Sebring 12 Hours again, now together with Swiss Jo Siffert.

Herrmann missed the win in the 1969 24 Hours of Le Mans with a Porsche 908 by only 120 meters, but it was he who finally scored the long-awaited first overall victory at the Le Mans 24 Hours for Porsche in 1970. He was assigned to Porsche Salzburg, the Austria-based factory-backed team owned by the Porsche family, which mainly entered cars painted red and white, the Austrian colors. In heavy rain, he and his team mate Richard Attwood survived with their Porsche 917K #23 as the best of only seven finishers.

Half jokingly, he had promised to his wife before the Le Mans race that he would retire in case of a win there. The 42 year old announced his retirement on TV, after having driven the winning car in a parade through Stuttgart from the factory to the town hall.

Using his contacts, Herrmann built a successful company for automotive supplies. He was kidnapped once in the 1990s and kept in a car trunk for many hours before escaping.

During his World Chmpionship career, he participated in 19 Grand Prix, achieving one podium, and a total of 10 championship points.

Bill Holland
World Championship Years Active: 1950-1953
World Championship Teams: Deidt, Kurtis Kraft

Born in Philadelphia, Pennsylvania on the 18th December 1907, Bill Holland was an American race car driver competing n Sprint Cars, Midgets, Indy Car and NASCAR.

Holland won the first ever automobile race at Selinsgrove Speedway in 1946, and almost took victory at the 1947 Indy 500, but slowed and allowed teammate Mauri Rose to pass him seven laps from the end, mistakenly believing that Rose was a lap down. He finished the years sconf I nthe AAA National Championship – hsi highest ever position.

He took Indy 500 honours in 1949 – his last win in Indy Car, the year before the race was part of the World Championship. He would only make two starts as part of the World Championship; 1950 – where he finished second and again in 1953, where he retired due to Cam Gear issues.

During 1951 and 1952 he made eight starts in NASCAR, which placed him on the AAA Indy Car blacklist for a period of time. He failed to win any of the races he was entered, his best placing was 4th at North Wilkesboro.

Holland died from complications of Alzheimer's disease on the 19th May 1984 and was inducted in the National Sprint Car Hall of Fame in 2005.

During his World Champiionship career, Bill Holland participated in two Grand Prix, finishing on the podium once, scoring six points.

World Championship Years Active: 1971 - 1983
World Championship Teams: March, Shadow, Penske, Ligier, ATS,
Lotus, Tyrrell, Osella

On the 10th July, 1946, Jean-Pierre Jacques Jarier was born at Charenton-le-Pont, near Paris. He came from a family which ran a small hotel. After school he was studying economics when he discovered the Montlhery racing circuit in the southern suburbs of Paris and he started racing motorcycles soon afterwards.

At 21, by promising to give up bike racing, he managed to convince his mother to sell her Peugeot road car in order to buy him a Renault 8 Gordini with which to race. The Renault 8 Gordini was the car which enabled many young Frenchmen to discover motor racing cheaply and realise their talent before moving on to the more expensive single seaters. He had impressive results in Formula France, before moving up to French Formula Three, finishing 3rd overall in 1970.

For 1971 he moved to the Shell Arnold European Formula Two team. He peaked with two 3rd places, and also made his Grand Prix debut at Monza when the team rented a March 701. However, the team dropped him midway through 1972 for financial reasons.

For 1973 he signed to the March Engineering Formula Two team, and was also given a Formula One seat by the outfit. Formula One was difficult in the uncompetitive 721G, but Jarier stormed to the Formula Two title with eight wins.

Jarier won the 1000 km Nürburgring race in 1974 with Jean-Pierre Beltoise. The pair drove a Matra-Simca 670C.In 1974 Jarier concentrated on Formula One, signing with the Shadow Racing Cars team. He became team leader following the death of Peter Revson, finishing 3rd at the Monaco Grand Prix on his way to 14th overall.

1975 began with a bang, as he put his Shadow DN5 on pole position for the Argentine Grand Prix, only for a component to break in the warm-up, preventing Jarier from taking the start. He repeated the feat at the Brazilian Grand Prix, and then dominated the race until a fuel metering unit failed, ending his race. Bad luck and poor reliability would curse his season, though the Shadow team fell from the pace as well. His only points-scoring finish was for 4th place in the shortened Spanish Grand Prix.

Jarier spent 1976 with Shadow Racing Cars, qualifying 3rd in an updated version of the previous year's car, the DN5B and setting fastest lap at the opening Brazilian Grand Prix, before spinning off on James Hunt's oil. However, this was a false dawn, and the car became uncompetitive, Jarier failing to score any points.

He switched to the ATS team in 1977, driving a Penske. He scored a point in his first race for the team, and then had one-off drives for Shadow and Equipe Ligier when the German team elected to miss the final races of the year. He also dabbled in sports cars, winning two races in an Alfa Romeo T33 with Arturo Merzario, and coming second at the Le Mans 24 Hours with Vern Schuppan in a Mirage.

His second year at ATS in the in-house HS1, was less successful, and he was fired after an argument with team principal Hans Gunther Schmidt after failing to qualify the car for the Monaco Grand Prix. He was briefly rehired for the German Grand Prix, only to miss the grid again, and again argue with Schmidt, leaving once more. However, at the end of the year he was signed by Team Lotus to take the seat left by Ronnie Peterson's death. He set fastest lap at the United States East Grand Prix, running 3rd before he ran out of fuel, and then took pole and dominated at the Canadian Grand Prix before an oil leak ended his race.

These showings saw him signed by Tyrrell Racing. He was a regular points-scorer over two seasons with the team, with his best results being two 3rd places, achieved at the 1979 South African Grand Prix and the 1979 British Grand Prix.

He began 1981 with a temporary assignment for Ligier, standing in while Jean-Pierre Jabouille returned to fitness, for two races. He then drove with Osella beginning midway through the season, giving some respectable performances for the small, underfunded team.

The following season saw a full season with Osella, with Jarier securing the team's best-ever finish with 4th at the San Marino Grand Prix, a race boycotted by the majority of British teams. While the rest of the year would be difficult, Jarier was instrumental in keeping the team's morale up following the death of Riccardo Paletti at the Canadian Grand Prix. The following year saw a full season with Ligier, but after a good run at Long Beach ended with a collision with Keke Rosberg, he seemed to lose hope, and finished the season without points.

During the 1983 season, he became grossly unpopular with the other drivers due to his bad behavior as a back marker on the track during races. Following this, Jarier retired from motorsport, but was tempted back to drive in the French Touring Car Championship until the end of the 1980s and then switched to Porsches for 10 years although in recently he has competed in the FIA GT series with a Chrysler Viper. Jarier introduced himself to a new generation by contributing major stunt work to the film Ronin, directed by John Frankenheimer who also directed the 1966 classic, Grand Prix.

During his World Championship carrer Jean-Pierre Jarier was entered into 143 Grand Prix, finishing on the podium three times, scoring 31.5 points.

World Championship Years Active: 1980 – 1991
World Championship Teams: Shadow, Spirit, Tyrrell, Toleman, Ferrari, McLaren, Ligier, Onyx, AGS, Footwork

Stefan Nils Edwin Johansson was born on the 8th September 1956 in Växjö, Sweden. His route to Formula One was via the British Formula 3 Championship, which he won in 1980 driving for future McLaren team boss Ron Dennis' Project Four team. He made his Formula One debut with the Shadow Racing Team at the 1980 Argentine Grand Prix when he was still a Formula Three regular. He failed to qualify for the race and the next race in Brazil and he was not seen in Formula One again until 1983 after spending 1982 in the European Formula Two Championship with Spirit Racing where he finished eighth overall, his best finish being third at Mugello in Italy.

Johansson's first Formula One race with Spirit was at the non-championship 1983 Race of Champions at Brands Hatch where he failed to finish due to failure of the Honda engine on lap four. His qualifying time was almost 20 seconds off the pole time set by 1982 World Champion Keke Rosberg in his Williams-Cosworth but his times in the race morning warm-up session were among the fastest. He moved up to 17th place before pulling into the pits with ending failure. Spirit continued to test and develop the 201C and Johansson re-entered Formula One at the 1983 British Grand Prix at Silverstone where he qualified the car in a credible 14th position. He raced in a further five Grands Prix in 1983 with a best finish of seventh in the Dutch Grand Prix at Zandvoort.

Stefan Johansson was replaced at Spirit by Mauro Baldi for the 1984 season when the team lost its Honda engines to Williams.He joined Tyrrell at the British Grand Prix as a replacement for the injured Martin Brundle. He then went on to Toleman for the end of season Grands Prix, finishing fourth in the Italian Grand Prix at Monza as a replacement for the team's regular driver Ayrton Senna who was stood down by the team for the race for breaking contract and signing with Lotus for 1985.

Johansson signed a contract with Toleman for 1985 but it fell through when Toleman failed to secure a tyre agreement. Instead Johansson started again with Tyrrell as a replacement for the suspended Stefan Bellof before being called up to Ferrari when René Arnoux was mysteriously sacked after the first race of the season in Brazil. He led his second race with Ferrari at their 'home' race, the San Marino Grand Prix, and two laps from home passed Senna's out of fuel Lotus to the delight of the Tifosi and would probably have won if his Ferrari 156/85 had not run out of fuel just half a lap later.

His role at Ferrari for the 1985 season was primarily to back up Michele Alboreto's championship challenge, though he did finish 2nd to the Italian at Canada and backed it up with 2nd in the next race at Detroit.

In 1986 he often outpaced Alboreto, despite the Italian being the teams lead driver. The V6 turbo in the Ferrari F1/86 lacked nothing in power compared to the Honda, BMW, Renault and TAG-Porsche engines, but the car itself proved to be difficult, with both drivers complaining through the season about lack of downforce and the cars reluctance to drive well on all but the smoothest of circuits. Johansson finished the 1986 Drivers' Championship his best ever in 5th place while Alboreto, who finished 2nd in 1985, could only manage 9th place.

He was replaced at Ferrari by Austrian Gerhard Berger for 1987, and he moved to McLaren as number two driver behind double and reigning World Champion Alain Prost. McLaren weren't as competitive in 1987 as they had been from 1984-1986, with Prost only adding three wins to his tally (and beating the record of 27 Grand Prix wins held by Jackie Stewart with his 28th win in Portugal) and failing to successfully defend his Drivers' Championship.

Further podium finishes did follow for the Swede and Johansson finished sixth in the Drivers' Championship. Stefan Johansson's position at McLaren was considered by many as just a stop gap signing by team boss Ron Dennis who had failed to lure Ayrton Senna from Lotus due to him being under contract until the end of 1987 and always intended signing the mercurial Brazilian for 1988.

Despite 11 podiums in three seasons, Johansson was still winless and was not wanted by a top team. He had hoped to join Williams in 1988 as a replacement for the departing 1987 World Champion Nelson Piquet, but Williams signed Riccardo Patrese instead.

He joined Ligier for 1988, ironically alongside the man he replaced at Ferrari, René Arnoux, but the team's first non-turbo powered car since 1981 was totally uncompetitive scoring no points and more often than not failing to qualify. The French teams low point of the year was when both Johansson and Arnoux failed to qualify for the French Grand Prix at Paul Ricard.

Better was to follow in 1989 as he was signed to lead the new Onyx team. Their car was temperamental and didn't always qualify, but Johansson finished a surprise and popular third in Portugal for his podium finish. He fell out with new team owner Peter Monteverdi in early 1990 and was duly sacked, making further appearances for AGS and Footwork in 1991.

During his Formula One career Johansson had participated in sports car races such as 24 Hours of Le Mans, and had won two World Sportscar Championship races in the 1980s the Mugello round in 1983, driving a Joest Racing Porsche 956 with Bob Wollek, and the 1988 Spa Francorchamps race in a Sauber C9 with Mauro Baldi.

For 1992 he moved over to CART Championship Car, winning the Rookie of the Year title with two third places, ahead of Belgium's Eric Bachelart. His first pole came at Portland the next year, but as in Formula One he never won a race. From 1992 to 1996, he started 73 races and had his best season overall in 1994, finishing in 11th. During this time, he competed in the 1993-1995 Indianapolis 500. At the 1996 Molson Indy Toronto race, he was involved in an accident that claimed the life of fellow driver Jeff Krosnoff and track marshall Gary Avrin. After making wheel to wheel contact, Jeff's car hit the barriers and also a tree and lamp post that was too close to the track. Krosnoff died instantly of the injuries sustained from hitting the lamp post.

After retiring from CART at the end of the 1996 season he returned to Sports Car racing. During 1997 he recorded two major race wins, at the 12 Hours of Sebring driving a Ferrari 333 SP and at Le Mans where he drove a Joest Porsche.

In 1997 Johansson founded a successful Indy Lights team running Fredrik Larsson and Jeff Ward; in 1998 its drivers were Guy Smith and Luiz Garcia, Jr.; for 1999 the seats went to Scott Dixon and Ben Collins.

During 1998 and 1999 Johansson raced for various sports car teams before forming Johansson-Matthews racing with an American businessman called Jim Matthews in 2000. They competed in the American Le Mans Series using a Reynard 2KQ prototype. Unfortunately this wasn't a successful vehicle in its original form and the partnership dissolved.

In 2001 Johansson campaigned an Audi R8 prototype with backing from Gulf Oil and the assistance of Mike Earle's Arena team. That year he raced in the European Le Mans Series, the American Le Mans Series and at Le Mans itself. His co-drivers were Guy Smith and Patrick Lemarie. At Le Mans Smith was replaced by Tom Coronel.

2002 saw Johansson back in an Audi R8 but this time one run by the Miami based Champion Racing team. His co-driver was ex Formula One driver Johnny Herbert and they competed in the American Le Mans Series.

For 2003, he returned to CART as a team owner, running American Spirit Team Johansson with Jimmy Vasser and Ryan Hunter-Reay as drivers. This was one of many new teams for the 2003 CART season. The team was under-funded, and although Hunter-Reay scored a fluke win in the wet conditions at Australia, it folded at the end of the season.

After only competing in a couple of celebrity races and occasional outings in the works Zytek in 2004 Johansson returned to full time racing in 2005 driving the Chip Ganassi run New Century Mortgage sponsored Lexus Riley Daytona Prototype in the American Grand-Am Rolex Sports Car Series. With co-driver Cort Wagner he scored his best finish, a second place, at Mont Tremblant in Canada, they finished the year in fifth place in the championship.

In 2006 as well as the Grand Prix Masters series, Johansson has made occasional appearances in Grand-Am for the Cheever and CITGO teams, and has continued an association with the works Zytek team in the Le Mans Series.

2007 saw Johansson competing in a Highcroft Racing Courage-Acura in the LMP2 class of the American Le Mans Series, sharing with David Brabham. He was due to race a Zytek at Le Mans in 2007, but the team could not rebuild the car in time after a test-day accident, and Johansson made a last minute deal to drive a works Courage.

Johansson took part in the inaugural Speedcar Series in 2008, where luck once again deserted him as the victim of a lot of other drivers' accidents. For 2008 Johansson did not have a full-time sports car drive, but had some outings planned in the Highcroft Acura ARX-01 in the ALMS and a place with the Epsilon Euskadi team at Le Mans.

Outside the cockpit, Johansson has a number of business ventures (including managing several successful drivers such as Scott Dixon) and is a keen artist – he is particularly known for his watch designs.

In his Grand Prix career, Johansson was entered in 103 reaces, achieved 12 podiums, and scored a total of 88 championship points.

Karl Kling
World Championship Years Active: 1954 - 1955
World Championship Teams: Mercedes-Benz

Karl Kling was born on the 16th September 1910, in Giessen, Germany the third son of the headmaster of the Pestalozzi School there. Entranced from infancy by motoring, at 16 Karl began a mechanical apprenticeship with the local Mercedes agent Neils und Kraft.

He found his way into motorsport via his first job as a reception clerk at Daimler-Benz in the mid-1930s, competing in hillclimb and trials events in production machinery in his spare time. During the Second World War he gained mechanical experience servicing Luftwaffe aircraft, and after the cessation of hostilities he resumed his motorsport involvement in a BMW 328.

Kling was instrumental in developing Mercedes' return to international competition in the early 1950s. In 1951 Mercedes had sent Kling to Argentina to drive one of their three-litre supercharged Grand Prix cars alongside the pre-war champion Hermann Lang and the new Argentine star Juan Manuel Fangio. Kling did well, and the next year took his place in the team. His win in the 1952 Carrera Panamericana road race, driving the then-experimental Mercedes-Benz 300SL was a defining point in assuring the Daimler-Benz management that motorsport had a place in Mercedes' future.

In 1953, while Mercedes prepared for an onslaught the next year on both Formula 1 and the sports car World Championships, Kling drove for Alfa Romeo. At the Nurburgring, Kling crashed heavily into a concrete bridge parapet, breaking his ribs and shoulders. Even so, he recovered sufficiently to drive, albeit unsuccessfully, for Porsche in the Pan Americana.

He was called up to the revived Mercedes Grand Prix squad in 1954 he finished less than one second behind the legendary Juan Manuel Fangio on his Formula One debut, taking second place in the 1954 French Grand Prix at the fast Reims-Gueux circuit.

This promising start was not to last, and with the arrival of Stirling Moss at Mercedes in 1955 Kling was effectively demoted to third driver. However, away from the World Championship, Kling took impressive victories in both the Berlin Grand Prix and the Swedish Grand Prix.

He left the Formula One team at the end of the season, to succeed Alfred Neubauer as head of Mercedes motorsport. He was in this post during their successful rallying campaigns of the 1960s, occasionally taking the wheel himself. On one such occasion he drove a Mercedes-Benz 220SE to victory in the mighty 1961 Algiers-Cape Town trans-African rally.

He died on March 18, 2003 only a few weeks after Manfred von Brauchitsch, who had preceded him as the oldest surviving Grand Prix driver. It wass said, that he was born too late and too early. Too late to be in the successful Mercedes team of the '30s and too early to have a real chance in 1954 and 1955.

Karl Kling competed in eleven Grand Prix during his World Championship carrer, scoring 17 points and finishing on the podium twice.

Nicola Larini
World Championship Years Active: 1987–1997
World Championship Teams: Coloni, Osella, Ligier, Modena, Ferrari, Sauber

Botn on the 19th March, 1964 in Lido di Camaiore, Italy, Nicola Larini began car racing in Formula Italia in 1983, then moved up to Formula Abarth in 1984, placing third overall in the championship. He also started in Italian Formula Three the same season, winning races the following yer.

In 1986 he won the title for Coloni in a Dallara, and briefly drove for the same team in Formula 3000 the following year. His rapid ascendancy continued when Coloni entered the final two European rounds of the 1987 Formula One season. Larini failed to qualify for the Italian Grand Prix, but got into the Spanish Grand Prix, only to retire early on.

For the 1988 season he was signed by the Osella Formula One team, and drew good notices for his valiant performances in the hugely uncompetitive car, with a best result of 9th in the Monaco Grand Prix. He would continue with Osella in the 1989 season, their much-improved car suffering from the lottery of pre-qualifying. However, Larini continued to shine, running 6th at the San Marino Grand Prix until a hub failure, and running third at the Canadian Grand Prix until an electrical failure.

The 1990 season saw a move up the grid to the Ligier team, but the well-funded French team were at a creative dead-end and the car was a distinct midfielder. A brace of seventh places were Larini's best results in a low-key year, although he easily outshone Philippe Alliot in the other Ligier.

Larini then moved to the new Modena team for the 1991 season, once again having to face pre-qualifying. He got through in the opening round, the United States Grand Prix, and held on for seventh place, but the team would develop acute financial difficulties, and were unable to progress. As a result, Larini would only qualify for four more races.

For the 1992 season, he was out of luck for a Grand Prix drive, but was signed by Ferrari to develop their active suspension system. Larini kept

140

his racing instincts sharp by winning the Italian Touring Car Championship for Alfa Romeo, and was called up to the Ferrari Formula One team for the end of the year, replacing Ivan Capelli to race-test the active suspension car. He made a fair impression, but started both races from the back of the grid for technical reasons. However, 1993 saw more Ferrari testing and touring cars, this time taking the DTM title in Germany for Alfa Romeo.

In 1994, he would have another chance with Ferrari in Formula One, replacing the injured Jean Alesi early in the season. He qualified seventh at the Pacific Grand Prix, but along with Ayrton Senna was eliminated at the first corner by Mika Häkkinen. Then at the San Marino Grand Prix he took second place, but his first points score was overshadowed by the tragic deaths of Roland Ratzenberger and Ayrton Senna. It was back to touring cars with Alfa for the rest of the year, with Larini placing third in the German series.

Alfa would drop off the pace for the next two years, with Larini placing sixth in the German series in 1995, and 11th in the Italian series in 1996. However, 1997 would see his Ferrari connections land him a seat with Sauber, who were using rebranded Ferrari engines. Larini scored a point on his return at the Australian Grand Prix, but left after five races after a series of disagreements with Peter Sauber.

Since then Larini has been a stalwart in touring cars, for Alfa Romeo for many years, and since 2005 for Chevrolet in WTCC. In November, 2009, he announced that he was quitting his professional racing driver career, but will not stop racing completely.

During his World Championship carrer, Nicola Larini was entered into 75 Grand Prix, scoring seven points and one podium.

JJ Lehto
World Championship Years Active: 1989-1994
World Championship Teams: Onyx, Scuderia Italia, Sauber, Benetton

Jyrki Juhani Järvilehto was born on the 31st January 1966, in Espoo, Finland. Like many racing drivers he began in karts at age 8, winning numerous events, before graduating to Formula Ford at the early age of 15. A switch to single seaters saw him dominate the Scandinavian Formula Ford. He then won the British and European Formula 2000 championship in 1987 and went on to win the coveted British Formula 3 title in 1988.

In 1989 Lehto drove in Formula 3000 for Pacific Racing. The season wasn't successful and he didn't score any podium finishes. Järvilehto didn't participate in the last race at Dijon-Prenois.

In 1989 Lehto tested for Ferrari before making his Formula One debut for the Onyx team as a late-season replacement for Bertrand Gachot. Though he failed to prequalify for his first race at Estoril he impressed with his speed in the tough sessions and made his first start in the following meeting. In the wet season finale at Adelaide he ran as high as 5th before retiring with waterlogged electrics.

He stayed with the team for 1990, but over the summer Onyx were sold to Swiss racer turned businessman Peter Monteverdi. Lehto, marked by many as a star of the future, was paired with Gregor Foitek but financial difficulties hampered his season, leading to the team's withdrawal after the Hungarian Grand Prix.

For 1991 he was signed by the ambitious Scuderia Italia team, financed by Beppe Lucchini with a Dallara chassis, Judd V10 engines and Emanuele Pirro in the second car. Due to poor results in 1990 the cars had to prequalify but soon established themselves as decent midfield runners.

In the wet San Marino Grand Prix Lehto impressed by lasting in a race of attrition to finish 3rd, scoring his first F1 points. He impressed elsewhere but did not score again through poor reliability and bad luck. He stayed with the team in 1992, now paired with Pierluigi Martini and using

Ferrari V12 engines but the new Dallara B192 chassis had severe handling problems. Lehto's best result was 7th at Spa, his worst a failure to qualify at the Hungaroring.

He landed the second seat alongside Austrian Karl Wendlinger, at the new, much-anticipated Sauber team for 1993, running Ilmor engines. The season started very well as Lehto survived a late downpour at Kyalami to score 5th place on the team's debut, then finished 4th at Imola despite a late engine failure. However, after a collision with Wendlinger at Monaco his relationship with both his team-mate and Sauber became frosty and his season tailed off with no more points scored.

For 1994 he saw off competition from Michele Alboreto and Luca Badoer to land the second seat at Benetton alongside Michael Schumacher. However, he injured his neck testing the new B194 in pre-season with test driver Jos Verstappen taking his place for the first two rounds of the championship.

Lehto returned to the cockpit for the ill-fated San Marino Grand Prix despite some question marks over his fitness. He qualified 5th but stalled on the grid, his car being struck from behind by Pedro Lamy's Lotus. This led to the safety car period which may have contributed to the death of three-times world champion Ayrton Senna as he run over debris from the accident.

Despite running 3rd in Spain before an engine failure and scoring a point in Canada,it was clear his injuries had not healed fully and he was replaced once again by Verstappen for the French Grand Prix. He returned to the cockpit for the Italian and Portuguese rounds in place of the suspended Schumacher but did not impress and was released entirely soon afterwards when the team signed Johnny Herbert. This freed him up to drive in the last two rounds for Sauber - Wendlinger's own injuries had failed to heal and his previous replacement Andrea de Cesaris was unreachable. Lehto's final Formula 1 drives were again mediocre.

After his Formula One career stalled, Lehto racing in the DTM in 1995 and 1996. Even though rated highly, victories eluded him, but this loss was probably made up by his successes in GT and sports car racing.

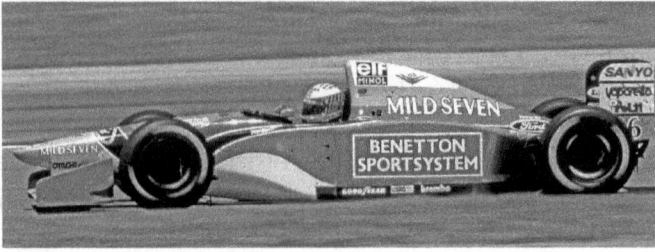

Letho before his engine expired at Barcelona in 1994

He was a late addition to the 1995 edition of the 24 Hours of Le Mans in a McLaren F1 GTR, but he won the race outright, at his third attempt, sharing the car with Yannick Dalmas and Masanori Sekiya. Lehto was an integral part of the win, gaining the lead for the team by driving a few stints during the rainy night. While others were driving cautiously, Lehto was seen to be sliding the car, lapping at times 30sec faster than everyone else.

He had three more guest appearances in the same car the next year, winning another race, before he got picked up by BMW to join the factory squad in the inaugural FIA GT season, partnering Steve Soper. Even though success came initially easily, including a win in front of his home crowd at the Thunder In Helsinki event, the might of Mercedes-Benz caught up with the McLarens and left Lehto conceding the title to former DTM rival Bernd Schneider.

After an unsuccessful 1998 campaign as a Mercedes-Benz factory driver in the American-based single-seater CART series with Team Hogan, Lehto stayed Stateside but returned to the BMW camp, which entered their V12 LMR sportscar racer in the American Le Mans Series, ALMS. Even though he ended up winning four races, Lehto lost the title on the account of a formality (he was not awarded the points gained for winning the 12 Hours of Sebring because he did not have an American racing license at that time). 2000 proved less successful as the near-unbeatable Audi R8 entered the scene.

BMW and Lehto stayed in the ALMS series for 2001, but stepped down to the GT-class with the controversial M3 GTR. The team was virtually unbeatable but Lehto lost out in the championship to the driver he shared the car with, Jörg Müller, as the latter had more fastest laps and laps in the lead to his name.

2002 started with unemployment, but he was picked up by Cadillac as an addition to their Northstar LMP sportscar programme at Le Mans and in the ALMS series. Although the car was not on the pace of the Audi R8s or Panoz LMPs, the car's fortunes did seem to turn for the better when it started to notch up regular podium finishes in the second half of the year. Cadillac's mother company General Motors pulled the plug on the project, leaving Lehto again without a job if it had not been for Champion Racing, who offered him a drive in their Audi R8.

Lehto won four times in 2003, but it was not until the factory Audi squad left the ALMS series that he was finally able to reap full rewards in 2004 and score his first championship success since his 1988 title in the British Formula Three, picking up six victories on the way.

A disappointing second half of the 2005 season prevented him from scoring double championship success, but nonetheless he managed to end his last year in full-time racing on an impressive note when winning both the 12 Hours of Sebring and the 24 Hours of Le Mans again.

In 2006 it was announced the Solaroli team would purchase two Porsche RS Spyders to be entered in the ALMS series. One car would be driven by Lehto, partnered by Johnny Herbert. However, nothing ever materialised.

Lehto did show up at the 2007 edition of the 24 Hours of Daytona to team up with Colin Braun and Max Papis in the Krohn Racing Pontiac-Riley. His first participation in the event was not a success though as the car suffered from a misfire, and after having spent a long time in the pits, finished 17th.

In 2008 he made an unexpected return to the race tracks when he showed up at the Malaysian Grand Prix to drive in the Speedcar support.

JJ Letho was enetered into 70 Grand Prix during his World Championship carrer, finishing on the podium just once, earning 10 points.

Stuart Lewis-Evans
World Championship Years Active: 1957-1958
World Championship Teams: Connaught, Vanwall

Stuart Nigel Lewis-Evans on the 20th April 1930, in Luton, Bedfordshire, England. After leaving school in Bexleyheath he served a three year apprenticeship at Vauxhall Motors, did his National Service as a despatch rider. He began racing in 1951 with a Cooper MkV 500 Formula 3 car, encouraged by and sometimes racing against his father, Lewis "Pop" Evans.

For 1952, Lewis-Evans embarked on a busy season both at home and on the continent with the Mk V. Significant results included second in the London Trophy and Holiday Special at Brands on 14th April, winning the International Trophy at Silverstone on 10th May. This was followed by wins at Brands Hatch and Chimay and a string of podium places.

Over the winter of 1952-'53, the Mk V was modified to capitalise on Stuart's slight build (he was no more than 5'4" and under 9 stone) by producing a 'lowline' body; to keep the car competitive with the latest factory Mk VII. At the Easter Brands Hatch meeting, Stuart took a second in the Easter 25 and Open and third in the Handicap then, on the 3rd May, second in the Senior Final and third in the Seniors V Juniors Handicap A trip to France yielded a win at Orleans on 31st May but he failed to finish the final at Amiens a week later. Later in the season he had several drives in the Francis Beart prepared 'Mk VIIa' Cooper in which he continued to shine, including taking the Redex Trophy at Crystal Palace.

For 1954 Stuart and Les Leston were signed up as Cooper Works Team Drivers in the new Mk VIII. Stuart was second at Kirkistown in March and could only manage third in the Ashmead Tankard at Caste Combe to the Revis of Reg Bicknell and Ivor's private Cooper. At Brough on 17th April, Stuart dominated beating Charlie Headland in his heat and the final and second on the handicap final, and again at Brands on Easter Monday winning the Open Challenge and Senior Finals.

He could only manage a lowly tenth place at Silverstone Daily Express Race on the 15th but improved for a fifth in the Seniors at Brands on 7th June and second in the Seniors on 4th July. On the 10th at Oulton he won his heat of the Beart Trophy but failed to finish in the final and the Grand Prix only brought a lowly thirteenth but at Fairwood on 24th Stuart took third. Back at Brands on 2nd August Stuart took second in the Open Challenge Final. At Crystal Palace on 18th September, he was pipped for second by Bicknell in the Redex Trophy, Bueb winning, then at Brands on 3rd October, he won his heat, with "Pop" second but failed to finish the Open Final and was disqualified from the Senior race. Stuart's year finished with a second to Ivor in the Christmas Trophy at Brands on 27th December.

For 1955, Stuart continued to run his Mk VIII privately and then a Mk IX. Things started badly failing to finish at Kirkistown on 19th March and Snetterton on the 26th but improved a little with a sixth in the Earl of March Trophy at Goodwood, then a win over Don Parker at Charterhall on 16th April and third at Ibsley on the 30th after a tussle with Don. At Brands on 1st May, Stuart won the first final beating George Wicken and Don Parker, then at Silverstone on 7th May in the 50 Mile Race, he took pole and set fastest lap before finishing third to Ivor and Jim after flying over the bank at Copse, on the 29th he took fourth in the Sporting Record Trophy at Brands and fifth in the Redex Trophy at Crystal Palace the following day.

Back at Brands in July, Stuart won the final of the Sporting Record Trophy ahead of George Wicken and Ivor and at Aintree, for the Grand Prix he was denied by a misfire after a race long duel with Jim Russell but could only manage fifth at Crystal Palace on the 30th. A DNF at Snetterton on 13th August was followed by another win in the John Bull Trophy at Oulton Park ahead of Ivor, David Boshier-Jones and Jim and a disappointing sixth at Aintree on 3rd September and a fourth in the final of the Beart Trophy at Brands on the 4th. In the Gold Cup at Oulton on the 24th, Stuart took fifth, Boshier-Jones winning.

1956 started brightly with a second to Tommy Bridger at Snetterton on 25th March and another second to George Wicken at Brands on 3rd April and yet another second at Aintree on the 21st, this time to Colin Davis.

Stuart was second again at Brands in the Sporting Record Trophy to Russell and the symmetry continued in the Redex Trophy on the 21st May to Bueb, with a joint lap record, and at Silverstone to Jim again. It was the same story in the Midsummer 100 at Aintree on 23rd June. Bizarrely, Stuart was awarded joint first with Russell at Mallory Park on 7th July, breaking the run. In the Grand Prix race on the 14th, he took fourth then back to second at Brands on 6th August and finally an outright win in the John Bull Trophy at Oulton over Russell, Parker, Boshier-Jones, Bueb and Allison. Lewis-Evans failed to finish at Snetterton on 2nd September then took fourth in a very close battle at Goodwood, the following week. Another DNF followed at Brands the next day, after winning his heat, then a second to Jim in the Gold Cup on the 22nd and a win on 14th October back at Brands.

In his first Formula One race, the 1957 Monaco Grand Prix, Lewis-Evans finished fourth in an inferior Connaught Type B, beaten only by multiple winners Fangio and Brooks, and Masten Gregory in one of the dominant Maserati 250F cars. Ferrari gave him a drive at Le Mans where he drove two thirds of the race to finish 5th overall

His performance in the Connaught brought him to the attention of Tony Vandervell, owner of the rising Vanwall team, and by the next Grand Prix Lewis-Evans was driving the third Vanwall. The 1957 Vanwall was fast when its engine held together, but not always reliable. Lewis-Evans took his first F1 win at the year's non-championship Moroccan Grand Prix, and pole position at the final World Championship event, the Italian Grand Prix.

The 1958 Formula One season would prove to be a much better year, at least initially, for the entire Vanwall team. Principal drivers Stirling Moss and Tony Brooks took three victories each, and Lewis-Evans added to the team's points haul with podium finishes in the Belgian and Portuguese events. He also took pole position at the Dutch Grand Prix, but failed to finish in the race. This was not his only retirement of the year - indeed his only other finish, although points-scoring, was a fourth place at the British Grand Prix.

He also drove Aston Martin in endurance events, Elva and Willment in short sports car races, the B R P Cooper-Climax in F2 in which he did consistently well, and kept the faith with a now ailing Formula 3 whenever his other commitments permitted.

Lewis-Evans crashed heavily at the dusty Ain-Diab circuit during the season-ending Moroccan Grand Prix. On lap 42 his Vanwall's engine seized and sent him lurching into barriers at high speed, and his car burst into flames. He was airlifted back to the UK in Tony Vandervell's Viscount airliner and was admitted to Sir Archibald McIndoe's East Grinstead specialist burns unit, but died in hospital of his burns six days after the accident.

His death cast a pall over Vanwall's victory in the 1958 International Cup for F1 Manufacturers, an achievement to which Lewis-Evans had contributed significantly.

Stuart Lewis-Evans participated in 14 World Championship Grand Prix, finishing on the podium twice and socring 16 points.

John Love
World Championship Years Active: 1962-1972
World Championship Teams: Cooper, Brabham, Lotus, March, Surtees

Born on the 7th December 1924, in Bulawayo, Southern Rhodesia, John Maxwell Lineham Love served in World War II before starting to race motorcycles in the 1950s.

Love then turned to racing a pre-war Riley Special sports car before buying an ex-works Jaguar D-type. Using this he was able to score better results and he finished sceond in the Angolan Grand Prix in 1959 and took on the visiting Europeans in the South African GP at East London in 1960, in which he finished seventh. That summer he tried racing in Europe, driving a Lola Formula 2 car at Chimay before returning to Africa, where he won the Angolan GP in his D-Type.

In 1961 he went back to Europe and raced in Formula Junior for Ken Tyrrell alongside South African Tony Maggs. The pair were very successful and in 1962 Love was taken on to race Tyrrell's Mini-Coopers in the British Touring Car Championship where he won the title. He also raced in Formula Junior but a bad crash at Albi left him with a badly broken arm, so he decided to return to Africa and concentrate on his John Love Motors garage business.

Nevertheless, he became a regular contestant in the South African Grand Prix and was leading the 1967 event at Kyalami in his Climax-engined Cooper when a misfire prompted him to make a precautionary stop for extra fuel and he dropped back to finish second behind the works Cooper-Maserati of Pedro Rodríguez.

Love would dominate racing in southern Africa in the 1960s, winning the South African Formula One Championship six times in succession from 1964 to 1969. He would also win his home race, the Rhodesian Grand Prix, six times. Love owned the Jaguar dealership in Bulawayo and had his own stock car racing team in the 1980s. He died of cancer in 2005.

During his World Championship carrer John Love was entered to ten Grand Prix, finishing on the podium once, scoring six points.

Tony Maggs

World Championship Years Active: 1961 – 1965
World Championship Teams: Lotus, Cooper, BRM

The son of a wealthy farmer and businessman, Anthony Francis O'Connell "Tony" Maggs was born on the 9th February 1937 in Pretoria, South Africa. He impressed in Formula Junior that year driving Gemini machinery, claiming his first victory in a British Formula Junior race in a John Davy Championship round at Snetterton in October. Later that month finished third in the following round behind Peter Arundell and Jim Clark.

He shot to fame in Ken Tyrrell's Formula Junior Cooper-Austin team in 1961, sharing the European Championship with Jo Siffert. He was invited into the Formula One team for 1962–1963, finishing second in the French Grand Prix both years, but was dropped at the end of 1963.

He completed the 1965 South African Grand Prix and later drove in some Formula Two races later in 1965 before an accident at Pietermaritzburg in a Lotus 22 twin-cam resulted in the death of eight-year-old spectator Michael Twyman.

Thereafter Maggs quit racing, concentrating instead on farming in the Zontspanberg region of the Northern Transvaal, surviving a light aircraft accident some years later in which his farm manager was killed.

Tony Maggs started 25 world championship grands prix, scoring 26 points and finishing on the podium three times.

Umberto Maglioli
World Championship Years Active: 1953 – 1957
World Championship Teams: Ferrari, Maserati, Porsche

Umberto Maglioli was born on the 5th June 1928, in Bioglio, Vercelli, Italy and was noticed in motor racing for the first time in 1951 when he and his mentor Giovanni Bracco drove a stock Lancia Aurelia B20 to 2nd OA in the Mille Miglia. After he won the 1953 Targa Florio, he was called into the Scuderia Ferrari and proved "worthy" in January 1954 when he took the win in the 1000 Kilometers of Buenos Aires.

By this point Maglioli had already had his first experiences in Formula One driving: He took part in his home Grand Prix at Monza in 1953. But Maglioli never became that successful in piloting single seaters as he did with the sports cars, hence his Formula One entries were only a few

He finished third in the 1954 Italian Grand Prix (sharing with Froilan Gonzalez) and third in the 1955 Argentine Grand Prix (sharing with Giuseppe Farina and Maurice Trintignant). In 1956 he had three races in a Maserati 250F and his final Grand Prix outing came at the Nurburgring in a 1.5-liter Porsche the following season.

Umberto Maglioli left the Scuderia Ferrari in 1956 and found a new home at Porsche; he stayed with the Germans for more than a decade, his last great victory dating 1968 when he won the Targa Florio in a Porsche 907/8 which he shared with Vic Elford.

He passed away on the 7th February 1999.

During his World Championship carrer, Umberto Maglioli was entered in ten races, finishing n the podium twice with a total score of 3.5 points.

Willy Mairesse
World Championship Years Active: 1960 - 1965
World Championship Teams: Ferrari, ENB, Lotus, Scuderia Centro Sud

Willy Mairesse was born on the 1st October 1928 in Momignies, right on the Franco-Belgian border in the province of Hainaut, Mairesse did not start competing until he was 25 when he joined a friend in a Porsche 356 on the Liege-Rome-Liege race in 1953. Having got a taste for the sport he entered his own Peugeot 203 the following year and in 1955, using the same car, he finally won the 1300cc Class. The following season he acquired a Mercedes 300SL and started racing as well as rallying, and finished third in the GT race supporting the German Grand Prix at the Nurburgring. The same year he won the Liege-Rome-Liege and caught the attention of the Equipe Nationale Belge, which was being run at the time by Ferrari importer Jacques Swaters. He drove for the team in 1957, 1958 and 1959 in sports cars but had few results beyond a second place in a Ferrari Berlinetta in the 12 Hours of Reims.

A battle with fellow countryman Olivier Gendebien on the Tour de France automobile in 1959 brought Mairesse to the attention of Enzo Ferrari and he was signed as a Ferrari driver for 1960. At the French GP he qualified fifth and at Monza in September he finished third in a Ferrari 1-2-3. That year he placed well on the Targa Florio and won the Tour de France automobile. He won the Tour again in 1961 and finished second at Le Mans and raced three times in F1.

Mairesse and Mike Parkes of England finished second to Phil Hill and Olivier Gendebien at the 1961 24 Hours of Le Mans. Driving a Ferrari, Mairesse and Parkes also eclipsed the previous Le Mans record, covering 2,758.66 miles.

Mairesse qualified fifth for the 1962 Belgian Grand Prix at Spa, Belgium. The pole was won by Graham Hill in a BRM. During the event Mairesse and the Lotus of Trevor Taylor dueled for more than an hour, passing and repassing a number of times each lap. The two cars came together at more than 100 miles per hour in the long, sweeping, left-hand Blanchimont Turn. Mairesse car went off to the left, careening into a hillside behind a ditch, and caught fire after flipping over. He was thrown out of his Ferrari and his shoes and the legs of his trousers were torn off. He was conscious, despite numerous scrapes, cuts, and burns. Mairesse was loaded into an ambulance and transported to a hospital. In a race in which only twelve of twenty-one starters finished, Mairesse came in fourth in the 1962 Italian Grand Prix. He was only a car length ahead of Giancarlo Baghetti.

In the 1963 12 Hours of Sebring Mairesse and Nino Vacarella placed second after Ludovico Scarfiotti and John Surtees. Thereafter, Surtees and Mairesse led for the 15 hours of the first 18 hours of the 1963 24 Hours of Le Mans before the car caught fire while Mairesse was driving. Mairesse escaped injury. Mairesse car crashed during the 1963 German Grand Prix. The Ferrari turned over multiple times after swerving off the track. He was rushed to the hospital with a broken arm. He did not return to racing until the end of 1964

He was triumphant in the non-championship Grand Prix of Angola in 1964, run at Luanda. Mairesse and Jean Beurlys of France finished third at the 1965 24 Hours of Le Mans. Masten Gregory and Jochen Rindt captured the 1965 24 Hours of Le Mans. Mairesse and Beurlys finished third in a Ferrari 275 GTB winning the GT category in its debut at Le Mans.

In April 1966 Surtees and Parkes won the 1,000 kilometer Monza Auto Race. Mairesse and Herbert Mueller of Switzerland came in third in a Ford sports car, two laps behind. He won the Targa Florio again in a Scuderia Filipinetti Porsche 906 but spent less time racing and concentrated on building up a business he had started. His last major result was at Le Mans in 1967 when he finished third. A year later, driving a private Ford GT40, he suffered a serious accident when the door latch of the car failed and the door flew up. Mairesse lost control and hit the wall and spent the next two weeks in a coma. He never fully recovered from his injuries and, sadly, committed suicide in a hotel room in Ostend in September the following year.

During his World Championship carrer, Willy Mairesse was entered into 13 Grand Prix, finishing on the podium once scoring seven points.

Robert Manzon
World Championship Years Active: 1950 – 1956
World Championship Teams: Gordini, Ferrari

Robert Manzon was born on the 12th Apri, 1917 in Marseille, France and started his working life as a mechanic before being a distributor of diesel engine parts. He was fond of car racing but World War II put an end to his hopes of becoming a driver, at least for a few years!

In 1947, at the age of 30, he bought a Cisitalia D46 to participate in the Robert Benoist Cup. Despite it being his very first race: he finished 3rd behind Wimille and De Saugé/Sommer, but ahead of Schell and Amédée Gordini himself. In fact, his first season was so good that Amédée Gordini, the main French racing car manufacturer of the time, decided to hire Manzon.

The following year began with a 2nd place in Perpignan with the Cisitalia and a 3rd in Geneva, Manzon's first race with a Gordini. Unfortunately, both results were to become the best ones of the entire season as he faced the same problems that hampered him during his career with Gordini: the cars were light, fast but unreliable. Yet, he did his best but the results were not as good as they should have been regarding the value of the man.

However, Robert Manzon quickly gained the reputation of a quick and tenacious driver. Moreover, his technical skills were really appreciated while he also proved his courage by saving Trintignant's life when Pétoulet's Gordini made a looping. The driver fell on the track while his car drove as far as an embankment, then back to the track towards the floored Trintignant. As Trintignant relates in his biography: "At this moment Manzon arrived at about 200km/h. If he had passed over me, he could have gotten out of this situation. But he did not hesitate to hit my car, risking his own life to save mine. Heaven thank him for his generous act and he was not injured. Ten years later I have not forgotten - these are things that cannot be forgotten – and I am still saying 'Thank you Manzon'." 1949 was similar to 1948 - retirement was followed by retirement.

In 1950 the first World F1 Championship saw the light. Manzon took part in the Monaco GP. Unfortunately he was among the nine drivers who had an accident at the Tabac bend. He even suffered a jaw injury but not seriously.

He finished 3rd at the dangerous Bremgarten track in Switzerland in a non-championship race and 4th in the French GP. This was an excellent performance given the poor reliabilityof his Gordini.

Early 1951 proved to be a disappointing experience. From March to June he took part in seven races: he retired in six of them! 1952 can be regarded as one of Manzon's best seasons. He was 3rd on the Swiss GP grid and challenged Taruffi in this first Championship race at Bremgarten. Unfortunately a holed radiator forced him to give up, handing Taruffi an easy win. One month later, at Le Mans, Amédée Gordini had a single goal: victory. So he decided to team Manzon with Behra. This team was considered a favourite for the 1952 race. Then, three hours after the start, the Jaguars retired and Manzon-Behra became the leaders. Gordini really thought his dream was coming true but it lasted "only" nine hours: at 3 AM the French drivers had to retire.

The season ended in Italy where Manzon qualified 4th, just behind his friend Maurice Trintignant. Robert drove a good race, going up and down between 6th and 3rd place, fighting with Farina and Bonetto, until mid-race, when he was forced to pit, once again missing an opportunity to score three or four points.

1954 was better than the previous year. Manzon was hired by Louis Rosier to drive a Ferrari 625, even though he drove for Lancia on some occasions. In July he finished 3rd in theFrench Grand Prix after a tremendous fight with Bira's Maserati. He passed the prince a few yards from the line, both lapped by the unbeatable Mercedes cars of Fangio and Kling. Both Manzon and Bira scored their very last Championship points.

At the end of 1954 Amédée Gordini contacted Robert Manzon to convince him to "return home" for 1955. Manzon accepted. Nevertheless, the situation had not changed - the team were still in dire straits and unable to manufacture a competitive car. The results were poor as the French driver's best result was a 5th place in Bordeaux, a minor F1 race.

1956 was his very last season, as he was 39 and unwilling to accept the dangers. He continued with Gordini, and the season proved to be as troublesome as the previous years; things could not improve given the difficulties of the French team. In Monaco he was about to finish 5th but the engine of his car broke ten laps from the end. His team mate, Hermano Da Silva Ramos, took this opportunity to score the only points he ever scored in a F1 Championship, the last points scored by a Gordini. At Le Mans, Manzon and Guichet retired after seven hours while they were 6th.

He participated in 29 Formula One World Championship Grands Prix, debuting on May 21, 1950. He achieved 2 podiums, and scored a total of 16 championship points. He is the last living racing driver to take part and score points in the first season of F1.

Onofre Marimon
World Champtionship Years Active: 1951 - 1954
World Championship Teams: Maserati

Onofre Agustín Marimón was born on the 23rd December, 1923 in Zárate, Buenos Aires, Argentina. He took part in numerous sport car races including the Le Mans 24 Hours and Mille Miglia, with a best result of 6th at the 1000km in Buenos Aires for Maserati in 1954.

After some privately funded Grand Prix races in 1951, Marimon joined the works Maserati team in 1953. He stood in for Fangio in some early-season non-championship races, and when Fangio left to join Mercedes he found himself leading the team. He finished an excellent third in the British Grand Prix, ahead of Fangio, and seemed destined for great things, but he was killed instantly in a crash at the Nurburgring during practice for the German Grand Prix in 1954.

His Maserati left the Nürburgring race course at the Breidscheid curve near the Adenauer Bridge after he lost control attempting to improve his qualifying time. He died at the bottom of a steep and treacherous incline.. He was pinned underneath the car as it came to rest on its top with the wheels spinning in the air.

He participated in 11 Formula One World Championship Grands Prix, debuting on July 1, 1951. He achieved 2 podiums, and scored a total of 8 championship points.

Jack McGrath
World Championship Years Active: 1950 – 1955
World Championship Teams: Kurtis Kraft

Born in Los Angeles, California on the 8th October 1919, John James "Jack" McGrath grew up in South Pasadena, California, and was a major player in the "mighty midgets" at Los Angeles' Gilmore Speedway in the late 1940s. McGrath won the first CRA (California Roadster Association) championship in 1946 and was dubbed "King of the Hot Rods." His efforts, along with those of friend and teammate Manuel Ayulo, helped establish track roadsters as viable race cars. The west coast roadsters evolved into sprint cars in the early 1950s.

Major wins at the AAA national level included the 1951 Syracuse and Langhorne 100 mile races, the 1952 Syracuse 100, and the 1953 Milwaukee 200. He finished the 1952 and 1953 AAA championship seasons in second place, and led the first 44 laps of the 1954 Indianapolis 500.

McGrath's storied 26-lap duel with Bill Vukovich in the ill-fated 1955 Indianapolis 500 ended when the magneto on his Hinckle Special Kurtis 500C's Offenhauser engine failed on lap 54. Fellow Californian and two-time Indy winner Vukovich died three laps later in a chain-reaction crash while in the lead.

"The Splendid Splinter" himself was killed in the final AAA dirt track race of the 1955 season at Manzanita Speedway in Phoenix, Arizona.

Jack McGrath competed in six Grand Prix, finishing on the podium twice and scoring 9 points.

Carlos Menditeguy
World Championship Years Active: 1953 – 1960
World Championship Teams: Gordini, Maserati, Scuderia Centro Sud

Carlos Alberto Menditeguy was born in Buenos Aires on the 10th August 1914. Menditeguy was a talented all-round sportsman who was judged to be amongst the world's top six polo players when he came to Europe on the back of the Fangio/Gonzalez bandwagon of the early 1950s. Wild and fearless behind the wheel, he was also brutally hard on the machinery. He was an Argentine Grand Prix regular but never spent a full season on the Championship trail. His best result was third in the 1957 Buenos Aires race.

After the 1960 Argentince Grand Prix, Menditeguy concentrated on other sports. In polo he reached the highest possible handicap of 10, before becoming a sucesful horse trainer.

Menditguy died on the 27th April, 1973 after an operation for treatment after a heart-attack, but he was also suffering from diabetes and Parkinson's.

He entered 11 Formula One World Championship Grands Prix, achieving one podium, and scoring a total of nine championship points.

Stefano Modena
World Championahip Years Active: 1987 - 1992
World Championship Teams: Brabham, EuroBrun, Tyrrell, Jordan

Born on the 12th May, 1963 in Modena, Italy, Stefano raced in the Italian Formula Ford national series for two seasons before joining Euroracing in his domestic Formula 3 series in 1985, placing 15th in an Alfa Romeo engined Ralt.

For 1986 he switched to Team Seresina's Reynard chassis and scored three wins to finish 4th overall, also placing 2nd at the Monaco support race and winning a round of the European series at Imola. In 1987 he joined Onyx for the Formula 3000 series, winning three rounds and being crowned as champion.

Modena was offered a one-off drive for Brabham in the final race of the 1987 Formula One season. While he impressed by qualifying 15th at Adelaide his inexperience with the turbo charged BMW engine saw him stop three times to replace flat-spotted tyres before retiring with exhaustion before mid-distance. He was intent on becoming a full-time Grand Prix driver for 1988, testing for Benetton before the season. However, for a full-time drive he had to join the new EuroBrun team. The car was not competitive however, and Modena was consigned to run near the rear of the field for the year.

1989 saw Brabham reform after a sabbatical in 1988, now owned by Swiss businessman Joachim Luthi but featuring a lot of the same staff as in 1987. Modena was offered one of the seats, driving alongside Martin Brundle. Equipped with Pirelli qualifying tyres Modena frequently qualified well, starting inside the top 10 on eight occasions despite using a Judd V8 engine.

However, the car wasn't reliable - though Modena's sole points finish would come with 3rd place at the Monaco Grand Prix. Before the 1990 season Luthi would be imprisoned for fraud and Brabham endured a difficult year with ownership problems.

He finally got his big break when he was signed as replacement for Ferrari-bound Tyrrell team leader Jean Alesi. With a healthy group of sponsors, 1989 spec Honda V10 engines, Pirelli tyres and a development of the successful 020 chassis much was expected of the combination, with some predicting race wins.

While his season started off with 4th place at Phoenix many of the front runners had retired without Modena getting near them. The wet conditions at Imola saw similar attrition allowing Modena to reach 3rd place before transmission failure. The following race at Monaco saw an even better performance as he qualified on the front row alongside World Champion Ayrton Senna, harrying the McLaren driver until being held up in traffic and suffering a violent engine failure.

A steadier run in Canada was rewarded with 2nd place after Nigel Mansell retired on the final lap. After that Modena's form dropped off badly as Pirelli struggled to develop a consistent race tyre while the heavily Honda engines made the 020 chassis difficult to balance. While Modena continued to qualify frequently in the top half of the grid he struggled in races, only scoring one more point for 6th place at the Japanese Grand Prix.

The season was considered a huge disappointment, and Modena left Tyrrell for Jordan the following season. The team had made a strong debut in 1991 and many considered Modena was lucky to land a drive with them. However, their car was hindered by the underpowered Yamaha V12 engine and Modena struggled all season. He failed to qualify for four races and became unpopular with his team for his lack of mechanical sympathy and moody behaviour compared to team-mate Mauricio Gugelmin. Despite scoring the team's only point of the year at the final round in Australia he was unable to find a drive in Grand Prix racing for 1993.

Instead he drove for Alfa Romeo in the Italian and German touring categories from 1993 to 1999, winning occasional races but never looking like winning a title. After a year with Opel in 2000 he retired from motorsport.

Stefano Modena participated in 81 Formula One Grands Prix. He achieved 2 podiums, and scored a total of 17 championship points.

Tiago Monteiro
World Championship Years Active: 2005 – 2006
World Championship Teams: Jordan, MF1

Tiago Vagaroso da Costa Monteiro was born on 24th July 1976 in Porto, Portugal and was inspired by his father to begin racing, and drove in the 1997 French Porsche Carrera Cup. He took five wins and five pole positions to become B-class champion and rookie of the year. In 1998, he competed in the French F3 Championship, finishing 12th overall and taking the rookie of the year award. He continued in the championship in 1999, taking one win and three other podium positions to finish sixth overall.

In 2000, Monteiro again competed in French F3, this time finishing second in the championship after taking four wins throughout the season. He also competed in the single Formula 3 European Championship double-header race, finishing second overall with one win at Spa-Francorchamps. He also competed in a couple of one-off events, coming second in the Korea Super Prix and ninth at the famous Macau Grand Prix.

In the Lamborghini Super Trophy, he achieved the fastest lap at Magny-Cours, and took pole position and the fastest lap at Laguna Seca. In 2001, Monteiro again finished second overall in the French F3 Championship after taking six pole positions, four wins and four podiums. Also competing in the French GT Championship, he managed four pole positions, two class wins and five podium finishes in the GTB class. A one-off entry in the Formula France series saw him win both races, and in the Andros Trophy, he did one fastest lap with a best finishing position of fourth.

In 2002, he stepped up to the F3000 Championship with the Super Nova team, taking five top-ten finishes on his way to 12th in the championship standings. He also completed the Renault F1 Driver Development Scheme, and had his first taste of a Formula One car, testing with the Renault team at Barcelona. In 2003, he joined Fittipaldi Dingman Racing for the Champ Car World Series, achieving a pole position in Mexico City and leading two races. He finished the year with 10 top-ten finishes, scoring 29 points to rank 15th overall in the championship. Monteiro was signed up as an official Minardi F1 test driver for the 2004 season, but also competed in the Nissan World Series with Carlin Motorsport. He was named Rookie of the Year after finishing second in the championship behind Heikki Kovalainen, and was ranked fifth in Autosport magazine's top ten drivers in the Formula One "breeding ground" championships.

Ater the Midland Group bought Jordan Grand Prix, Monteiro was announced as a full-time race driver alongside Indian Narain Karthikeyan for the 2005 season.In the United States Grand Prix he achieved his first podium finish in controversial circumstances when all but three teams pulled out due to concerns over tyre safety (the Michelin-equipped teams pulled out of the race, not taking their place on the grid. The Bridgestone teams were the only ones to run). Monteiro finished third out of just six drivers.

At the podium ceremony, at which none of the scheduled dignitaries were present, Ferrari drivers Michael Schumacher and Rubens Barrichello quietly accepted their awards, and quickly exited. However, Monteiro stayed behind to celebrate his first podium finish alone amid the booing fans, a decision which although initially controversial, was later met with some sympathy from the Formula One fraternity.

Shortly before the 2005 Turkish Grand Prix, Monteiro suffered toothache that was severe enough to prevent him taking part in the race. However, his team principal Colin Kolles, a qualified dentist, performed emergency root canal surgery, and Monteiro was fit enough to race, which saw him finish 15th following a collision with Juan Pablo Montoya, which resulted in the Colombian running wide on the penultimate lap and losing second place to Fernando Alonso, thus preventing Montoya's McLaren team scoring its first 1–2 finish since the 2000 Austrian Grand Prix.

In 2006 Midland re-signed Monteiro to partner Dutchman Christijan Albers. The two endured a largely uncompetitive season, with their M16 car not even scoring a single point, and the pair were regularly outpaced during the year by Toro Rosso and the occasional Super Aguri. In the 18 races, Monteiro retired from six, with his best finish being at the wet-dry

Hungarian Grand Prix where he finished ninth, just outside the points-scoring positions with Albers finishing behind in tenth.

It was announced later that year that Monteiro would not be driving for the newly-renamed Spyker team in 2007. The highly-rated German Adrian Sutil was instead signed on a multi-year contract.

Monteiro then joined the SEAT Sport team and would drive in the World Touring Car Championship (WTCC) with a SEAT León. He was forced to wait until the second round of the 2007 season at Zandvoort to make his debut, as the contract was signed a few days before the season opener in Curitiba. However, he took three podium finishes and a pole position during a successful first season in which he was ranked 11th overall.

In 2008 driving the TDi version of the SEAT León, he took his first win at Puebla in Mexico, and later in the season he won the second race on home ground at Estoril in Portugal. He stayed with SEAT in 2009, and scored two podiums in Valencia and Brno en route to finishing 9th overall in the drivers standings, contributing to SEAT winning the manufacturers championship.

Monteiro raced with the semi-privateer SR Sport team in the 2010 WTCC season driving a SEAT León TDI, following the withdrawal of SEAT Sport at the end of the previous season. For 2011, he again drove for SUNRED Engineering, where he was partnered by rookies Aleksei Dudukalo and Pepe Oriola, as well as 2010 teammates Michel Nykjaer, Fredy Barth and Gabriele Tarquini. He remains with the team for 2012 under the "Tuenti Racing Team" banner.

Monteiro joined the Honda Racing team from the 2012 Race of Japan and then for 2013, racing the new Honda Civic with team mate Gabriele Tarquini.He scored the first podium finish for the Honda Civic in the WTCC at the 2012 Guia Race of Macau, finishing third in race one.

Tiago Monteiro competed in 37 World Championship Grand Prix, finishing on the podium once, scoring seven points.

Gianni Morbidelli
World Championship Years Active: 1990 - 1997
World Championship Teams: Scuderia Italia, Minardi, Ferrari, Footwork, Sauber

The son of Giancarlo Morbidelli, the founder of Morbidelli motorcycle company, Gianni Morbidelli was born on the 13th January 1968 in Pesaro, Italy. He starting karting in 1980, spending six years until he became the EUR-AM championship winner, before moving to Italian Formula Three.

He became Italian Formula 3 and Formula 3 European Cup champion in 1989, as well as winning two races in Italian Touring Cars. He then moved to the Scuderia Italia Formula One team, doing the first 2 races of the 1990 F1 season as stand-in for Emanuele Pirro, before concentrating on Formula 3000. He won a single race and finished 5th in the 1990 championship, as well as undertaking test driver duties for Scuderia Ferrari for that year.

Resuming his F1 career at the end of the 1990 season, Morbidelli competed in the final two races of the season with Minardi, where he remained until the end of 1992. He briefly joined Ferrari for the 1991 Australian Grand Prix, drafted in after Alain Prost left the team, where Morbidelli earned his first Formula One points, earning half a point for 6th after a rain-shortened race.

A lack of sponsorship led to him leaving Minardi to rejoin Italian Touring Cars for 1993, where he drove an Alfa Romeo 155 to two wins for Alfa Corse, before being hired by Footwork Arrows for 1994. He managed four point-scoring positions in two years with the team, including his only podium place finish in the 1995 Australian Grand Prix, earning third place in a race of high attrition. Morbidelli became Footwork Arrows' most successful driver, with a total of eight points for the team.

Morbidelli also competed in the Italian Superturismo Championship for 1995, scoring two race wins, and, after spending a year out in 1996 testing for Jordan, gained another podium that year. Back in Formula

166

One for 1997, he raced in several mid-season events for Sauber as a replacement for Nicola Larini. He scored no points and was not classified in the championship for that year. His unsuccessful season, and two injuries by separate testing accidents, led to Morbidelli retiring from Formula One racing.

In 1998 he drove for Volvo in the British Touring Car Championship, but was not as competitive as his team-mate Rickard Rydell, who won that year's title. His only competitive showing was in the summer meeting at Thruxton, where he charged from near the back of the back to finish fourth, passing many cars in the process. Morbidelli then spent several years in various European touring car series', with a high point in the 2001 European Touring Car Championship, where he raced the BMW 320i to fifth place in the championship, winning the last race at Estoril. Morbidelli raced in the Italian round of the 2004 season in a SEAT Toledo, but scored no points and did not contest in further meetings.

He then drove a Lamborghini in several grand tourer races in 2005, and moved back to touring cars for 2006. Competing in the World Touring Car Championship for N-Technology, he managed two second places in an Alfa Romeo 156. Not as competitive as when he was driving the BMW, he moved back to GT racing for 2007, winning two races in the ADAC GT Masters series.

He has had considerable success in the Italian Superstars Championship, where Morbidelli won the title with both Audi RS4 and BMW M3 three years in a row from 2007. The short-lived Speedcar Series gave him another championship title, where he won the 2008–09 championship. The season featured a close fight with defending champion Johnny Herbert, with Morbidelli finishing one place ahead in the final round to win the title. Another Superstars title followed in 2013 with Audi Sport Italia.

During his Formula One carrer, Gianni Morbidelli wasentered into 70 Grand Prix, finishing on the podium once scoring eight and a half points.

Roberto Moreno
World Championship Years Active: 1982 - 1995
World Championsahip Teams: Lotus, AGS, Coloni, EuroBrun, Benetton, Jordan, Minardi, Andrea Moda, Forti Corse

Roberto Pupo Moreno was born on the 11th February, 1959 in Rio de Janeiro, Brazil. A friend since childhood with Nelson Piquet, he first raced in Formula One as a stand in for Nigel Mansell at Lotus at the 1982 Dutch Grand Prix after Mansell broke his wrist in the previous Grand Prix at Canada. Underprepared, Moreno failed to qualify. It took his reputation a while to recover from this poor showing, but in 1987 he was called up to replace Pascal Fabre for the AGS team at the 1987 Japanese Grand Prix. In the following Australian Grand Prix, he drove the ungainly JH22 to 6th place for his, and the team's, first ever point.

Following his Formula 3000 Championship in 1988, he signed a testing contract with Ferrari, who helped him land a racing drive with Coloni. The car was never competitive, however, and Moreno only made the grid four times.

Initially, 1990 seemed to be even less promising, with Moreno signing for the nosediving EuroBrun outfit, qualifying for just 2 out of 14 races. However, shortly after being informed the team would not be competing in the last two rounds of the season, he was contacted by Benetton to drive their second car, with Alessandro Nannini having lost a hand in a helicopter crash.

Moreno finished an excellent 2nd on his Benetton debut in the 1990 Japanese Grand Prix, behind childhood friend and team-mate Nelson Piquet, although this result was helped by most other top cars dropping out, Alain Prost and Ayrton Senna famously colliding at the first corner.

For 1991, Benetton signed Moreno full-time. However, the Benetton B191, on Pirelli tyres, was not as competitive as anticipated, and Moreno's best results were 4th place at the Monaco Grand Prix and the Belgian Grand Prix, a race in which he set the fastest lap.

The latter would be his last race for the team before he was controversially paid off and dropped in favour of Michael Schumacher.

There are rumours to this day that Moreno was purposely driving within himself for the whole season in order to not show Piquet up. As it was, Moreno was offered the vacant Jordan drive for the 1991 Italian Grand Prix and the following race in Portugal, and raced for Minardi in the final race of the season.

Moreno in the 1991 Benetton-Ford

For the 1992 season, he found himself back with the minnows, signing for Andrea Moda. The outfit had risen from the ashes of Coloni, and after two non-starting races with Alex Caffi and Enrico Bertaggia, decided to start over with Moreno and Perry McCarthy. Moreno and McCarthy faced an uphill struggle, with the uncompetitive team scrambling to even get to most races. Moreno would only qualify the under-tested, under-funded car once, for the Monaco Grand Prix, before the team collapsed following team owner Andrea Sassetti's arrest at the Belgian Grand Prix.

He spent the next two years racing Italian and French Touring Cars, and also attempted to qualify for the 1994 Indianapolis 500. 1995 saw a return to Formula One, with the ambitious Forti team. Moreno's Brazilian heritage helped him land the drive. Sadly, their car was laughably slow, and Moreno's best result was 14th in the Belgian Grand Prix. He would exit Formula One crashing into the pitlane wall at the Australian Grand Prix.

1996 would see Moreno resume his Champ Car career, as he raced a Payton-Coyne Lola-Ford, finishing 3rd at Michigan. For 1997 he drove for three teams, earning the epithet "Supersub", with his best result of 5th at Detroit in a Newman-Haas Swift-Ford. 1998 was more barren, with just three drives, though he came 6th at Twin Ring Motegi in the Project Indy Reynard Motorsport-Mercedes.

The following season again saw him take two different teams (Newman/Haas and PacWest), with two 4th places his best. In 1999 he also made his first Indy Racing League start at Phoenix International Raceway finishing 6th and returned to the Indianapolis 500 after a 13 year absence finishing 20th for Truscelli Team Racing. 2000 finally saw him land a full-time drive in the Patrick Racing Reynard Motorsport-Ford, and he led the series for much of the distance, eventually ranking 3rd overall.

Moreno won his first Champ Car race at Cleveland, and in a scene scarcely seen in motor racing, the emotional Moreno wept openly. It had been his first race victory since his Formula 3000 victory twelve years earlier. He won again for Patrick Racing at Vancouver the following year, but was less consistent and dropped to 13th in the standings.

In 2003 he drove for Herdez Competition, taking his Lola-Cosworth to 2nd at Miami, and announced his retirement from motorsport at the end of the year.

In August 2006, Moreno became the first driver to test the new Panoz-built Champ Car. After running thousands of miles of testing in the Panoz DP01, Moreno got a chance to race it at the 2007 Grand Prix of Houston, substituting for the injured Alex Figge at Pacific Coast Motorsports.

Roberto Moreno participated in 75 Formula One Grands Prix, achieved 1 podium, and scored a total of 15 championship points

Mike Nazaruk
World Championship Years Active: 1951 - 1953
World Championsahip Teams: Turner, Kurtis Kraft

Originally from upstate New York, Mike Nazaruk was born on the 2nd October 1921. He moved to Long Island to find work with Grumman Aircraft, and settled in North Bellmore, near East Meadow and Hempstead. What he also found there within walking distance was Freeport Stadium, a busy one-fifth-of-a-mile oval where the Midgets of the American Racing Drivers Club filled the stands on a regular basis.

By 1948, Nazaruk was racing midgets in what was the Golden Age of Midget Racing, and Freeport Stadium was the hub of the Midget world.

By 1949, the so-called "Midget craze" was dying, and drivers as well as owners began looking for another way to make a living. Luckily for him, his team boss Mike Caruso was also fancying the leap to AAA, and got one of his Midgets "stretched" into a Sprint Car, complete with a supercharged Midget engine! The car was a little bit late in getting ready, but when it was there was no stopping "Iron Mike" and his little hand grenade: in the first six starts, they collected three wins, two seconds and one third place finish, besides two fast times in qualifying!

In five years, he would win nineteen AAA Big Car main events and finish in the top 5 in points six times, alongside fourteen AAA Midget feature wins.

If the 1951 "Indy 500″ had been the "Indy 600″ instead, he might've become the first rookie winner since George Souders, but even so the pundits were thoroughly impressed. His second place would be his bestfinisah at Indy, at a time when the race was part of the World Championship. Within a year, he would team up with millionaire car owner Lee Elkins, perhaps the nuttiest eccentric ever to own a racing car, commencing a love/hate relationship that took them both to the brink of despair, at times.

He was always at his best during the really long grinds, the 100-lappers on dirt as well as on asphalt, the latter due to his early training at Freeport, no doubt. But still, nobody could believe how quickly and easily he took to the high-banked ovals of the Midwest, where he was soon to become a real master of the art.

He'd use the same attitude, a kind of macho stance, to intimidate other drivers, whom he would look straight in the eye, with an icy stare, and declare "Don't get between Nazaruk and the checkered flag – you won't like what happens!" But, most famously, he was the same kind of tough bastard against himself: with his super-aggressive style of driving, he crashed quite frequently, but he never once missed a race through injury, even when lesser men would have considered retirement from the sport!

In 1953 he was thrown from his flipping Sprint Car at the Minnesota State Fair, except for his left foot which got entangled in the cockpit, so that Mike got dragged along down the track, hanging from the car like a rag doll from the hand of weeping toddler – a hush fell over the crowd, fearing the worst.

Amazingly, when he came to, he was found to have broken no bones at all, but basically he had been skinned alive; and twisted every joint in his body. When they dressed his wounds at the hospital, he was told to rest for a week, at which he exclaimed "Oh no, I can't do that!", rose to his feet and walked gingerly out the door, calling for a taxi to the track, from where he single-handedly drove back to his seasonal residence in Indianapolis, a trip of 600 miles! Arriving there on Tuesday morning, he had barely time to take a nap and change, then it was off to Cincinnati, two hours away, for a 100-lap Midget race on Wednesday, which he won , and a five-hour trip to Detroit on Thursday, finishing third in a 50-lapper there. Then a day's rest before a 500-mile round trip to Du Quoin, and a pair of 100-mile dirt track races there over the weekend, winning with the Midget again, and qualifying on pole for the Champ Car race – "Iron Mike" indeed!!!

At the end of 1954, driver and team owner had their "final" bust-up, and Mike made a deal to run Ted Nyquist's new Sprint Car in the East, rattling off a string of wins to celebrate the fact. After several years of concentrating on the asphalt high-banks of the Midwest, Nazaruk's return to the dirt bullrings of the East must at least in part have been influenced by the comeback of Langhorne to the AAA schedule, after several years as an "outlaw track".

At the end of April 1955, Mike was on his way from Indianapolis, where he was slated to drive Ed Walsh's roadster, to Langhorne for another Sprint Car race, stopping at Mutt Anderson's place in Xenia. Anderson was the Elkins crew chief, hired when Nazaruk had recommended him after preparing his winning Midget several times, and the two were having "reconciliation talks" – the Nyquist car was a good ride for the East, but Mike wasn't going to miss out on the Midwest season!

Like everyone else that weekend, Anderson noticed Mike's heavy flu, and asked him to take a rest. "Aw, it's just a lousy thirty-miler, and you know, I need the money. I'll be passing again late Sunday night, and take a nap in the car so I don't wake you up and the family. See you on Monday morning!" But when Mutt looked in his driveway on Monday, he didn't need the confirmation that came in later that day.

At Langhorne, on a lightning fast track this time, a distinctly on-form Charlie Musselman had been leading the first half of the race in record time. His defences weakened by the flu and the medication, Mike still wasn't going to settle for second, and pushed into the lead in a heart-stopping move, even edging away a bit, but looking hairier by the minute! Then, it happened – Musselman, still following at about a hundred paces, couldn't believe his eyes: Nazaruk never lifted when Nyquist's Hillegass went out of control, and banged the wall not once or twice, but three times before barrel-rolling out of the premises, crushing and ripping the driver's body apart before ejecting it into the countryside. It was not a pretty sight, but at least he didn't feel anything.

Mike left the world exactly like he had lived every day of his professional life: full-bore, no quarters asked and none given. He also left a profound impression on those who had worked with, or driven against him.

Mike Nazaruk took place in three World Championship races, coring eight points and finishing on thep odium once.

Jackie Oliver

World Championship Years Active: 1967 - 1977
World Championsahip Teams: Lotus, BRM, McLaren, Shadow

Keith Jack Oliver, better known as Jackie Oliver, was born on the 14th August 1942 in Chadwell Heath, Essex, England. Oliver began a long career in motorsport in 1961, driving a Mini in British club saloon racing. He then upgraded to a Lotus Elan and entered GT racing, scoring some excellent results, and then having a difficult time in Formula Three, where his natural speed was blighted by mechanical failures.

For 1967 he was drafted into the Team Lotus Formula Two team, which also saw him making his Grand Prix debut in the F2 class at the German Grand Prix, where he came 5th overall and won the F2 class.

The following season he was called up by Colin Chapman to take over the works F1 seat for Team Lotus after the death of Jim Clark. His contract did not include an F2 drive. In discussions with Tony Rudlin, a failed racing driver, at that time responsible for running the Herts and Essex Aero Club for ex-world motor cycling champion, Roger Frogley, a deal was struck to run in the club's colours. Lotus supplied and ran the car, supplied the mechanics and generally acted as competition managers while Rudlin was team manager.

The F2 team was reasonably successful although not running full Team Lotus spec. At the end of the year the team was invited to compete in the four races making up the Argentine Temporada. The Herts and Essex Team finished third overall in the series. The F1 season would turn out to be difficult, with Oliver struggling for finishes. He led the British Grand Prix until an engine failure, and would only finish twice, his best result being 3rd place at the season-closing Mexican Grand Prix.

With Jochen Rindt signing for Lotus for 1969, Oliver was out, switching to BRM. He was to suffer disappointing two years at the Bourne team, which would effectively kill off his Grand Prix career. In two years he would muster just four finishes, with his only points scores being 6th place in the 1969 Mexican Grand Prix, and 5th in the 1970 Austrian

Grand Prix. The vast majority of his other races saw the BRM break down.

His best results in these seasons would come from endurance racing, in John Wyer's Gulf Ford GT40, winning the 12 Hours of Sebring and 24 Hours of Le Mans events with Jacky Ickx in 1969, and the 24 Hours of Daytona and the 1000 km Monza in 1971 with Pedro Rodríguez.

In 1969, he would debut in CanAm, initially for Autocoast in the TI-22, and then for Don Nichols' Shadow team. 1971 saw him out of a full-time Formula One drive, though he had three drives in a third McLaren. For the next year he concentrated mainly on CanAm with Shadow, though he would take a one-off drive for BRM at the British Grand Prix, where he retired.

For 1973, Shadow entered F1, and Oliver was nominated as team leader. The Shadow DN1 proved a difficult chassis, and once again his season was blighted by mechanical errors. However, in the Canadian Grand Prix he ran well, and many believe he actually won the race, but the lap charts were thrown into confusion by a rain shower meaning multiple pit-stops, and a staggeringly inept deployment of a pace car by the organisers. As it was, Oliver was classified 3rd, his only points finish of the year.

1974 saw Oliver concentrate on CanAm, taking the series title for Shadow. He was becoming more involved in the management side of Shadow, but would compete in Formula 5000 for the team for three seasons, and even briefly returned to F1, finishing 5th in the 1977 Race of Champions, and taking 9th in the Swedish Grand Prix.

At the end of 1977 he left Shadow along with financer Franco Ambrosio, designers Tony Southgate and Alan Rees, and engineer Dave Wass to form the Arrows Grand Prix team, also taking the young Riccardo Patrese to the new team.

Arrows would become famous for having the longest losing streak in Formula One history, 382 races with no wins. However, the team would always have well-presented cars which would usually be competitive, if not front-runners, and would often give breaks to talented drivers -

besides Patrese, Thierry Boutsen, Gerhard Berger, Marc Surer and Martin Donnelly would all drive for the team early in their career.

In 1990 Oliver and Rees - the only two founders left - agreed to sell the team to Japanese businessman Wataru Ohashi, the boss of the Footwork Group. He continued to invest heavily, hiring designer Alan Jenkins and concluding an expensive engine deal with Porsche for a supply of V12 engines. Ohashi also funded the construction of a state-of-the-art 40% rolling road windtunnel in the old Arrows factory.

The Footwork-Porsche program was a disaster and in 1992 Arrows began a relationship with Mugen Honda. Unfortunately the economy in Japan had taken a downturn and 18 months later Ohashi was forced to stop supporting the team. He agreed to lease the team back to Rees and Oliver and in 1994 the pair regained their old team, having paid a great deal less than they had sold it for. The team struggled for money in 1995 and in early 1996 Rees and Oliver agreed to sell it to Tom Walkinshaw. Oliver gave away control but retained 49% of the shares and took on the role of Sporting Director. There was hope of good results in 1997 when Walkinshaw did a deal for Yamaha engines, Bridgestone tires and signed up Damon Hill, and although the team came close to victory in Hungary, the package was not very successful. The team struggled through 1998 and in January 1999 was sold to a new consortium: Oliver left the board to retire.

Jackie Oliver was entered into 51 World Championship Grand Prix, finishing on the podium twice and scoring 13 points.

Mike Parkes
World Championship Years Active: 1959 – 1967
World Championship Teams: Fry, Ferrari

Michael Johnson Parkes was born on the 24th September, 1931 in Richmond, Surrey, England. His father was a charter pliot and flying instructer who would later become managing director of Avis, and as such Mike was surrounding by engineering equipment from a young age.

After leaving school, Mike became an engineering apprentice for Humber-Hillman, during which he achieved a Higher National Certificate in Mechanical Engineering. Upon completion of his apprenticeship, Parkes worked in the experimental department of the Roots Group where his work included early development of the Hillman Imp compact car.

He started racing in 1952, initially using his own road car – an M.G. After a few years racing on the British club scene, he was invited to take part in the 1958 Le Mans 24 Hours race by Lotus boss Colin Chapman, as a reserve driver – however he did not actually get to race.

Racing a Formula Two specification Fry-Climax, Parkes made his Grand Prix debut attempting to qualify for the 1959 British Grand Prix. Following this, he started to make his name in Sports and GT cars, including some notable perofrmances in privetly run Jaguars and Sunbeams.

With follow 'Nearly Man' Willy Mairesse, he came in second in the 1000km Nürburgring race in May 1962. Their Ferrari placed after the winning car of the same marque driven by Phil Hill and Olivier Gendebien. The race was 44 laps. Parkes finished a mere car length behind Graham Hill in the 28th Royal Automobile Club tourist trophy race in August 1963. Umberto Maglioli and Parkes drove one of the Ferraris which claimed the top five qualifying positions for the 1964 12 Hours of Sebring.

Parkes and Maglioli, working together for the first time, finished a considerable distance ahead of the Ferrari of Ludovico Scarfiotti and Nino Vaccarella.Parkes teamed with Jean Guichet in a Ferrari to capture

177

the 1,000 km Classic of Monza, Italy in April 1965. Parkes and Guichet led from led most of the in their Ferrari prototype after taking the lead from John Surtees and Ludovico Scarfiotti.

Parkes and Guichot placed 2nd to Surtees and Scarfiotti in a 620-mile race at the Neurburgring in May 1965. The winning pair led the full 44 laps. It was a 4th consecutive victory for Ferrari. Surtees and Parkes were in a Ferrari prototype in their victory in a 620-mile Monza sports car event in April 1966

Parkes secured 2nd place in the 1966 French Grand Prix at Rheims driving a Ferrari. Jack Brabham won the race and his teammate, Denny Hulme, came in 3rd, in a Brabham Repco. Parkes won an international Formula One race at Silverstone by one third of a lap over Brabham in April 1967. This event was the last prior to the 1967 European rounds of the Formula One World Championship, which began at the 1967 Monaco Grand Prix.

Parkes' Formula One career ended after he broke both legs in a crash at the 1967 Belgian Grand Prix. He established the Filipenetti racing team in Modena during 1970, using his contacts within the Italian motor industry. However the backing was not there and Parkes last competitive came in 1973 in a De Tomaso Pantera.

From here he then took up a development role with Lancia, working specifically on the Stratos rally car. Despite Lancia being based in Turin, Parkes still loved living in Modena, and on his way to Turin one Sunday evening in August, his Lancia Beta HPE aquaplaned off the road at a notorious accident spot. Mike Parkes was killed instantly.

He participated in 7 Formula One World Championship Grands Prix, achieving two podiums, and scored a total of 14 championship points.

Reg Parnell
World Championship Years Active: 1950 – 1954
World Championship Teams: Alfa Romeo, BRM, Ferrari, Maserati, Cooper

Born in the Derbyshire hillsides in England o nthe 2nd July, 1911, Reginald Parnell came from a family which ran a garage business in Derby. When Donington Park opened in 1933 Parnell was a spectator and he decided to try his hand at racing. In 1935 he bought an old Bugatti. He soon sold the car and acquired an MG Magnette but in 1937 he lost his racing licence after an accident in practice for a race at Brooklands. He was overtaking Kay Petre when he lost control, crashing into her Austin and causing it to roll. Petre suffered serious injuries. This meant that he was unable to race.

The outbreak of war meant that the best years of his career were wasted. He returned to racing as soon as he could in 1946 in a variety of different machines, notably a Maserati 4CL and then an ERA, before participating in the very first Formula One World Championship Grand Prix, at Silverstone, in 1950 where he finished third. He raced a wide selection of different cars, and his other World Championship Grands Prix included two races for BRM: one in the Ferrari "Thinwall Special" owned by Tony Vandervell, who was later to run the Vanwall team; one in a Cooper-Bristol; and a couple for the Scuderia Ambrosiana team, the first in a Maserati and the other in a Ferrari. He won many non-championship races until his retirement from racing in 1957.

After his racing carrer finished, he became the team manager of Aston Martin, a move which led him to oversee a famous 1-2 at Le Mans in 1959 when Roy Salvadori and Carroll Shelby led home Maurice Trintignant and Paul Frere. The company then decided to enter F1 and Parnell led the team but at the end of 1960 the programme was abandoned.

For 1961, the Samengo-Turner brothers (Paul, William & Fabian) asked Reg Parnell to take over the management of the Yeoman Credit Racing Team sponsorship deal from Ken Gregory of the British Racing Partnership.

During the 1961 Formula One season he ran two Cooper T53 Low-Line–Climax cars for John Surtees and Roy Salvadori, who between them collected a handful of championship points. For the 1962 season the team was renamed Bowmaker-Yeoman Racing, and in place of the Coopers ran Lola Mk4 chassis, again powered by Climax engines. Surtees and Salvadori remained with the team, but Salvadori had a nightmare season, failing to finish a single race. Surtees fared much better, however, scoring 19 points and finishing in fourth place in the drivers' championship.

During the season he also gave Reg Parnell his first podium finishes as manager – with second places in both the British and German events – and took pole position at the season-opening Dutch Grand Prix.

He was in the process of building a car when he died from peritonitis at the age of only 52 after a routine appendix operation went wrong.

During his World Championship carrer, Reg Parnell was entered into seven Grand Prix, finishing tnhe podium once, scoring nine points.

Cesare Perdisa
World Championship Years Active: 1955 – 1957
World Championship Teams: Maserati, Ferrari

Cesare Perdisa was born in Bologna, Italy on the 21st October, 1932. In 1954 Perdisa began racing a Maserati in the Sport category; driving a Maserati A6GCS he triumphed at the Bologna Raticosa, in the Italian University championship, the Coppa della Consumana, the Portugal GP and a came second in the Supercortemaggiore Grand Prix at Monza. In 1955 he claimed the Shell GP at Imola and the 6-hour night race in Bari.

Victories in these categories paved the way for Perdisa to become an official Maserati driver. At the wheel of a 250F he came a great third at Monte Carlo in the F1 World Championship. He raced again for Maserati but objections to his racing by his father precluded further notable results.

Significantly younger than the majority of the drivers around at the time, Perdisa often gave his car to his more experienced team-mates when they encountered troubles.

This happened, for example, on the 11th lap of the 1956 Belgian Grand Prix, Stirling Moss lost the right rear wheel of his Maserati. Moss brought his car to a stop and ran a quarter of a mile back to the pits where he took over Perdisa's Maserati, which he drove to the finish.

In March 1957 Perdisa withdrew from the upcoming 12 Hours of Sebring after the death of his team-mate Eugenio Castellotti. Castellotti died at the Modena Autodrome when he crashed a Ferrari he was testing for the event. Although Perdisa initially claimed he was giving up racing for some time because of the shock he experienced when Castellotti died, he subsequently retired for good

Perdisa passed away in Bologna on the 10th May, 1998

He participated in 8 Formula One World Championship Grands Prix, achieveing 2 podiums, and scored a total of 5 championship points.

World Championship Years Active: 2011 – to date
World Championship Teams: Sauber, McLaren

Born in Guadalajara, Jalisco, on the 26th Janaury 1990, Sergio Pérez Mendozais is the youngest child of Antonio Pérez Garibay and Marilú Pérez (née Mendoza). Pérez began his career at the age of 6 years in karting in 1996. In his first year of competition he achieved four victories in the junior category at the end of the year and claimed the runner-up spot in the category. In 1997, Pérez participated in the Youth Class (karts), where he was the youngest driver in the category and earned a win, five podiums and finished fourth in the championship.

The following year, he returned to compete in the junior category, where he had eight wins; and at the end of the campaign, he became the youngest driver to become champion of the category. He also participated in several races in Shifter 125 cc, and competed in Master Kadets, where he finished on the podium.

In 1999, he raced in the 80 cc Shifter category, where he took three wins and finished third in the championship. Pérez also became the youngest driver to win a competition in the category, after obtaining special permission from the Federation to participate in the 80 cc Shifter.

In 2000, he raced in the Shifter 80 cc Championship, and also participated in three races in the Shifter 125 cc category which was part of the Telmex Challenge. However, Pérez was not satisfied with the results and the following season, was up for another championship, this time on the 125cc Shifter Regional, and once again was the youngest driver to compete in the category. With all these achievements, the Mexican driver caught the attention of scouts for Scuderia Telmex.

With six wins in 2002, Pérez finished as the national runner-up in the Shifter 125 cc category, and participated in the global race Shifter 80 cc, in Las Vegas, where qualified fifth and finished in 11th place.

In 2003, he was leading both championships in the 125 cc category, but withdrew from the last seven races, which proved to be a disappointment in his title aspirations. However, he finished in third place in Telmex

Challenge, in addition to winning the Cup runner-up in Mexico. In the same year, he was also invited to attend the Easy Kart 125 Shootout, where he competed against drivers from around the world and managed to qualify in first place to eventually take the checkered flag, while he was the youngest in the category.

Pérez competed in the United States-based Skip Barber National Championship in 2004. Driving for a team sponsored by Mexican telecommunications company Telmex, he finished eleventh in the championship. He moved to Europe for 2005 to compete in the German Formula BMW ADAC series. Pérez was allowed to reside in a restaurant owned by his team manager for four months. He finished fourteenth in the championship, driving for Team Rosberg, and improved to sixth position the following year.

Pérez switched to the British Formula Three Championship for 2007. Pérez relocated his personal residence to Oxford. He competed in the National Class – for older chassis – with the T-Sport team, winning the championship by a comfortable margin. In the process, he won two-thirds of the races and a similar proportion of pole positions, and finished all but two races on the podium.

For 2008, he and T-Sport graduated to the premier International Class of the championship, where he was one of the few drivers to be equipped with a Mugen Honda engine. After leading the championship early in the season, he eventually finished fourth in the drivers' standings.

Pérez drove for the Campos Grand Prix team in the 2008–09 GP2 Asia Series season, partnering Russian driver Vitaly Petrov. He was the first Mexican driver to compete at this level of motorsport since Giovanni Aloi took part in International Formula 3000 in 1990. He won his first GP2 Asia Series race at Sakhir, winning from lights-to-flag in the sprint race having started from pole position. He added a second win at Losail, during the sprint race of the night meeting in Qatar.

He moved to Arden International for the main 2009 GP2 Series season, driving alongside fellow Formula Three graduate Edoardo Mortara. Pérez finished twelfth in the standings, with a best result of second coming at Valencia. In the off-season, he contested two rounds of the 2009–10 GP2 Asia Series for Barwa Addax, ahead of a 2010 main series campaign with the team

The Sauber Formula One team announced that Pérez would join them in 2011, replacing Nick Heidfeld. Pérez became the fifth Mexican to compete in Formula One, and the first since Héctor Rebaque competed between 1977 and 1981.

He passed the chequered flag in seventh place in his first race, the Australian Grand Prix, impressing observers by stopping to change tyres only once, becoming the only driver in the field to make fewer than two stops However, both Sauber cars were subsequently disqualified for infringing technical regulations.

Pérez failed to repeat the result in Malaysia where body parts flew off Sébastien Buemi's Toro Rosso car and into the electrical system of Pérez's Sauber, forcing his retirement.

During the third part of qualifying for the Monaco Grand Prix, Pérez lost control of his car upon exiting the circuit's tunnel section, swung to the right and crashed into the barrier, before sliding across the chicane and hitting the TecPro barrier with a heavy side impact. Pérez was seen holding his hands around his head in an attempt to protect it just before the final impact. The session was suspended, and marshals and medical personnel extricated Pérez from his car. A Sauber team spokesman confirmed that Pérez was conscious and able to talk after the accident, and had been taken to the circuit's medical centre. He suffered a sprained thigh and concussion, and did not take part in the race the following day, on medical grounds. After taking part in the first practice session of the Canadian Grand Prix, Pérez did not feel well enough and decided not to take any further part, and was replaced by Pedro de la Rosa.

Pérez returned for the European Grand Prix and finished eleventh after attempting to run the race on a one-stop strategy.

Pérez started the 2012 season with eighth place at the Australian Grand Prix, losing several places on the final lap due to excessively-worn tyres. In the second round at Malaysia, he went on to battle with Fernando

Alonso for the win. In the dying laps of the race he was able to close the gap to 0.5 seconds, but was not able to make the pass as he went wide at turn 14 and fell back, finishing 2.2 seconds behind Alonso in second. Many observers praised the performance of Pérez during the race despite his late-race error, taking Sauber's best result as an independent team.

Pérez took his third podium at the Italian Grand Prix. On Saturday, he failed to qualify for Q3, and was twelfth on the grid. On Sunday, he put in a storming drive to climb through the field to second place, passing on track, among others, Kimi Räikkönen, Nico Rosberg, Felipe Massa and Alonso. Unlike most of the drivers in the field, Pérez started the race on hard tyres and changed to the medium tyres on lap 29, allowing him to lead the Grand Prix for five laps. As a result, Pérez and his car's outstanding tyre management got him well into the points, and ultimately, to a podium finish. Ultimately, Pérez finished the season in tenth place in the Drivers' Championship with 66 points, 6 more than team-mate Kobayashi.

Lewis Hamilton's decision to leave McLaren for Mercedes in 2013 allowed Pérez to be confirmed as Hamilton's replacement. In the season-opening race in Australia, Pérez qualified 15th and finished in 11th position, later describing the weekend as "difficult" for himself and the team as a whole. Pérez started the Malaysian Grand Prix from ninth on the grid, and finished the race in the same position, scoring his first points for McLaren. Pérez also achieved the fastest lap of the race, having pitted for fresh tyres.

His season with McLaren became more difficult and by the end of the year it was announced he would be replaced for 2014, with Perez being reported to have a drive secured with the Force India team.

So far, Sergio Perez has been entered into 58 Grand Prix, finishing on the podium 3 times and scoring 129 points.

Henri Pescarolo
World Championship Years Active: 1968 – 1976
World Championship Teams: Matra, March, Williams, BRM, Surtees

The son of a surgeon, Henri Pescarolo was born in the Calvados region in northern France on the 25th September, 1942. He was in his third year of medical school when motor racing got in the way.

It was 1964 and the French magazine Sport Auto had put together a series of races for Lotus Sevens which Ford France had purchased and donated to regional racing clubs. Ten thousand would-be racing drivers applied. This was eventually whittled down to 19 drivers with Pescarolo representing Paris. He won the first race at Montlhery but the competition was intense since it included Johnny Servoz-Gavin, Patrick Depailler and Jimmy Mieusset. Mieusset ended up as champion although Pescarolo won the hillclimb award.

He got his chance in Formula 3 at the end of 1965 with Matra and in 1966 was team mate to Servoz-Gavin and Jean-Pierre Jaussaud. Servoz-Gavin won that year but in 1967 Pescarolo took the title and moved into Formula 2 in 1968 with Matra. His career was stopped temporarily in the spring of 1969 when he suffered facial burns after crashing a Matra sports car at Le Mans but he was soon back in action. Following his accident we started sporting a destictive beard, which he still has to this day to partially cover the burns.

In 1968 and 1969, he competed in three F1 races for Matra, before doing a full season in 1970. The high point of this period was third place at Monaco. He moved to Frank Williams' team in 1971, finishing fourth at the British GP.

A poor season in 1972 saw him switching his attention to sports car racing with Matra and he won the Le Mans 24 Hours in 1972, 1973 and 1974 – his 1972 drive was partnered with ex-Formula One Champion Graham Hill.

His single-seater career revived briefly with Ron Dennis's Rondel Racing in F2 which was followed by a season of F1 with the Motul-sponsored BRM team. Although he returned to F1 again in 1976 with a rented Surtees he never made a big impression.

Pescarolo holds the record for Le Mans starts with 33 and has won the race on four occasions as a driver. He raced at Le Mans for the last time in 1999. He has yet to win the race as a team owner, coming very close in 2005 with the Pescarolo C60H. His team did manage to win the LMES championship in the same year. His team was also second at Le Mans in 2006, followed by a third in 2007 behind a pair of diesel-powered prototypes.

In sports car racing he was enormously successful with 22 major victories including the Daytona 24 Hours in 1991. In the 1990s he competed on the Paris-Dakar Rally on eight occasions and became an important figure in the Filiere Elf, picking young drivers and helping to train them.

Henri Pescarolo participated in 64 Formula One World Championship Grands Prix. He achieved one podium, and scored a total of 12 championship points

Nelsinho Piquet
World Championship Years Active: 2008 – 2009
World Championship Team: Renault

Your father has won two Formula One World Chmapionships before you are even born and adds a third one whilst you are still wearing nappies! You have the chance to do anything you want to do – so what do you choose? You try to follow in your father's footsteps of course. Although unfortunetly you fail and end up leaving Formula One in shame. Sounds like a tall tale? Actually it's all true.

Nelson Ângelo Tamsma Piquet Souto Maior was bornon the 25th July 25, 1985 in Heidelberg, West Germany only a few days after his father, Nelson Piquet, finished second in the British Grand Prix for Brabham. He is also known as Nelson Piquet Junior or Nelsinho Piquet.

Piquet's parents separated soon after he was born, and he lived in Monaco with his Dutch mother, Sylvia Tamsma, until he was eight years old. He then moved to live in Brazil with his father.

His racing career started in 1993 in Brazilian karting, where he would stay until 2001 when he moved to Formula Three Sudamericana. His father's wealth enabled him to race for his own team, a practice he continued until he left GP2 Series. He raced in part of the 2001 season there, staying for 2002 winning the championship with four races to go. In 2002 he also raced one race of Brazilian Formula Renault.

In 2003, Piquet moved to the UK where he joined the British Formula Three Championship and formed the Piquet Sports team. He went on to finish the championship in 3rd place with six wins, five podiums and eight pole positions. A test with his father's former team, Williams, followed.

In 2004, Piquet won the British Formula Three Championship. He became the youngest driver to have ever won the championship at 19 years and 2 months. He also did further running for Williams.

In 2005, Piquet took part in the A1 Grand Prix for A1 Team Brazil, winning both the Sprint and Main races at the first event of the season at

Brands Hatch, as well as scoring a point for the fastest lap. He also drove for the HiTech/Piquet Sports in the GP2 Series, winning his first race at Spa Francorchamps in Belgium, and tested for the BAR-Honda Formula 1 team. In 2006, Piquet gained second place in the championship to British driver Lewis Hamilton in his second year of GP2.

He was signed as test driver for Renault Formula One team for the 2007 season, and was promoted to the race team for 2008, alongside returning double World Champion Fernando Alonso.

The first race of the 2008 season in Australia saw Piquet start 21st and damage his car in a collision on the opening lap, before ultimately retiring on lap 31. This was exactly the same result as his father achieved in his first race at the 1978 German Grand Prix.

Piquet was under increasing pressure from his Renault team over the course of the 2008 season, and there was speculation he would lose his race seat if he did not improve. Renault did nothing to quell the rumours, publicly urging him to improve after the Turkish Grand Prix and suggesting after Monaco that he lacked confidence. Despite the pressure, the young driver responded well. Piquet scored his first points in F1 with a 7th place finish at the 2008 French Grand Prix passing his twice-World Champion team mate Fernando Alonso in the last few laps.

At the German Grand Prix, he finished ahead of the Ferrari of Felipe Massa to claim second place to Mclaren's Lewis Hamilton and his first podium finish, after being the only driver on a one-stop strategy which, with the help of the Safety Car segment, gained him several positions.

Despite rumours that he was on his way out, Renault decided to keep Piquet by signing him to a one-year contract. Alonso continued as his teammate hoping to elevate Renault into title contention once again. Piquet had a disappointing start to the 2009 season, failing to make past the first qualifying session in any of the first three races

Later, at the 2009 German Grand Prix, Piquet out-qualified his team-mate for the first time. However, following the 2009 Hungarian Grand Prix, he still had not scored any points in the 2009 season. In August, Piquet confirmed that he had been dropped by Renault. After losing his drive, it emerged that he had, under instruction from senior members of the team, crashed deliberately at the 2008 Singapore Grand Prix to help his teammate, Fernando Alonso, win the race. Piquet made statements to the Fédération Internationale de l'Automobile (FIA) that it had been deliberate, and he had been asked by Renault team principal Flavio Briatore and engineer Pat Symonds to stage the crash

On 21 September, on conclusion of the FIA hearings, Piquet Jr, who was 23 at the time of the 2008 Singapore GP, said "I bitterly regret my actions to follow the orders I was given... My situation at Renault turned into a nightmare. Having dreamed of being a Formula One driver and having worked so hard to get there, I found myself at the mercy of Mr Briatore. His true character, which had previously only been known to those he had treated like this in the past, is now known. Mr Briatore was my manager as well as the team boss, he had my future in his hands but he cared nothing for it. By the time of the Singapore GP he had isolated me and driven me to the lowest point I had ever reached in my life. Now that I am out of that situation I cannot believe that I agreed to the plan, but when it was put to me I felt that I was in no position to refuse."

Unable to secure an F1 drive, Piquet decided to move to NASCAR for 2010. Piquet ran well during his first season, especially on 1.5 mile tracks, finishing 10th in points as well as being a finalist for Most Popular Driver and runner-up to Joey Coulter for Rookie of the Year.

Piquet signed with Turner Motorsports for 2012 after KHI folded. He drove the full season in Trucks and part-time in the Nationwide Series in 2012, scoring his first win in a NASCAR-sanctioned series in March at Bristol Motor Speedway, winning his first-ever K&N Pro Series East start.

Piquet then scored his first win in NASCAR competition, winning the Nationwide Series Sargento 200 at Road America; he was the first Brazilian driver to win a NASCAR national touring series event.

During his Formula One carrer, Nelshino Piquet took part in 28 Grand Prix, finishing on the podium once, scoring 19 points.

Tom Pryce
World Championship Years Active: 1974 – 1977
World Championship Teams: Token, Shadow

Thomas Maldwyn Pryce was born in Ruthin, Wales on the 11th June 1949 in Ruthin, Denbighshire, Wales to Jack and Gwyneth Pryce. Jack had served in the Royal Air Force, as a tailgunner on a Lancaster bomber, before joining the local police force. Gwyneth was a district nurse.

He took an interest in cars while driving a baker's van at the age of 10, before informing his parents that he wanted to be a racing driver. After he left school at 16, Pryce's mother insisted on him taking an apprenticeship as a tractor mechanic at Llandrillo Technical College, giving him "something to fall back on", as she put it, if his career as a racing driver was not successful.

Pryce's first steps into motor racing came at the Mallory Park circuit in Leicestershire when he was 20 years old. Pryce was put through his paces by Trevor Taylor, an ex-Team Lotus driver and old team mate of Pryce's childhood hero Clark. He later became a star in the Formula 5000 series. From there, Pryce went on to compete in the Daily Express Crusader Championship, a series run by Motor Racing Stables for racing school pupils using Lotus 51 Formula Ford cars. Races alternated between the Brands Hatch and Silverstone circuits, Pryce made his debut at the former. "The races were £35 a time. But I sold my Mini and my parents offered all the help and encouragement I could wish for" Pryce recalled in an interview in 1975.

The prize for the overall winner of the series was a Formula Ford Lola T200 worth £1,500. The series was decided at the last round, held at Silverstone, the day before the 1970 Formula One International Trophy. Pryce qualified on the third row for the race, which was held in rainy weather. Jack Pryce remembered that his son was rubbing his hands in delight: "he always loved racing in the rain". The early part of the race was led by a driver called Chris Smith but then heavy rain started and Pryce was able to catch up to Smith and overtake him before winning the race by a comfortable margin.

Pryce continued to make a name for himself during 1971, entering a new twin-seater Sportscar category called Formula F100, which he won with what was described by motorsports author David Tremayne as "embarrassing ease". He then moved up to Formula Super Vee, driving the then choice car a Royale RP9, before making his Formula Three debut for the same manufacturer at Brands Hatch.

In that race at Brands Hatch, Pryce took an unfancied Royale RP11 to first place in the Formula Three support race for the 1972 Formula One Race of Champions against many established Formula Three drivers such as Roger Williamson, Jochen Mass and James Hunt. A run with Royale's Formula Atlantic works team was also in store for Pryce during 1972, where he took pole position for the final three rounds of the championship and won the final round at Brands Hatch.

Following an invitation to test one of his cars, Pryce found himself racing in the Formula Two series with Ron Dennis' Rondel Racing outfit, his best result for the team came at the Norisring where he was leading the race until a brake failure meant he had to give up first place to team mate Tim Schenken. At the end of 1973, Pryce won the Grovewood award for his efforts during the year.

Pryce started his career in Formula One with the small Token team and made his debut for the team at the BRDC International Trophy, a non-championship Formula One event held at Silverstone, but lack of an airbox and an engine cover, along with his shortage of experience in the car, made him the slowest driver of the 16 competitors during qualifying: 26 seconds slower than James Hunt's Hesketh in pole position. He then made his only World Championship start for them at the 1974 Belgian Grand Prix.

Shortly after an impressive performance at the Formula Three support race for the 1974 Monaco Grand Prix, Pryce joined the Shadow team.. Pryce qualified fourth in his second Grand Prix for the team in France, but a collision with James Hunt meant yet another early exit. Later in the season, Pryce received 100 bottles of champagne for finishing fastest in the practice session for his home Grand Prix at Brands Hatch. He went on to qualify on the fourth row of the starting grid.and scored his first points in Germany in only his fourth race. Pryce later claimed two podium finishes, his first in Austria in 1975 and the second in Brazil a year later. .At the start of the 1975 season, Pryce's future was subject to much speculation. Rumour linked him with a drive at Lotus, the team run by Colin Chapman, who had been keeping an eye on Pryce's progress throughout 1973 and 1974. At the time, Lotus was experiencing financial difficulties and reports suggested that Shadow and Lotus would swap Pryce and Swede Ronnie Peterson. The trade was viewed as a good acquisition for both teams, as Pryce was considered a driver of the same ability as Peterson, but would cost Lotus less, while Peterson could attract sponsorship to the relatively new Shadow team. The deal never materialised, however, although Shadow team manager Alan Rees claims that it came very close to being completed.

At the non-championship Race of Champions held at Brands Hatch. Pryce qualified on pole position and, following a poor start, passed Peterson and Jacky Ickx before closing an eight second gap to race leader Jody Scheckter, whose engine failed while Pryce harried him, letting Pryce through to become the first Welshman to win a Formula One race. Pryce showed other signs of promise during the season, most notably in Monaco and Britain where he qualified on the front row of the grid, the latter being in pole position.

Pryce also achieved his first World Championship podium finish, in extremely wet conditions at the Austrian Grand Prix and finished in the points four more times. The highest of those came in Germany where he finished fourth, despite the fact that while he was running second behind Carlos Reutemann fuel had been leaking into the cockpit of his DN5 during the final laps around the very long Nürburgring, reportedly "searing his skin and almost blinding him with fumes". The Welshman later received the Prix Rouge et Blanc Jo Siffert award, named after the Swiss Formula One driver, for this achievement.

During 1975 Pryce married Fenella, more commonly known as Nella, whom he met at a disco in Otford in 1973.

Prior to the start of the 1976 season, Pryce and Dave Richards, future head of the Prodrive motorsports engineering company, entered a Lancia

Stratos in the Tour of Epynt, a rally event contested by many established rallying names. Unfortunately for Pryce, he crashed into a bridge only 10 miles into the first stage, but he still competed in the afternoon stages after his car was rebuilt.

Once the Formula One World Championship season got under way Pryce instantly added a second podium finish to his tally, at the first round in Brazil. This came at the expense of continuing team mate Jarier, who was caught out by oil on the track from James Hunt's McLaren. Both Shadows enjoyed reasonable competitiveness during the next two races at Kyalami and Long Beach. However, changes in car regulations, meaning that teams had to lower their airboxes and mount the cars' rear wings further forward, along with revised Goodyear tyres, meant the Shadow DN5B lost much of its competitiveness although Pryce achieved a second points scoring finish of the season in Britain.

The new Shadow DN8 was not introduced until the twelfth round at Zandvoort, where Pryce qualified the new car in third, and finished the race only one place lower in fourth: it would be the last points scoring finish of Pryce's career. The Welshman finished his last full season 12th in the Drivers' Championship with 10 points, 59 points behind World Champion James Hunt.

Pryce started the first race of 1977 in Argentina in ninth place and stayed with the leading group until a gear linkage failure on the 45th lap of the 52 lap race. Following a long pit stop to fix the fault, he was not classified. Pryce qualified 12th for the second round in Brazil, but on lap 34 retired from the race, while running in second place, as the result of an engine failure.

Pryce's Shadow DN8 before his gear linkage failed in Argentina, 1977

Tom Pryce began his final race weekend, the 1977 South African Grand Prix at Kyalami, by setting the fastest time in the Wednesday practice session, held in wet weather. Pryce posted a time of 1 minute 31.57 seconds with the next best, the eventual 1977 World Champion Niki Lauda, a full second slower. The weather dried up prior to the Thursday session, and he slipped back down the grid to fifteenth place, almost two seconds slower than James Hunt's pole position time.

The Welshman's Shadow DN8 made a poor start to the Grand Prix and by the end of the first lap was in last place. Pryce started to climb back up the field during the next couple of laps, overtaking Brett Lunger and team mate Renzo Zorzi on lap two, and Alex Ribeiro and Boy Hayje the following lap. By lap 18 Pryce had moved from 22nd to 13th place.

On lap 21, Zorzi pulled off to the left side of the main straight, just after the brow of a hill and a bridge over the track. The Italian was having problems with his fuel metering unit, and fuel was pumping directly onto the engine, which then caught fire. Zorzi did not immediately get out of his car as he was experiencing trouble in disconnecting the oxygen pipe from his helmet.

The situation caused two marshals from the pit wall on the opposite side of track to intervene. The first marshal to cross the track was a 25-year old panel beater named William. The second was 19-year old Frederik Jansen Van Vuuren, commonly known as Jansen Van Vuuren, who was carrying a 40 lb fire extinguisher.

George Witt, the chief pit marshal for the race, said that the policy of the circuit was that in circumstances involving fires, two marshals must attend and a further two act as back-up in case their extinguishers were not effective enough. Witt also recalled that both Bill and Van Vuuren crossed the track without prior permission. The former only just made it safely across the track, but the latter did not. As the two young men started to run across the track, four cars driven by Hans-Joachim Stuck, Pryce, Jacques Laffite and Gunnar Nilsson were exiting the final corner and coming onto the main straight.

Pryce was directly behind Stuck's car along the main straight; Stuck himself sensed Van Vuuren and moved to the right to avoid both marshals, narrowly missing Bill. From his position directly behind Stuck, Pryce could not see Van Vuuren and was unable to react as quickly as Stuck had done..

Van Vuuren was thrown into the air and landed yards in front of Zorzi and Bill. He died upon impact, his body being literally torn in half by Pryce's car. The fire extinguisher he had been carrying smashed into Pryce's head, before striking the Shadow's roll hoop. The force of the impact was such that the extinguisher was thrown up and over the adjacent grandstand. It came to ground in the car park to the rear of the stand, where it hit a parked car and jammed its door shut.

The impact with the fire extinguisher had wrenched Pryce's helmet upward sharply, and he had been partially decapitated by the strap. Death was almost certainly instantaneous.

Pryce's Shadow DN8, now with its driver dead at the wheel, continued at speed down the main straight towards the Crowthorne corner. The car left the track towards the right, scraping the metal barriers before veering back onto the track after hitting an entrance for emergency vehicles. It then hit Jacques Laffite's Ligier, sending both Pryce and Laffite head on into the barriers.

Van Vuuren's injuries were so severe that, initially, his body was only identified after the race director had summoned all of the race marshals and he was not among them.

The eventual race winner was Austrian Niki Lauda, this being his first win since his near fatal accident during the 1976 German Grand Prix. At first he announced it was the greatest victory of his career, but when told on the victory podium of Pryce's death, he said that "there was no joy after that".

Pryce's death, particularly the horrific nature of it, was met with great grief from all those who knew him during his career, none more so than his wife Nella, his parents Jack and Gwyneth and the Shadow team. His body was buried at St Bartholomew's Church in Otford, near Sevenoaks, Kent, the same church where he and Nella were married two years earlier.

A Trust was established in 2006 to create a memorial to Pryce in Ruthin. A local artist was commissioned by Ruthin Town Council in 2008 to design a plaque and in February 2009, an auction of Formula One pit passes to fund its manufacture was announced. The memorial was unveiled on 11 June 2009, on what would have been Pryce's 60th birthday.

Pryce is the only Welsh driver to have won a Formula One race and is also the only Welshman to lead a Formula One World Championship Grand Prix: two laps of the 1975 British Grand Prix. Had it not been for his untimely death, it is certain that he would have been the only Welshman to win a World Championship Grand Prix.

During his World Championship carrer, Tom Pryce competed in 42 Grand Prix, finishing on the podium twice, scoring 19 points.

.

Brian Redman
World Championaship Years Active: 1968 – 1974
World Championship Teams: Cooper, Williams, Surtees, McLaren, BRM, Shadow

Born on the 9th March 1937 in Colne, Lancashire, England; Brian Herman Thomas Redman was the son of a grocery chain owner who enjoyed an expensive education at Rossall School, an educational establishment which boasts conductor Sir Thomas Beecham, Leslie Charteris (the author of The Saint novels) and Aston Martin owner Sir David Brown amongst its alumni.

His father owned 24 grocery stores in Lancashire while his maternal grandfather had made a fortune as a manufacturer of mops. After three years at a catering college Redman had to do his National Service with the East Lancashire Regiment. When he left the army he went into the family firm but after three months his grandfather died and Redman was put in charge of the mop business. In the end the business was sold and Redman went into the garage business with Mike Wood, a rally navigator that he knew, but that too was short-lived and Brian went back to the family firm.

In 1959 he began competing, starting out in club races with a Morris Minor. He graduated to a Jaguar XK120 and finally made an impact driving an E-Type Jaguar which was owned by Red Rose Motors team owner Charlie Bridges. He won 16 out of 17 races. Bridges bought him a Lola T70 sportscar for 1966 and he began to make an impact at international level. That year he was third in the Grovewood Awards behind Chris Lambert and Jack Oliver.

In 1967 he was offered a F2 drive by Red Rose Motors and made an immediate impression although it was in sports car racing that he scored his best result, partnering Jacky Ickx to victory for JW Automotive in the Kyalami Nine Hours at the end of the season. That earned him a drive with John Wyer's team in 1968 and sharing with Ickx he won at Brands Hatch and Spa. The year began with his F1 debut for Cooper at the South African GP.

He was then taken on by Ferrari to drive in F2 and did an impressive job at the Nurburgring. He was offered a works drive, which he declined. He finished fifth for Cooper in the Race of Champions and was a remarkable third in the Spanish GP. But at Spa he suffered a high-speed accident after a wishbone failure and he over vaulted the barriers. Redman suffered a serious break to his right forearm which required two steel pins. He was out of action for the rest of the year but returned at the start of 1969 as a driver for Porsche, teaming up with Jo Siffert and helping Porsche to win the World Sportscar title.

In 1970 he drove a Porsche 917K and a Porsche 908/03 with former works Aston Martin racing team manager John Wyer's Gulf-sponsored team, winning a handful of races with Jo Siffert, including the grueling Targa Florio in Sicily. The conservative Redman decided to retire from his dangerous profession, getting a job as a Volkswagen car dealership manager in South Africa in 1971. But this only lasted for 4 months, as he did not like the political atmosphere of South Africa; and he returned to his home county of Lancashire in Northern England. He didn't have a drive; although Wyer contacted Redman and offered him a drive in the Targa Florio. After being asked by Wyer to start the race, because he did not want Siffert and Pedro Rodríguez who had an intense track rivalry on the dangerous and demanding track at the same time; Redman crashed his and Siffert's Porsche 908/03 20 miles into the first lap and was injured.

Thinking his career was finished, he then found himself signing a one-race deal to drive for Scuderia Ferrari's sportscar team at the Kyalami 9 Hours race in South Africa that year. He and Clay Regazzoni won the race, and he then received a full-time offer from Ferrari for the 1972 season. He won a number of races and the Ferrari team won every race in the series that year except for Le Mans, an event they did not participate in. He also raced for Ferrari in 1973, winning the Nürburgring 1000km race with Jacky Ickx.

Redman then moved to the United States and then won the American F5000 championship three times in a row from 1974–1976 against considerable opposition, including Mario Andretti and Al Unser, driving a Jim Hall/Carl Haas entered Lola. But in 1977 he had a serious accident in his Lola F5000 car at the Mont-Tremblant circuit near St. Jovite; it took him 9 months to recover; but he returned to racing on a spectacular note by winning the 12 Hours of Sebring in 1978 driving a Porsche 935. Later in his career he achieved more success in endurance racing, winning the 1981 IMSA GT championship. His last year of professional racing was in 1989 at the age of 52; driving for the works Aston Martin team in the World Sportscar Championship. In the 1990s he was involved in the Redman-Bright F3000 team.

Brian Redman participated in 15 World Championship Grands Prix, scoring one podium in the 1968 Spanish Grand Prix He scored a total of 8 championship points.

Mauri Rose
World Championship Years Active: 1950 – 1951
World Championship Team: Deidt

Mauri Rose was born o nthe 26th May, 1906 in Columbus, Ohio. He began his driving career at a Bridgeville, Pennsylvania, board track on the fourth of July, 1927.

He made his way to Indianapolis first in 1932, and in 1933 he drove a modified Studebaker all the way to fourth place before falling out on the 125th lap with a failed engine. The following year, he finished second to "Wild Bill" Cummings by just 27 seconds. That close finish would torture him-and the machines that he drove-until victory finally came within his grasp several years later.

His greatest competitive success came through his association with Lou Moore. In 1941, he took Moore's Maserati-powered Elgin Piston Pin Special to the head of the field, but retired with ignition problems. When Rose threatened to find a relief ride with another team, Moore pulled in teammate Floyd Davis. Rose picked up the battle in 14th place. Forty-five miles and one of the greatest feats of Brickyard driving later, he had moved up to ninth and by 300 miles he was fourth. He took the lead at 425 miles and never looked back. Some later said it was half a victory, but Rose's keen ability could not be overlooked. "I had to drive harder to win in 1941 than I did in the other two," Rose recalled.

Following the four-year war interruption, Rose returned in 1946 to find his stature elevated at the Brickyard. While that year's race was cut short by a steering failure, the 1947 race was notable for its controversy. Rose was teamed with 39-year-old rookie Bill Holland, piloting Moore's Blue Crown Specials. Holland had a comfortable two-mile lead as the race entered its last 100 miles; it was time for Rose to make his move. As Rose pulled out to pass, Holland-misreading the pit-crew signals-waved Rose around, thinking he was a lap behind. But as Rose took the checkered flag, Holland immediately learned otherwise.

There was no doubt about the 1948 triumph, another Blue Crown 1-2 victory. Rose, Holland, and the Novi hope, Duke Nalon, let Ted Horn and Rex Mays spar for almost half the race. When Nalon made his move, Rose was in his wake. Better pit work on the next stop gave Mauri the lead over Horn and Nalon, after which he outraced every challenger save Duke and the Novi until Duke retired near the end of the race. As in 1947, Holland had to be content with second. In 1949 Rose was running in second place-to Holland-when, with eight laps to go, the car broke.

For 1950 he managed a third place finish; however he retired the following year after a blowout-induced rollover. He returned to engineering full-time with a number of enterprises, including General Motors, where he helped Chevrolet establish its presence in both hod-rodding and stock-car racing.

For the 1967 race, officials of the Indianapolis Motor Speedway invited him to drive the Chevrolet Camaro Pace Car.

While his career in racing was filled with success, Rose considered his most important accomplishment to be his invention of a device that made it possible for amputees to drive an automobile.

Rose died on New Year's Day, 1981. In 1994, he was posthumously inducted into the International Motorsports Hall of Fame.

Mauri Rose participated in 2 World Championship races. He finished on the podium once and scored 4 World Championship points.

Louis Rosier
World Championship Years Active: 1950 – 1956
World Championship Teams: Talbot-Lago, Ferrari, Maserati

Louis Rosier was born on the 5th November 1905 in Chapdes-Beaufort, France, he started out driving his father's wine truck before becoming an apprentice in a garage. He competed on motorcycles in hillclimb events, starting in 1927 with a Harley-Davidson, and then opened up his own garage - he enjoyed Renault and Talbot concessions - and a transport company in the city of Clermont-Ferrand. In 1938 he tried his hand at car racing with a few hillclimbs and a run in the Le Mans 24 Hours.

During the war he worked with the Resistance in his region and his wife and daughter were taken hostage and sent to Germany. After the war Rosier travelled to Germany to find them. In 1946 he went back to competition with a Talbot, beginning with the Monte Carlo Rally. He then acquired a Lago-Talbot Grand Prix car and began taking part in French national races, of which there were many at the time. His first major victory came at Albi in 1947 and at Forez in 1948. In 1949 he won the Belgian Grand Prix and the French Championship, a title he would win for the next four years.

Rosier was the owner and manager of a racing team, the "Ecurie Rosier". Originally setup to run Rosier's Talbot-Lago T26, and later evolved to an actual team running 250Fs and finally Ferrari 500s simultaneously for Rosier and another driver

Rosier finished 4th at Silverstone in a Talbot, in October 1948. The event was the RAC International Grand Prix, the first grand prix to be held in England since 1927. Rosier won the 1950 24 Hours of Le Mans in a blue Talbot. He teamed up with his son Jean-Louis Rosier who only drove two laps during the race, which means Louis won the race practically by himself. He finished one lap ahead of Pierre Meyrat who drove a car of the same marque. For 1952 he switched to a Ferrari 500 and continued to be a strong contender for the next two seasons. He went on racing F1 cars but also turned to sports cars and rallies, including a run in the Carrera Panamericana in 1953. In April 1956 Rosier finished 4th in a Maserati, in a 201 mile race at Aintree.

203

Louis Rosier was one of the key sponsors of the Charade race track. After WWII, Jean Auchatraire (president of the racing section of the local Automobile Club) and Louis Rosier promoted the idea of a race track around Clermont-Ferrand.

A set of preliminary designs were drawn up for a circuit of a length between 4 and 6 km, meeting the latest safety regulations with large parking capacity at a location just outside the city limits on a hilly landscape.

The Le Mans disaster in1955 brought the project to a halt. All race events were postponed. No further events were allowed to take place on temporary urban tracks. Racing events were only to be allowed on dedicated race-tracks, providing that they met a new set of rules. In Clermont-Ferrand, as was the case for many other new race tracks, new safety devices were being imagined and discussed, reviewed and assessed. But the concept of a "mountain race track" moved forward. It would be the only one of its kind in France.

Auchatraire, Rosier and Raymond Roche worked together to get the project accepted by the political community before searching for funding. But Rosier was killed at Montlhéry on 26 October 1956 and would not witness his project come to fruition. The racetrack was opened on 27 July 1958, with the name of its famous founder "Circuit de Charade Louis Rosier". Soon after, several champions participated in racing events on the track, each of them, including Stirling Moss, making very positive statements about the track and its surrounding.

Louis Rosier participated in 38 Formula One World Championship Grands Prix. He achieved 2 podiums, and scored a total of 18 championship points.

Paul Russo
World Championship Years Active: 1950 – 1959
World Championship Teams: Nichels, Kurtis Kraft

Born on the 10th April, 1914 in Kenosha, Wisconsin, Paul Russo started racing midget cars in 1934 and was the 1938 AAA Eastern Midget Champion. Russo won the first race held at the Nutley Velodrome in New Jersey in 1938

He drove in the AAA and USAC Championship Car series, racing in the 1940–1941, 1946–1954, 1956–1959 and 1962 seasons with 85 starts, including the Indianapolis 500 races in each year but 1951 and 1952. He finished in the top ten 49 times, with 3 victories: at Springfield (1950), Detroit (1951) and Williams Grove (1952).

Russo died on February 13, 1976 off the coast of Clearwater while in Florida for the Daytona 500 and is buried at Crown Hill Cemetery in Indianapolis.

Russo was inducted in the National Midget Auto Racing Hall of Fame in 1992.

Paul Russo participated in 8 World Championship races. He set 1 fastest lead lap, finished on the podium once and accumulated a total of 8.5 World Championship points.

Mika Salo
World Championship Years Active: 1994 – 2002
World Championship Teams: Lotus, Tyrrell, Arrows, BAR, Ferrari, Sauber, Toyota

Mika Juhani Salo was born on the 30th November, 1966 in Helsinki, Finland. His interest in racing was nurtured by his father, who liked racing and worked next to a go-kart track.

"When it all started I was four years," Mika Salo told Speedcafe.com, "I lived near a race circuit in Finland. My father was a bit interested and he took me to the circuit that was near his workplace. There were some rental cars and I got to try one. I can't remember what happened but I liked it. By five I was already racing so he bought me a used, old go-kart. I started racing straight away in some club championship races. I was younger than anyone else because there were no other five year olds to race against, but I kept winning all the time. I guess I was good at it."

In 1989, Salo competed in the British Formula Three Championship, racing for Alan Docking Racing. He raced with the Reynard Toyota package which was not the season's best. Staying with Alan Docking Racing for 1990 and moving to a more competitive Ralt chassis, he raced against countryman and fierce rival Mika Häkkinen in Formula Three, finishing second to him.

In 1990, Salo was caught driving under the influence in London. Subsequently the chance of him gaining a FIA Super Licence necessary to compete in Formula One was destroyed in the short-term. He then moved to Japan in an attempt to revive his damaged reputation.

After a few years racing in Japan he made his first Formula One start at the penultimate round of the 1994 season in Japan for the ailing Lotus team. He was kept on for the season's finale in Australia. Following the collapse of Lotus following the end of the season, Salo moved to Tyrrell for 1995. He was to spend three years with the team, scoring points several times. In the 1997 Monaco Grand Prix he completed the whole (rain-shortened and -slowed) race without refuelling, taking fifth place ahead of the faster Giancarlo Fisichella as a result. Despite a promising 1998 with Arrows, he had no full-time drive in 1999.

In 1999, following an injury to BAR driver Ricardo Zonta, Salo did get a short-term drive with the team for three races whilst the Brazilian recovered. However a greater opportunity arose when Michael Schumacher broke his leg at a crash during the 1999 British Grand Prix. Salo was selected as his substitute to partner Eddie Irvine at Ferrari.

In his second race in Ferrari at the 1999 German Grand Prix Salo led for part of the race and would have scored a Grand Prix win but team orders demanded that he give the lead to Irvine, who at the time was fighting for the championship with Mika Häkkinen. Following the race, Irvine handed his victory trophy over to Salo as a gesture to show his gratitude. He also finished third at Monza, ahead of Irvine.

Salo was back full-time in 2000 with Sauber, taking 11th in the championship, although he left the team at the end of the season to join the new Toyota team in preparation for its Formula One entry in 2002. He scored two points for Toyota in their first season, becoming the first driver since JJ Lehto at the 1993 South African Grand Prix to score points on a team's debut by finishing sixth at the 2002 Australian Grand Prix. He retired from Formula One at the end of 2002, after surprisingly getting fired from Toyota.

His first post-Formula One race came at the 2003 12 Hours of Sebring, driving the UK-entered Audi R8, the same car he was due to race at the 24 Hours of Le Mans if it had not run out of fuel already after the first hour. He raced in four CART races for PK Racing during the same year, his best finish being third in Miami in his second series start.

Because of his strong links with Ferrari he was picked up to be part of the development program of the Maserati MC12 GT racer. He made his FIA GT debut in 2004, narrowly losing the 24 Hours of Spa-Francorchamps in a Ferrari 575. After that he entered the last four races of the season in the Maserati, winning two races and finishing second once.[citation needed]

2005 was a year somewhat lost in the doldrums with only two participations with the Maserati MC12 in the ALMS GTS-class, a competition where the car turned out to be not even half as competitive as in the FIA GT series.

For 2006, Salo returned to racing full-time, signing with AF Corse in the FIA GT to drive the Ferrari F430 and later on in the year with Risi Competizione in the ALMS. He was victorious in class in the 24 Hours of Spa and finished third in the FIA GT2 Drivers' Championship with 61 points, while his efforts in the ALMS contributed to Risi's Teams' Championship cup. In the following year he continued with Risi Competizione in the ALMS and took the GT2 class honours in the 12 Hours of Sebring and the championship along with teammate Jaime Melo. They won a total of eight races out of twelve in the class. In addition, he won the RAC Tourist Trophy with Thomas Biagi when substituting for Michael Bartels, driving a Maserati MC12 once more.

Salo raced again in the ALMS for Risi Competizione in 2008. Although he was not successful in defending his previous year's titles, he won the GT2 class in the 24 Hours of Le Mans, coming in 18th overall.

In 2009, he joined the Risi Ferrari team at the blue-riband races only, the 12 Hours of Sebring, the 24 Hours of Le Mans and the Petit Le Mans event, winning all three of them. Having won these enduro races all more than once, Salo felt he was ready for a new challenge. He set his mind on NASCAR, and had his first test with Michael Waltrip Racing at the half-mile New Smyrna Speedway in November 2009.

In 2012 Salo competed in the Gold Coast 600 V8 Supercar championship event with co-driver Will Davison. The pair won the second of the races and Salo performed well as one of the best international drivers against more experienced regular local drivers.

During his Formula One career, Mika Salo was entered into 111 Grand Prix, during which he achieved two podiums, and scored a total of 33 championship points.

Roy Salvadori
World Championship Years Active: 1952 – 1962
World Championship Teams: Ferrari, Connaught, Maserati, BRM, Cooper, Aston Martin, Bowmaker-Yeoman Lola

Born in Dovercourt, Essex, Egnland on the 12th May 1922, Roy Francesco Salvadori was born to parents of Italian descent. After working as a car dealer, Salvadori began his motor-racing career in 1949 at the wheel of a 2.9-litre Alfa Romeo and graduated to Formula One via a succession of other cars, including a Frazer-Nash owned by Tony Crook and a 2-litre Maserati sports car that he drove for Sidney Greene's Gilby Engineering team.

He made his Formula One debut in a Ferrari 500 in the 1952 British Grand Prix before joining the Connaught team the following year, only to retire in every one of the five grands prix he contested.

From 1954 to 1956 he drove a Maserati 250F owned by Greene, taking a succession of good placings in predominantly non-championship Formula One events, and was then invited to drive for the works Cooper team. His best Formula One season came in 1958, when he was the fourth-placed driver, achieving second place in the German event and third in the British.

His best year on the circuit was 1958, when he was runner up in the German Grand Prix, third in the British Grand Prix at Silverstone and fourth in the overall drivers' championship.

In 1959 he shared the winning Aston Martin DBR1 at Le Mans with the American driver Carroll Shelby. In Formula One that year, Salvadori drove the front-engined factory Aston Martin DBR4 – but it was eclipsed on arrival by the new generation of rear-engined machines. Following his success at Le Mans, in 1960 Salvadori returned to the 24 hour race in another Aston Martin DBR1, alongside Jimmy Clark, finishing a good third behind two Ferraris.

Salvadori's efforts after that were to be frustrated. By the time he negotiated a contract to drive a Cooper for the independent Yeoman Credit squad in 1961, Colin Chapman's ultra-lightweight Lotus designs were beginning to rule the Formula One roost. However, in the 1961 US

Grand Prix, he was gaining on the leading Lotus in the closing stages when his engine failed.

In 1962 he drove a Lola for the Bowmaker team, but found himself outclassed by John Surtees. A bad crash at 130mph in Australia led him to retire from Formula One.

After retiring from driving he returned to running his car dealership. Salvadori then became involved in the original Ford GT40 programme, though when the early car proved unstable at high speeds he left the programme, refusing to take a fee. In 1966 and 1967 he managed the Cooper F1 team. After that he returned to the motor business before retiring to Monte Carlo, where his flat overlooking the Grand Prix finishing straight became a venue for glamorous Grand Prix parties.

Roy Salvadori passed away on the 3rd June, 2012. He participated in 50 Formula One World Championship Grands Prix, debuting on 12 July 1952, and achieved two podiums, scoring a total of 19 Championship points.

Takuma Sato
World Championship Years Active: 2002 – 2008
World Championship Teams: Jordan, BAR, Super Aguri

Takuma Sato was born on the 28th January, 1977 in Tokyo, Japan. In 1996, he started karting and in 1997 won the Kanto region championship. That same year he entered Suzuka Racing School, where he won a scholarship for the All-Japan Formula 3 Championship. He chose, however, to move to Europe to pursue his ambition of reaching Formula One.

He won the British Formula 3 title in 2001 and began competing in Formula One in 2002, with the Honda-powered Jordan team, and was paired with Giancarlo Fisichella. His low point was a tremendous crash in Austria, caused when Nick Heidfeld lost control of his Sauber under braking and hit the side of Sato's car, punching a hole in the side of the cockpit.

He scored a podium finish at the 2004 USGP at Indy and finished eighth in the championship driving for BAR Honda that year.

Sato was retained by BAR-Honda for the 2005 season, but the 2005 car was not as close to the front of the pack as the previous year's design. Sato missed the Malaysian Grand Prix with illness, and both drivers were disqualified from the San Marino Grand Prix and the entire team banned from the two subsequent races for using cars which were underweight when all fuel was removed. The Court did not find that this was deliberate.

For 2007 he moved into the Super Aguri team, established by former Fornula One driver Aguri Suzuki and funded by Honda. .At the 2008 Canadian Grand Prix, Sato finished sixth after having a race that had seen him move from the middle of the grid to a high of fifth, passing Ferrari's Kimi Räikkönen before a pit-stop error dropped him back to eleventh. He moved up five places in the last 15 laps, passing Toyota's Ralf Schumacher and then on lap 67 the McLaren-Mercedes of world champion Fernando Alonso (this was met with cheers around the track).

In late 2008, Sato took part in tests at Jerez with Scuderia Toro Rosso, to become a candidate to fill the seat vacated by Sebastian Vettel. He was competing against former Toro Rosso driver Sébastien Bourdais and Red Bull Racing test and reserve driver Sébastien Buemi for one of the two race seats.Sébastien Bourdais eventually won the race seat and in March 2009 it was announced that Sato would not be the reserve driver for the Red Bull team.

He signed with KV Racing Technology to drive in the 2010 IndyCar Series season finishing in 21st place, he signed for the same team for 2011.

For 2013, Sato joined A.J. Foyt's team, driving the #14 car vacated by Mike Conway. In the third race of the season at Long Beach, Sato scored his first IndyCar win, in his 52nd start in the series, making him the first Japanese driver to win an IndyCar race.

Takuma Sato was entered into 92 Grand Prix during his Formula One carrer, scoring 44 points and finishing on the podium once.

Harry Schell
World Championship Years Active: 1950 – 1960
World Championship Teams: Cooper, Talbot-Lago, Maserati, Gordini, Ferrari, Vanwall, BRM

Harry O'Reilly Schell was born on the 29th June 1921, in Paris, France. The son of expatriate American and sometime auto racer Laury Schell; his mother was the wealthy American heiress Lucy O'Reilly. O'Reilly was an auto racing enthusiast who had met Laury while visiting France; they soon became familiar names on the rallying scene together.

She became heavily invested in the Delahaye concern, first campaigning sports cars for them and then championing the development of a Delahaye Grand Prix car, which she ran under the Ecurie Bleue banner. Frenchman René Dreyfus won the 1938 Pau Grand Prix for the team in a shock upset over Mercedes, but the Delahaye project failed to raise the necessary backing and was never developed to its full extent.

Shortly before the outbreak of the Second World War, Schell's parents were involved in a road accident in which Laury was killed and O'Reilly severely injured. When France was occupied by Germany, Schell and his mother returned to America, where Schell took on the running of two Delahayes at the 1940 Indianapolis 500. Having already volunteered in the Finnish Air Force during their Winter War with Russia in 1939, Harry then earned a commission in the United States Tank Corps when America entered the Second World War.

Schell went on to race in Europe, driving Coopers in Formula 3, Formula 2 and even the Formula One World Drivers' Championship upon its inception in 1950. His first appearance was in a Cooper powered by a J.A.P. V-twin engine at Monte Carlo; it ended in an accident at the harbor chicane that involved the majority of the field.

In the following years he raced in Formula 2 for HWM and Gordini, while enjoying a playboy lifestyle. In the mid 50s he drove for Maserati and finished second in the Rome GP and third at Aintree

In the 1954 Spanish Grand Prix, he took the lead from the start in his private Maserati and drove off into the distance before spinning out of first place and then retiring with a transmission failure.

He twice stood on the podium with a high of second in the 1958 Dutch Grand Prix, won the Caen Grand Prix of 1956, and balanced those with periodic sports car outings. He partnered with Stirling Moss in securing a second place at the 1957 12 Hours of Sebring, and took third place at the same event in 1959.

His most notable spells in Formula One came for B.R.M., Vanwall, and the Maserati factory effort as a subordinate to the five-time champion Juan Manuel Fangio. He also drove for Scuderia Ferrari for a single run at the 1955 Monaco Grand Prix.

At the 1956 French Grand Prix, he relieved an ill Mike Hawthorn after his own Vanwall had gone out with an early engine failure and drove back into second position. The Ferrari team, operating under the assumption that Schell was a lap adrift, had been caught out, and a dramatic fight for the lead ensued, but Schell's effort went for nought as he was forced to make a lengthy pit stop soon after

By the start of 1960, and nearing 40, Schell's prospects appeared dim, and he campaigned a private Cooper run under his family's Ecurie Bleue banner. That changed, however, when he was contracted by the British Racing Partnership team before the start of the European Grand Prix season for a full program of events, to be teamed with Tony Brooks and the up-and-coming Chris Bristow in year-old Coopers.

Schell died in practice for the non-championship International Trophy event at Silverstone in 1960, when he crashed his Cooper at Abbey Curve. Schell was driving at approximately 100 mph when his car slid into the mud on the side of the track and lost a wheel. The Cooper somersaulted and penetrated a safety barrier, causing a brick wall to collapse.

Harry Schell was entered into 57 World Championship Grand Prix, finishing on the podium twice.

Tim Schenken
World Championship Years Active: 1970 – 1974
World Championship Teams: Williams, Brabham, Surtees, Trojan, Lotus

Timothy Theodore Schenken was born on the 26th September 1943, in Sydney, Australia. His Schenken started out in racing with an Austin A30 at the Templestowe hillclimb on the outskirts of Melbourne. He was obviously quick and managed to get his hands on a Lotus 18 single-seater in which he began winning events and then titles. In 1965 he decided to head for Britain and was soon making an impression in Formula Ford and then in Formula 3, winning the British titles in both disciplines in 1968.

In 1970 he received the call he had been waiting for and made his F1 debut with Frank Williams. In 1971 he was taken on by Ron Tauranac to race alongside Graham Hill at Brabham. That year he finished on the podium in Austria. At the same time he was racing in Formula 2 events for Ron Dennis's Rondel Racing and finished fourth in the series

He had a great deal of success in Sports Cars racing for Ferrari. In 1972 he won the Buenos Aires 1000 km and Nurburgring 1000 km races, finished second in the Daytona 6hour, Sebring 12hour, Brands Hatch 1000 km and the Watkins Glen 6hour, and finished third at the Monza 1000 km and Zeltweg 1000 km races. 1973 saw him finish second at the Vallelunga 6hour and Monza 1000 km races.

In 1974 he co-founded Tiga Race Cars in Britain with New Zealander Howden Ganley, whose cars had great success in the Sports 2000 category, and constructed cars for a number of over formulae. During this period Schenken acted as a team owner and a manager in various different categories before selling his shares in 1984 when he returned to Australia.

In 1975 and 1976 he finished second in the Nurburgring 1000 km and then in 1977 he won the Nurburgring 1000 km race for a second time. At Le Mans in 1976 he finished second in the GT Class and was 16th overall. In 1975 he was runner up in the European GT Championship and finished third in the championship in 1976.

He continued to drive in sports and touring car races, notably as a member of the Broadspeed Jaguar works team in the 1977 European Touring Car Championship before retiring when he returned to Australia.

He is currently employed each year as the Race Director for the Australian V8 Supercar Championship Series. He also is a director of the Confederation of Australian Motor Sport, the Clerk of the Course at the Australian Grand Prix and was the Clerk of the Course for the inaugural 2008 Singapore Grand Prix.

He participated in 36 Formula One World Championship Grands Prix, achiving one podium, scoring a total of seven championship points.

Dorino Serafini
World Championship Year Active: 1950
World Championship Team: Ferrari

Teodoro - "Dorino" - Serafini was born in Italy, in the small town of Pesaro on 22nd July, 1909. From his young age he started racing motorcycles, his most successful being a Benelli of 175cc. He remained loyal to Benellis up to 1933, when he switched to another Italian make, MM.

The combination Serafini-MM in 175cc soon became the one to beat, and by the end of the year Serafini had won enough races to be crowned Italian Champion. In 1935 he "jumped" to 500cc racing driving a Bianchi. 1936 would surrender a second Italian Championship to him, this time in the 500cc series. With few things left to prove on home soil, he accepted the offer in 1938 to become works driver for Gilera, mainly in charge of developing their powerful 4-cylinder supercharged machines. Come 1939, and Serafini, now used to the bike, had a fantastic year winning the Grand Prix of Sweden, Germany and Ulster to become European Champion of 1939.

At the end of the war, not being a youngster anymore and using his motorbike record as a calling card, Dorino started racing cars. In July 1947, on two consecutive weekends, he took the wheel of a Cisitalia D46 and took part in the I Coupe de Petites Cylindrées at Reims and in the IX Grand Prix de l'Albigeois, obviously at Albi. Details are scarce, but he retired in both races.

Later in the year Serafini was entered by Scuderia Milan at the wheel of one of their Maseratis 4CL on the XIII Grand Prix de Comminges to be held at St Gaudens. His performance was a blistering one as he led the race from the start, signing the fastest lap of the race on the early stages. However all that came to an abrupt end in a shocking way when Serafini found that both the steering wheel and the column came away in his hands! He hit a tree head-on and was very seriously injured, his ribs, arms and legs broken, while also suffering some burns.

His comeback to single-seaters was the final race of the 1948 Formula Two season, on the Circuito de Firenze, For 1949, Serafini drove an OSCA in several F2 races and, at the end of the year received an offer from Ferrari to join the Scuderia and drive for the team together with Ascari and Villoresi.

The following season was busy, as he drove in sportscars and single seaters for Ferrari. He also drove at Le Mans, partnering Sommer. In sportscars, Dorino won both the Giro di Calabria and the Giro di Toscana and finished second in the Mille Miglia, where only Marzotto was able to beat him.

As a full member of the Scuderia, he also raced single-seaters, starting with an inauspicious retirement on the first lap - after qualifying last - on the Gran Premio di San Remo in April, where he drove a 125.

The Grand Prix des Nations at Geneva had marked the first appearance of the 4.1-litre Ferrari, and, driven by Ascari, gave the Alfa Romeo team their biggest fright for some time; the car lying second for 62 of the 68 laps before retiring with water pouring from an exhaust pipe. Villoresi also did well in the 3.3-litre car but had the misfortune of spinning on some oil and sustaining injuries in the resulting crash.

With Villoresi unable to recover in time for the Italian Grand Prix, Ferrari decided to offer Serafini his debut in the final race counting towards the World Championship. At some point there were talks of Sommer actually driving the car, but luckily for Serafini those ended in nothing.

The Ferrari team started practice for the Italian Grand Prix full of confidence, for Ascari had already recorded an unofficial lap time of 1 min 59.0 sec in the 4-litre Ferrari. Alfa Romeo was well aware of this and spent the two days of official practice trying to beat the time. Of the five cars entered though, only Fangio succeeded in breaking the two-minute barrier

At the start, the three Alfa Romeos out-accelerated the lone front-row Ferrari with Farina taking the initiative. Ascari, though, was not behind for long and at the end of the first sizzling lap he was right on Farina's tail, having passed Sanesi and then Fangio. For thirteen laps Farina held off the Ferrari challenge but then on lap 14 Ascari shot past the leading Alfa only to be overtaken two laps later. Ascari continued to hold out until lap 22 when the Ferrari's rocker gear broke. Two laps later it was Fangio's turn to retire when his gearbox seized. Sanesi was already out after his engine had blown up; the terrific pace was certainly taking its toll.

Now the remaining Alfas began their first stops for fuel and tyres and when Taruffi stopped, his car was handed over to Fangio. But it was not to be Fangio's day and on lap 35 he retired a second time when the engine dropped a valve. By then Ascari had walked back to the pits and taken over from Serafini, who was fighting with Fagioli for second place, when he stopped for tyres but Farina was now well over a lap ahead and even Fagioli, now in second place, was nearly half a minute away. The Lago-Talbots of Sommer, Étancelin and Rosier completed the first six.

By lap 50 Farina had made his second and final stop for fuel and was still nearly a lap ahead of Ascari so consequently he was able to ease off. Fagioli remained second until his fuel stop on lap 51 allowed Ascari to move ahead. For the remainder of the race there was no change on the leader board apart from Sommer retiring with gearbox trouble on his 49th lap. Farina went on to win the race at his own pace, the victory making him the first World Champion.

Really delighted about the performance of his third driver, Ferrari was reassured by his performances in October. First, on the Circuito del Garda, he followed Ascari to finish second in the last F2 race of the season. A fortnight later, the whole team travelled to Barcelona to take part in the X Gran Premio de Penya Rhin, at Pedralbes. Serafini qualified second and finished second again to Ascari. A final race in Argentina, for the Eva Perón Cup at Buenos Aires also resulted in second place for Serafini.

The 1951 season started in March with the non-championship Gran Premio di Siracusa. Serafini drove a 212, qualifying in third spot and finishing second to Villoresi: his third second place in succession in a Formula One race.

On April 8, Dorino qualified his usual 166/50 in third spot for the IX Grand Prix de Marseille, run to F2 rules. Villoresi won the race, and Serafini finished in fifth position. On April 22 he finally got his hands on a 375 for the VI Gran Premio di San Remo. Performing as usual, he qualified the car fourth and, you might guess, finished second yet again, this time to Ascari.

Next on the agenda was the Mille Miglia the combination Serafini-Ferrari was favourite for the win. However, the Ferrari had a brake fade and Serafini had to make an emergency move to avoid hitting a house. It was too late, and car and driver disappeared into the bottom of a steep riverbank. Thankfully, Serafini was alive.

In 1954 he tried to make a comeback, now at the wheel of his Lancia on the Brescia-Roma-Brescia race. He won the GT class and finished seventh overall, but had probably decided that his racing days were over.

49 years after the Martinsicuro accident, on the 3rd July, 2000, Dorino Serafini, just two weekends away from his 91st birthday, died peacefully in a hospital in his hometown, Pesaro.

He participated in one Formula One World Championship Grand where he finished second and scored 3 championship points, his points being halved as he shared the drive with Alberto Ascari. Serafini still holds the record for highest percentage of podium places per race, 1 podium in 1 race gives him a 100% score!

Johnny Servoz-Gavin
World Championship Years Active: 1967 – 1970
World Championship Teams: Matra, Cooper, Tyrrell

Born on the 18th January, 1942 in Grenoble, France, Georges-Francis "Johnny" Servoz-Gavin worked as a ski instructor in his teenage years, during which time he became known as "Johnny".

Aged 21, Servoz-Gavin started competing in national rally events but, after attending the Magny-Cours circuit racing drivers' school, decided that he wanted to race single seaters. He acquired a Brabham BT18 for the 1965 season, and his performances attracted the attention of Jean-Luc Lagardère, the Matra aerospace group's racing director.

By the late 1960s, Servoz-Gavin was a rising star, following in the footsteps of Jacky Ickx and Jean-Pierre Beltoise. He became French Formula Three Champion in 1966 driving a works Matra MS5, and in 1969 he won the European Formula Two Championship.

His Formula Three racing performances won Servoz-Gavin the attention of Matra, resulting in his moving into Formula One. His best season was 1968, particularly the 1968 Italian Grand Prix in which he finished second and scored six points, driving a Matra. He also impressed at the Monaco Grand Prix, entering as Jackie Stewart's stand-in, starting from the front row of the grid, and leading from Graham Hill at the start, until his race ended early after clipping a barrier and breaking a driveshaft in a similar incident to the one that resulted in the death of Lorenzo Bandini in the Monaco Grand Prix the previous year. The following season, he also scored a sixth place in the 1969 Canadian Grand Prix at Mosport Park, which secured him a place in history as the only driver ever to score a world championship point with a four-wheel-driven Formula One car, the Matra MS84.

Servoz-Gavin suffered an eye injury in an off-road event in the winter of 1969–70, and had been worrying that his eyesight had been damaged. Driving a March 701, he finished fifth in the 1970 Spanish Grand Prix at Jarama. Then after hitting a barrier again, and failing to qualify for the Monaco Grand Prix he decided to retire.

After his racing career was over, Servoz-Gavin lived on a houseboat and suffered serious burns when a gas bottle exploded on his boat in 1982.

He died on the 29th May 2006 as the result of a pulmonary embolism, following a period of ill health. He was 64 years old.

He participated in 13 Formula One World Championship Grand Prix between 1967 and 1970, failing to qualify in one. He achieved one podium, and scored a total of nine championship points.

Mike Spence
World Championship Years Active: 1963 – 1968
World Championship Teams: Lotus, BRM

MichaelSpence was born on the 30th December 1936, in Croydon, Surrey, England and began his motor sport career through involvement with his family's garage business in Maidenhead, Berkshire. After early outings in 1958, driving his father's Turner and an AC Ace sports car, Spence moved into open wheel racing in Formula Junior in 1959.

Immediate success at the wheel of his Emeryson earned Spence the opportunity to drive the car in the non-Championship 1961 Solitude Grand Prix less than two years later, although his gearbox failed after only six laps. However, later that year he finished an astonishing second in the Lewis-Evans Trophy race at Brands Hatch. These results prompted moves to the privateer Ian Walker Racing FJ team for 1962, driving a Lotus 22, and then to the works Lotus Formula Junior squad in 1963.

Despite disappointing results in his first Formula Junior season with a major team, with fourth place in the British Grand Prix FJ support race his best result, toward the end of 1963 Spence was called up to the Lotus Formula One team. Spence entered the 1963 Italian Grand Prix as replacement for Trevor Taylor, who was out through injury. Although he qualified his Lotus 25 in 9th spot, in the race the car's oil pressure faded, ending Spence's race on lap 73.

With Lotus signing Jim Clark and Peter Arundell as lead drivers for 1964, Spence spent most of the early season driving in Formula Two events. However, Arundell suffered a severe accident in an F2 race, and from the 1964 British Grand Prix onwards Spence moved up to partner Clark in the Formula One team. The rest of the season passed uneventfully, and despite Spence running second through much of the Italian Grand Prix, his best finish was fourth place at the season finale in Mexico.

1965 started promisingly, with Spence winning the prestigious Race of Champions at Brands Hatch, and taking third in the International Trophy at Silverstone. However, once the World Championship got underway the year continued where 1964 had left off, and Spence had only claimed two points finishes by the time the Formula One circus arrived once again at the season closing race in Mexico. Here his luck was to change, and he managed to secure his first and only podium finish, taking 3rd place behind American duo Richie Ginther and Dan Gurney. Unfortunately for Spence, this performance was not enough to save his seat at Lotus, and at the end of the season he found himself out of a drive.

Moving back into the privateer world, Mike Spence was signed by BRM for the 1966 Formula One season, but was seconded to the Reg Parnell Racing team rather than drive for the works squad. Driving the Parnell team's, by now elderly, Lotus 25, once again Spence was only able to scrape together two points finishes from World Championship rounds. Although, following the pattern from previous seasons, Spence performed rather better in non-Championship events, winning the South African Grand Prix.

In 1967 Mike Spence was promoted back into a works car, partnering Jackie Stewart in the full BRM team. Though he managed to score points in no fewer than five World Championship races during the season, none of these was with anything higher than fifth place. Mike Spence was due to remain with BRM for the 1968 season, although retirement at the season's first round in South Africa did not bode well, his race performances here and during the Race of Champions and International Trophy events belied a great potential for the season.

During 1967, Jim Hall hired Spence as part of his Chapparal sports car team. One of the most innovative engineers in 1960s motorsport, Hall pioneered many advances in racing technology. For 1967 the great advance was the addition of aerodynamic wings to the rear of his cars, generating extra downforce to improve grip levels and hence cornering speeds.

Driving the Chaparral 2F with regular partner Phil Hill Spence managed to make a great impression on the sports car scene. Fastest laps in the Sebring 6h and 1000km Spa races were just the prelude to a dominant win in the 1967 BOAC 500 race at Brands Hatch. Spence and Hill finished half a lap ahead of the Jackie Stewart/Chris Amon Ferrari 330P, who were themselves three laps ahead of anybody else.

For 1968 Spence moved to the Ford-backed Alan Mann Racing team. He became one of the few people ever to drive the ill-fated Ford P68 in competition, although an engine mount failure on his own entry, followed by a driveshaft failure on the team's second car during the race, prevented Spence from reaching the chequered flag.

Following Jim Clark's death in early 1968, Colin Chapman invited Spence back to Lotus as part of their Indianapolis 500 race team. Spence was due to race the revolutionary Lotus 56 gas turbine car. However, during practice at the Indianapolis Motor Speedway three weeks before the race, Spence misjudged his entry to turn one and collided heavily with the concrete wall. The right-front wheel of the Lotus swivelled backwards into the cockpit and struck Spence on the helmet. Mike Spence died in the hospital, from massive head injuries, a few hours after the accident.

The chief observer, Walt Myers, said that Spence was going too high on the turn every time around the track and that he had turned on the yellow light to warn Spence. In Spence's rookie driving tests, Chief Steward Harln Fengler had warned Spence about "unconventional cornering." Problem: coming in too low.

The next morning after the accident, the turbines were gone from the garages. USAC had them impounded for a thorough check. Nothing was found wrong with the three remaining cars; and Joe Leonard, Art Pollard, and Graham Hill drove them in the race, finishing 12th, 13th and 19th, respectively.

Coincidentally, another driver named Spence died in 1929 at the track and a spectator named Spence got killed by a tire that flew off a car in 1938.

Mike Spence participated in 37 Formula One World Championship Grands Prix. He achieved 1 podium, and scored a total of 27 championship points.

Rolf Stommelen
World Championship Years Active: 1969 – 1978
World Championshipe Teams: Brabham, Surtees, March, Lola, Hill, Arrows, Eifelland

Rolf Johann Stommelen was born on the 11th July 1943 in Siegen, Germany and came up through the ranks of racing in Germany in the early 1960s and ended up as a Porsche factory sports car driver in the late 1960s, winning the Targa Florio in 1967 with Paul Hawkins in a Porsche 910.

Stommelen won the pole position for the 1969 24 Hours of Le Mans in a Porsche 917 a year after finishing third in a Porsche 908. He took part in the German Grand Prix that year, in a Formula Two specification Lotus 59B, finishing a credible eigth.

In 1970, he made his full time Formula One debut with Brabham with sponsorship obtained from the German magazine "Auto Motor und Sport" and raced both sportscars (Toj and Porsche works teams) and Formula 1 throughout the 1970s.

In 1971 he moved on to join Rob Walker's Team Surtees, which was sponsored at the time by Brooke Bond Oxo. It was not a great year and Stommelen scored only three World Championship points.

In 1972 he joined Gunther Hennerici's new Eifelland team which bought a March 721 and handed it over to Luigi Colani, who created a futuristic but not very successful bodywork. The car appeared at eight F1 races before Henerici sold his caravan business. The new owners were not interested in continuing in racing.

Stommelen was back at Brabham in 1973 and then in the 1974 Austrian GP replaced the injured Guy Edwards in the Embassy Hill team. This led to a drive in 1975 when the team debuted the new Lola F1 car. In Barcelona the GH1 was leading the race when the rear wing failed. The car went into the barriers and bounced back into the road causing Carlos Pace to crash. The Hill car then hit the barrier on the other side of the track and flew over it. Five people were killed and Stommelen was very seriously injured.

After his recovery, Stommelen returned to sports car racing, winning races for Alfa Romeo and also winning the 24 Hours of Daytona a further three times.

In 1976 Stommelen had the honor to drive the maiden race of the Porsche 936 at the 300 km Nürburgring race. With a black body and without the air-intake, the 936 of this race became known as the black widow. He qualified second, between the factory Renault Alpine A442 of Patrick Depailler and Jean-Pierre Jabouille on first and third. The Renault team was eager to win at Porsche's home soil. On the racing day in hard rain, Stommelen managed to overtake the Renault in front right after the start. Now in the lead, he rushed towards the Nordkehre, braked and let deliberately room for the Renaults in pursuit to overtake. The Renaults, wanting to take back the lead after 2 of 300 km, rushed past Stommelen into the water puddles and crashed into the catch-fences in tandem, with Stommelen taking back the lead again. After the sixth lap, the throttle cable of the 936 stuck in the "open" position. But instead of giving up, Stommelen continued the race by turning off the master switch at the bends to brake, and turning on the master switch again after the bends to accelerate throughout the rest of the race, mastering an unbelievable second place at the end of the race.

In 1978 he was given the task by the Porsche factory to pilot the mighty Porsche 935 "Moby Dick" in Martini Colors. The 78 "Moby Dick" had a 3.2 liter Turbo Engine that produced 845 HP and Stommelen recorded 235 mph on the Mulsanne Straight.

During the season he also signed for the new Arrows Formula One team, alongside Riccardo Patrasse, however he failed to score any points and retired from Formula One at the end ofthe season.

He continued at Le Mans with the Porsche 935, nearly winning the 24 hours of Le Mans with Dick Barbour and actor Paul Newman as co-drivers in 1979 in a Porsche 935, only to be set back by a 23 minute long pit stop caused by a stuck wheel nut. The Team would not have come so far, if Stommelen had not been constantly 25 seconds faster than his team mates per lap.

In the 1980's he was still a sought after prototype pilot and raced successful on Kremer CK5, Lancia LC1 and Porsche 956.

Stommelen was killed in a vicious crash during an IMSA Camel GT event at Riverside International Raceway on 24 April 1983. He was running a John Fitzpatrick entered Porsche 935 with codriver Derek Bell. Stommelen had just taken over the car from Derek Bell and was running the car at second place when the rear wing broke due to mechanical failure at 190 mph. The car became uncontrollable, slammed against a concrete wall, somersaulted and caught fire.

Rolf Stommelen participated in 63 Formula One World Championship Grands Prix, achieving one podium, and scored a total of 14 championship points

Philippe Streiff
World Championship Years Active: 1984 – 1988
World Championship Teams: Renault, Ligier, Tyrrell, AGS

Philippe Streiff was born on the 26th June, 1955 in Grenoble, France. He started karting at the age of 14, winning both the junior and cadet categories in the Alps League Championship.At the age of 21 he build his first race car, before winning the Volant Motul competition at the Nogaro racing school at the end of 1977.

He began to race in Formula Renault in 1978 and won his first race at the French GP meeting at Paul Ricard in July that year. He finished only fifth in the series but knowing that he needed to move quickly he jumped into the European Formula 3 Championship in a privately-entered Martini-Renault. It was not until he switched to Toyota power that he became fully competitive and in 1980 he beat the Martini factory team at Zolder. Streiff then decided to return to Formula 3 in France and won the title in 1981 in an Ecurie Motul Nogaro Martini-Alfa Romeo.

This led to Streiff graduating to Formula 2, taking his Motul sponsorship to Henri Julien's tiny AGS team. He was a frontrunner in the series for the next three seasons, finishing in the top six in the series in all three years, but his only victory came in the very last Formula 2 race in the wet at Brands Hatch in 1984. That year he made his F1 debut with a third works Renault at Estoril.

In 1985 he drove for AGS in Formula 3000 but midway through the season was called in by Ligier to replace the accident-prone Andrea de Cesaris. When Ligier missed South Africa for political reasons Streiff went to Tyrrell for one event and then in Australia he finished third, crossing the line on three wheels after crashing into his team mate Jacques Laffite.

Streiff was signed by Tyrrell for 1986 thanks to support from Renault but the relationship was not a successful one and Tyrrell switched to Ford engines in 1987. Streiff stayed on but was overshadowed by Jonathan Palmer and with little hope of a top F1 drive Streiff decided to go back to AGS, which had by now graduated to F1.

He helped build the team into a sensible midfield operation but in pre-season testing for the 1989 season he crashed heavily in Rio de Janeiro and suffered neck injuries which left him paralysed.

Although the roll over bar of the AGS was ripped from the chassis, much has been made about the poor medical attention Streiff recieved in the imediate aftermath of the accident, with many observers believing it to be a major factor in him being a quadrapligic.

Although constant re-education work has reduced the effects of the handicap, Streiff remains handicapped from the waist down although this has not stopped him developing a successful business empire.

He was the organiser of the annual Elf Kart Masters at Bercy and recently opened Streiff Kart, a new permanent karting centre in the north of Paris. He runs a company which is converting vehicles for handicapped users and recently became the French importer for Gillet sports cars, which are built in a factory in Namur, Belgium.

Philippe Streiff was entered in 55 Formula One Grands Prix, finishing on the podium once, and scoring a total of 11 championship points.

Hans-Joachim Stuck
World Championship Years Active: 1974 – 1979
World Championship Teams: March, Brabham, Shadow, ATS

Son of the infamous pre-World War Two Auto Union driver Hans Stuck, Hans-Joachim Stuck was born on the 1st January 1951 in Garmisch-Partenkirchen, Germany. As a young boy, his father taught him driving on the Nürburgring.

In 1969 he started his first ever motor race at the Nordschleife. The following year, at just 19 years of age, he won his first 24 hours race at the wheel of a BMW 2002TI. He won there again in 1998 and 2004, too, each time with a BMW touring car.

In 1972, Stuck teamed up with Jochen Mass to drive a Ford Capri RS2600 to victory at the Spa 24 Hours endurance race in Belgium. His campaigns racing the BMW 3.0 CSL "Batmobile" were very successful in 1974 and 1975, in the German DRM as well as in the USA together with Ronnie Peterson. Later in the 1970s he raced the turbo-charged BMW 320i.

After some success in Formula 2 with a March-BMW, he also entered F1 with March. Stuck was quite successful at Brabham-Alfa in 1977, leading the 1977 United States Grand Prix at Watkins Glen in the rain, but was replaced by Niki Lauda for 1978. Stuck missed an opportunity to join Williams F1 just before this team became successful.

Stuck continued racing touring and sports cars all over the world, winning the 24 hours of Le Mans twice with a Porsche 962. Stuck says the 962 is the favourite racecar he has driven during his career, describing it has having the "perfect combination of power and downforce".

In the 1990s he tasted touring car success, winning the DTM Championship in 1990 with Audi, before returning to Porsche until the 24 hours of Le Mans in 1998. He resumed an official role with BMW after that. In 2006, Stuck raced in the inaugural season of the Grand Prix Masters formula for retired Formula One drivers. Stuck announced the end of his active career as a race driver after 43 years after the 2011

231

Nürburgring 24 hours, in which he participated with a Reiter Engineering Lamborghini Gallardo LP600+ GT3 together with Dennis Rostek and his sons Ferdinand Stuck and Johannes Stuck. Team Stuck[3] finished 15th overall following gearbox problems

Hans-Jochim Stuck participated in 81 Grands Prix. He achieved 2 podiums and scored 29 championship points.

Aguri Suzuki
World Championship Years Active: 1988 – 1995
World Championship Teams: Zakspeed, Larrouse, Footwork, Jordan, Ligier

Born in Tokyo, Japan on the 8th September 1960, Aguri Suzuki began racing karts in 1972, at the age of 12. In 1978 he won the Japanese kart championship and in 1979 made his debut in the Japanese Formula Three (All-Japan F3) championship. He continued in karting and in 1981 was again Japanese Kart Champion.

In 1983 he finished second in the All-Japan F3 series, driving a Hayashi-Toyota. He then turned to touring car racing and, driving for the Nissan factory team won the Japanese title in 1986. The same year he made his debut in Japanese F2 and drove in the Le Mans 24 Hours. In 1987 he finished runner-up in the Japanese F3000 series, winning one race. In 1988, driving a March-Yamaha he won the title.

In 1988, Suzuki raced in European F3000 with Footwork, before he debuted in Formula One at his home race, replacing the ill Yannick Dalmas in the Larrousse-Lola.

Zakspeed, who were using Yamaha engines, hired Suzuki for 1989, when he gained the unenviable record of failing to pre-qualify in all 16 races.

For 1990 and 1991, he drove again for Larrousse. Three sixth-places were dwarfed by 3rd place at Suzuka – the first ever podium for an Asian driver in F1 – which turned him into a local hero.

In 1992 and 1993, he was at Footwork alongside Michele Alboreto and then Derek Warwick, but both usually outperformed him. A one off drive for Jordan in the 1994 Pacific Grand Prix resulted in retirement. He shared a Ligier with Martin Brundle in 1995, but only scored one point in his races. A massive crash in practice at Suzuka, caused a neck injury, which saw him miss the race, and he immediately announced his retirement.

He later moved on to JGTC and remained involved in Japanese driver development. In 2000, with long term sponsor Autobacs, he would run the ARTA (Autobacs Racing Team Aguri) who despite winning the GT300 title in 2002, would expand to DTM a season later and launched Super Aguri Fernandez Racing with Adrian Fernandez, running cars in the IRL. Aguri still competes in both categories in Super GT, with team director/former driver Keiichi Tsuchiya managing the GT300 class, running the ASL Garaiya, a car his main sponsor helped to fund and develop. They race a Honda HSV-10 GT in the GT500 class.

From 2006 Suzuki ran the Super Aguri F1 Formula One team with the backing of Honda. He managed to put together his new team in just four and half months from his initial announcement on 1 November 2005. The team overcame the hurdle of its initial entry being rejected by the FIA after not securing financial guarantees before the entry deadline, and their acceptance was not formally confirmed until 26 January 2006. The team made its debut at the Bahrain Grand Prix on 12 March 2006. On 6 May 2008, after competing in the opening four races of the season, the team withdrew from Formula One due to financial problems

During his Formula One carrer, Aguri Suzuki was entered into 88 Grand Prix, finishing on the podium once and scoring 8 points.

Trevor Taylor
World Championship Years Active: 1959 – 1964
World Championship Teams: Cooper, Lotus, BRP, Shannon

Trevor Taylor was born in Sheffield, the son of a garage owner from Rotherham. He began his racing career in 500 cc Formula Three racing, initially in a Staride and later a Cooper-Norton.

1957 started badly with a DNF in the Earl of March Trophy but improved for a third and a second to Jim Russell at Silverstone on 18th May and, the following day at Snetterton, another third to Jim and Tommy Bridger. The Redex Trophy at Crystal Palace brought a fifth place then a win at Mallory on 22nd June followed by disappointment at Silverstone the following week, after winning his heat Trevor failed to finish in the final.

He bounced back at Mallory on 6th July, winning his heat and the final ahead of Boshier-Jones and Russell then took third in the prestigious Commander Yorke Trophy. Jim returned the favour at Snetterton on the 28th and, back at Mallory, a heat win was followed by failure in the final on 6th August then a third on the 17th. Snetterton brought another DNF and Goodwood on the 28th September, fifth ahead of Ivor Bueb with Lewis-Evans taking honours. The Gold Cup on 5th October brought a fourth then Brands, the next day, a sixth. Though still not quite on a par with the stars such as Jim Russell and Stuart Lewis-Evans, Taylor had established himself as a front runner.

Trevor took another step forward in 1958, finishing second to Stuart Lewis-Evans in the Earl of March Trophy followed by a DNF at Silverstone on the 4th May then wins at Mallory on the 11th and Brands on the 18th and a DNF at Crystal Palace, in the Beart Cooper, on the 25th. He was back on top at Brands on 8th June and Crystal Palace on 5th July, again in Francis Beart's car.

Disappointment followed in the Grand Prix, after scrapping with Lewis-Evans for the lead, he slowed and then retired and a further DNF in his heat at Brands on 4th August but he achieved his first win in the Commander Yorke Trophy at Silverstone on the 9th. He failed in his heat of the Lewis-Evans Trophy then took a second to Don Parker in the Archie Scott-Brown Memorial on 7th September. A DNF at Oulton Park was followed by second at Goodwood on the 27th and his year ended with a second to Tommy Bridger in the World Sports Trophy at Brands on 5th October. Ten victories in all earned Trevor the British F3 Championship for 1958

After a frustrating year in 1959 spent with his own Formula 2 Cooper, during which he attempted to qualify for the British Grand Prix, he received an invitation to run his own Lotus 18 as a second works car alongside Jim Clark the following season. Taylor and Clark shared the 1960 British Formula Junior title and Trevor retained it in 1961 before joining Clark in the Lotus Grand Prix team the following year. He managed a second place to Hill's BRM at Zandvoort, but suffered from some major accidents, many of which were definitely not his fault, and a succession of mechanical disasters, he gradually slipped further into Clark's shadow through to the end of 1963 when Chapman replaced him with Peter Arundell.

At the end of 1961 Taylor got a regular Formula One drive with Team Lotus and proved competitive with Clark and Moss in the South African series in December 1961. Taylor often proved competitive in non championship F1 races and performed well in the following years SA F1 races.

He was second in the 1962 Formula One season opening Dutch Grand Prix, having passed Scuderia Ferrari driver Phil Hill after a long duel.The 156 Ferraris of Hill and Baghetti being very unsuited to the circuit.

In the 1962 Belgian Grand Prix at Spa-Francorchamps Taylor was running second to Clark, fending off the attacks of Ferrari driver Willy Mairesse, when he missed a gear change. Mairesse brushed Taylor's Lotus and both drivers crashed. Taylor continued with Team Lotus in 1963, and on the fast Rheims circuit in the 1963 French GP, Taylor repeated the form he had shown at Spa the previous year, strongly contesting 2nd place with Jack Brabham, until his Lotus retired late in the race.

Taylor was rarely competitive on tight circuits, and generally other than the ultra fast Rheims, Spa and Italian slipsteam circuits, qualified in the upper midfield only on easier tracks like Watkins Glen and Kylami and team owner Colin Chapman suggested Taylor take a sabbatical after the end of the 1963 season.

In 1964 he joined Innes Ireland in the BRP-BRM team run by Alfred Moss and Ken Gregory, but netted only a sixth place finish at Watkins Glen. Financial pressures caused the team to close its doors at the end of the year and that was the end of Taylor's F1 career.

After 1964 Taylor enjoyed lesser forms of racing, and tested a Cosworth Formula One car in 1969 which was entered for Grands Prix but did not race.In that the opening year of F5000, Trevor Taylor was a strong contestant in the Guards Championship winning F5000 rounds in a Surtees TS5 in Holland, Denmark, Germany and Ireland and finished runner up to Peter Gethin in the 1969 F5000 series.

Taylor died in September 2010 at the age of 73 after contracting cancer.

Trevor Taylor participated in 29 World Championship Formula One Grands Prix, and made his debut on 18 July 1959. During his career he achieved one podium finish, and scored a total of eight championship points. Taylor is credited with inventing the yellow stripe that ran down the middle of Team Lotus cars during the 1960s.

Johnny Thomson

World Championship Years Active: 1953 – 1960
World Championship Teams: Kurtis Kraft, Kuzma, Lesovsky, Nichels, Del Roy

Known as "The Flying Scot," Johnny Thomson was born on the 9th Apri, 1922 in Lowell, Massachusetts, and was just 16 when he began racing Midgets in a V-8-powered car that he built to use at the race track which was just across the street from his home. Then, when America entered World War II, the graduate of the New England Aircraft School in Boston became a crew chief on a North American B-25 Mitchell Bomber that saw considerable service in Italy and he came home with five battle stars and the Distinguished Air Force Medal for bravery beyond the call of duty.

With the war over, Thomson picked up where he left off by winning 32 races in 1948 in the McLeod Offy and he was the United Car Owners Association's New England Midget Champion in 1948 & 1949. After that, he raced successfully with the American Racing Drivers Club and became the American Automobile Association's Eastern Midget Champion in 1952.

In 1953, Thomson began driving Sam Traylor's highly regarded jet-black Offy-powered Sprint Car and he and his pal Hinnershitz became the stars of the AAA Eastern Division. He also raced in some AAA Championship events and made his first start that year in the Indianapolis 500.

The 1954 AAA and 1958 United States Auto Club Eastern Sprint Car Champion had five 100-mile USAC National Championship victories on the venerable dirt-miles – in 1957 at Langhorne, Pennsylvania; then in 1958 at Springfield and DuQuion, Illinois; Syracuse, New York; and Sacramento, California. His 1957 victory at Langhorne from the pole was the first time that a 100-mile race had been run on a dirt track in less than one hour, as he averaged 100.174 mph in his winning yellow No. 44 D-A Lubricants Dirt Offy

In 1960, Thomson died at a sprint car event at the Great Allentown Fair when his car crashed through the fence and flipped into the infield.

Thomson was inducted in the National Sprint Car Hall of Fame in 1996 and the National Midget Auto Racing Hall of Fame in 1997.

Johnny Thomson participated in 8 World Championship races. He started on the pole once, set 1 fastest lead lap, and finished on the podium once, accumulating a total of 10 World Championship points.

Jos Verstappen
World Championship Years Active: 1994 – 2003
World Championship Teams: Benetton, Simtek, Footwork, Tyrrell, Stewart, Arrows, Minardi

Born on the 4th March 1972 in Montfort, Holland, Johannes Franciscus "Jos" Verstappen began karting at the age of 8, and was participating in national competitions not long after. In 1984 he became Dutch junior champion. He remained successful, and won two European titles and a large number of international races in 1989.

At the end of 1991 he made the transition to car racing. He drove in Formula Opel Lotus, and won the European championship in his first year. This was followed by an offer to drive in Formula Three with Van Amersfoort Racing, who also developed other drivers such as Christijan Albers, Tom Coronel and Bas Leinders. During that European winter season, he raced in New Zealand Formula Atlantic. Subsequently, in German Formula Three, he won several international competitions, including the 1993 Marlboro Masters and the German Formula 3 championship.

Verstappen first drove a Formula One car when he tested for the Footwork Arrows team alongside Gil de Ferran and Christian Fittipaldi at the Estoril circuit in Portugal. The test took place on September 28, 1993, two days after the 1993 Portuguese Grand Prix was held at the same circuit. Despite the large increase in power, Verstappen set a time that would have qualified him in the preceding race on only his fourth timed lap, and improved his time by more than a second after 65 laps. His best lap time of the day was 1:14.45, which was only 0.07 seconds slower than regular driver Derek Warwick had lapped during qualifying, and would have placed him tenth on the grid, a highly impressive performance for a first test.

After the test, Verstappen was contacted by every Formula One team except Ferrari and Williams, and was eventually signed as the Benetton team's test driver for the 1994 season.

After a crash in pre-season testing by regular driver JJ Lehto, Verstappen drove in the first two races of the season as a substitute, partnering Michael Schumacher and made his Formula One debut at the 1994 Brazilian Grand Prix. During the race he collided with Eddie Irvine, which triggered a multiple accident also involving Éric Bernard and Martin Brundle. Verstappen's car somersaulted, but he emerged unharmed.

At the Pacific Grand Prix Verstappen ran 6th but spun off on cold tyres immediately after a pit stop. Lehto was fit for the next race at Imola, but his performances in subsequent races were disappointing and he was rested by Benetton following the Canadian Grand Prix, allowing Verstappen to return to the race seat.

One of the most dramatic incidents affected Verstappen at the German Grand Prix. During his first scheduled pitstop during the race, fuel leaked onto the car after the fuel hose was disconnected, setting the car, with Verstappen in it, ablaze for a brief period. As was usual at the time, Verstappen had slightly opened the visor of his helmet for the pit stop, and he walked away with slight burns to his nose.

A high point in this season was Verstappen's third place during the next Grand Prix in Hungary, Schumacher having allowed Verstappen to unlap himself on the final lap to pass Martin Brundle's stricken McLaren-Peugeot. He took another third place at the Belgian Grand Prix due to Schumacher's post-race disqualification from victory, and a fifth place at the Portuguese Grand Prix

For the last two races of the season, Verstappen was replaced by the more experienced Johnny Herbert in a bid to win the Constructors' Championship for Benetton. The team was unsuccessful in this aim and the prize went to the rival Williams team.

In 1995 he was loaned to Simtek by Benetton team principal Flavio Briatore. Despite some strong showings, Verstappen only finished once in the five races he drove for the team due to technical difficulties. The team had deep financial troubles and went bankrupt after the Monaco Grand Prix.

Out of a race drive, Verstappen did some test driving with Benetton and Ligier. Briatore decided against taking up his option for Verstappen in 1996, signing Jean Alesi and Gerhard Berger to drive instead.

In 1996 he drove for the Footwork team and impressed in the early rounds, running 5th in Interlagos and finishing 6th in Buenos Aires. During the Belgian Grand Prix a part of the suspension of Verstappen's car broke off, causing him to crash heavily. He ended up with a prolonged neck injury.

Initially Verstappen featured strongly in Walkinshaw's plans for 1997 but the surprise availability of Damon Hill saw him dropped instead. His form in the second half of the season dropped off as development on the 1996 car ground to a standstill, TWR Arrows focusing instead on 1997.

In 1997 he went to the Tyrrell team but did not score any points, though he briefly ran 5th in the Canadian Grand Prix. The team suffered from an underpowered Ford Cosworth EDV V8 engine and a lack of funding leaving Verstappen and team-mate Mika Salo struggling towards the rear of the field. Verstappen's best result for the team was 8th at the wet Monaco Grand Prix.

Before the 1998 season Tyrrell were sold to British American Tobacco, who intended to rebrand the team as British American Racing in 1999 after one final season under the Tyrrell banner. Ken Tyrrell wanted to retain Verstappen alongside Tora Takagi but BAT insisted on taking the well-backed Ricardo Rosset alongside the young Japanese driver. Tyrrell himself left the team in disgust over the matter, leaving Dr. Harvey Postlethwaite to run the team.

Out of a regular drive for 1998, Verstappen tested for Benetton once again early in the year, but the team would not hire him as a permanent test driver for lack of sponsors. As an experienced, fast free agent Verstappen was a common name mentioned in pit lane gossip as a replacement for underperforming drivers.

He would eventually return to the series at the French Grand Prix, replacing Jan Magnussen at Stewart. However, the car was uncompetitive, the team struggled to run two cars to the same level and

Verstappen did not perform significantly better than his predecessor. Johnny Herbert was signed to partner Rubens Barrichello for 1999 and Verstappen was left casting around for a drive again.

Stuggling with the Stewart-Ford in 1998

Near the end of 1998 he became the test driver for the Honda Formula One project. He teamed up with old Tyrrell friends Rupert Manwaring and Harvey Postlethwaite, planning to test the new car in 1999 and join the series in 2000. All went well for the operation, with the testing hack showing well against upper-midfield teams such as Benetton and Williams in various test sessions until Postlethwaite died of a heart attack.

Not long after, Honda changed their plans from becoming a fully factory team to just an engine supplier and Verstappen was again without a Formula One seat. He tested for the Jordan team in case Damon Hill decided to retire before the end of the season, but this came to nothing when Verstappen's testing performance was underwhelming and Hill resolved to see out the season.

In 2000 he returned to Arrows, who had put together an impressive package including Supertec engines, a neat chassis with good straight-line speed and a bevy of sponsors. The car proved to be unreliable but its speed allowed Verstappen and team-mate Pedro de la Rosa to dice with the front runners at several circuits.

In his second race back at Interlagos he ran 6th before spinning due to a sore neck brought on by his lack of recent seat time. In the wet/dry Canadian Grand Pri, he drove superbly in the later stages to move into a strong 5th and score his first points since 1996. After the first corner accidents in Austria, de la Rosa and Verstappen ran 3rd and 4th but mechanical problems sidelined them both. Verstappen would score only once again, a strong 4th place at Monza, but overall had impressed with his strong, aggressive race performances.

For 2001 he was retained by Arrows. The Supertec engines were replaced by Asiatech units and de la Rosa was dropped on the eve of the season in favour of the Red Bull-backed Enrique Bernoldi.

The package was more reliable but less competitive. Highlights of the season included running 2nd at Sepang having started 18th, making a superb start and running well in changing conditions before dropping to 7th and later scoring the team's only point of the year for 6th at the A1-Ring. Less impressive were his performances at Interlagos, where he ran into the back of leader Juan Pablo Montoya just after being lapped and Montreal where he moved into the top 6 but asked too much of his brakes and crashed out on a day when points were possible.

Nevertheless he had re-signed to drive for Arrows in 2002 only to be dropped at the eleventh hour in favour of Heinz-Harald Frentzen. Later that year he almost signed a test contract with Sauber but he turned out to be physically too large for the car, which was smaller than its predecessor.

He returned to the cockpit in 2003 with Paul Stoddart's European Minardi team. With limited funds and underpowered engines it was a difficult season with little opportunity to shine. His best result was 9th at the Canadian Grand Prix, one place away from a point under the new scoring system.

At the Brazilian Grand Prix he had been running ahead of eventual winner Giancarlo Fisichella on the same strategy only to spin off on standing water, but generally the year was one to forget – and many noted that Verstappen was largely outperformed by rookie team-mate

Justin Wilson. At the end of the year he left the Italian team because he did not feel like driving in the rear-guard for another year.

Out of a drive for 2004 Verstappen was considered as a replacement for Giorgio Pantano at Jordan partway through the season but was unable to fit in the car and began looking for drives outside Formula One for the following season.

After two years of not participating in races, Verstappen was confirmed in July as driver of the A1 Team Netherlands managed by seatholder Jan Lammers's Racing for Holland, for the A1 Grand Prix series. They won the feature race at Durban.

On 27 September 2006, Verstappen split with A1 Team Netherlands after failing to secure payment guarantees. This resulted from Verstappen only being paid for the 2005/06 season a few weeks before the next season started. He was replaced by Jeroen Bleekemolen for the first race of the 2006/07 season at the team's home race at Zandvoort.

Verstappen announced that he would take part in the 2008 24 Hours of Le Mans race, as well as enter the 1,000 kilometre races in the Le Mans Series. Driving a LMP2-class Porsche RS Spyder fielded by Van Merksteijn Motorsport, Verstappen was partnered by team owner Peter van Merksteijn, Sr.. Jeroen Bleekemolen also joined the team for the 24 Hours of Le Mans race.

After winning the 1000km Catalunya and 1000km Spa, and finishing second in the 1000km Monza, Jos Verstappen won the LMP2 class of the 2008 24 Hours of Le Mans. With his victory at the 1000km Nurburgring, Verstappen clinched the LMP2 Drivers' title and Van Merksteijn Motorsport won the LMP2 Manufacturers' title. He also participated in the 2009 24 Hours of Le Mans in a Lola-Aston Martin.

Jos Verstappen participated in 107 Grands Prix. He achieved two podium places, and scored a total of 17 championship points which makes him the best performing Dutch race driver in Formula One to date.

Luigi Villoresi
World Championship Years Active: 1950 – 1954
World Championship Teams: Ferrari, Maserati, Lancia

Born in Milan, Lombardy Italy on the 16th May, 1909, Luigi Villoresi came from a prosperous family, Villoresi could afford to buy a car and began competing in local rallies at the age of twenty-two with a Lancia Lambda and a few years later acquired a Fiat Balilla with which he and his brother Emilio competed in the Mille Miglia.

In 1935, he raced in the Coppa Ciano, finishing third and went on to capture the Italian driving championship in the 1100 cc sports car class. The following year he and his brother purchased a Maserati which they drove individually in different races. Emilio was so successful that he was signed to drive an Alfa Romeo for Scuderia Ferrari in the 1937 season. Unfortunately, Emilio died while testing an Alfa Romeo factory racer at the Autodromo Nazionale Monza.

In 1938, Luigi Villoresi became part of the Maserati team, driving the 8CTF model that Maserati had designed to compete with the dominant German Silver Arrows. In 1939 he won the South African Grand Prix but the onset of World War II interrupted his racing career. At war's end, he returned to race for Maserati until 1949 when he signed again with Ferrari debuting in Formula One on 21 May 1950.

Villoresi finished second in the 1949 Buenos Aires Grand Prix-President Juan Peron Grand Prix. Villoresi won the first Grand Prix de Bruxelles, beating Alexander Orley of the United States.

Villoresi skidded on oil, penetrated a barrier, and killed three spectators at the Grand Prix des Nations race in Geneva. Nino Farina impacted Villoresi's car at high speed but was uninjured. Villoresi broke his left leg and suffered head injuries which were treated at a hospital.

Villoresi displayed his agility as a driver in the 1953 Italian Grand Prix at Monza. Giuseppe Farina made contact with the Maserati driven by Onofre Marimón as he was approaching the finish line. Villoresi made a brilliant manoeuvre while racing at over 100 mph. The crowd came to its feet to witness his quick thinking in pulling his car off the track at great speed. Villoresi then finished third after winner Fangio and Farina, who was two seconds behind at the end. The race marked the first time a Ferrari did not win an event in races counting toward the Formula One World Championship.

Already 41 years old, Villoresi served as an elder statesman for the Formula One team, notably as Alberto Ascari's mentor who became his closest friend. In 1954, he and Ascari joined the new Lancia racing team but Ascari's death in the spring of the following year profoundly affected Villoresi and his career went into steep decline.

Villoresi was critically injured while testing a Lancia Aurelia near Rimini, Italy in April 1954. He was riding with his mechanic when he skidded while attempting to avoid a Fiat driving in the opposite direction. Both Villoresi and his mechanic were pinned beneath the Lancia. A group of farmers came to their aid, using oxen to lift the car. Both men remained conscious. Villoresi sustained a number of deep head wounds, facial lacerations, and bruises all over his body. He was listed in serious, but not critical condition.

Villoresi retired from Grand Prix racing in 1957 after 31 Formula One championship starts without a victory but made it to the podium eight times while scoring a total of 49 championship points. Villoresi continued rally racing and won the Acropolis Rally in Greece in 1958 before retiring to a home in Modena.

Luigi Villoresi died in 1997 at the age of eighty-eight.

Derek Warwick
World Championship Years Active: 1981 – 1993
World Championship Teams: Toleman, Renault, Brabham, Arrows, Lotus, Footwork

Born on the 27th August, 1954, in Alresford, Hampshire, Derek Stanley Arthur Warwick began his career in British stock car racing under the Spedeworth organisation at tracks such as his local Aldershot Stadium.He won the Superstox English Championship in 1971 and the World Championship at Wimbledon Stadium in 1973.

Then he switched to formal racing with Formula Ford and in 60 starts won 30 races with 18 seconds. Graduating to Formula 3 he won the British title in 1978 battling Nelson Piquet, moved up to F2 to be second in the European contest, then made his F1 debut in 1981 with Toleman. He managed to qualify for only one race, the season finale at Las Vegas. Warwick had a mainly dismal 1983 season in the Toleman car, but bounced back, scoring points in the final four rounds of the championship.

He joined Renault in 1984 after Alain Prost left them at the end of 1983. Warwick, expecting to have a race-winning car, led the Brazilian Grand Prix, his first drive for them, only to retire because of a suspension failure. He finished in second place in both the Belgian and British Grands Prix in 1984 and placed seventh in the championship.

The turning point in Warwick's career was his decision to stay at Renault for 1985 and reject an offer to drive for Williams.The season was a poor one for Renault and the team withdrew from Formula One at the end of the year. Renault's withdrawal, and Ayrton Senna's refusal to let Warwick join him as team mate at Lotus, left Warwick without a team for the 1986 season. Following the death of Elio de Angelis in a testing accident in May, however, Warwick was invited to take his place at Brabham.

In 1987, Warwick moved to the Arrows team, ending the season with 3 points scored. The 1988 season saw an improvement on the Arrows performance due to the powerful Megatron engine and Warwick finished

7 times in the top 6, earning him 17 points and a respectable 8th position in the championship. In 1989, victory eluded Warwick on two occasions. The first was in the Brazilian Grand Prix, when a disastrous pit-stop cost him more than the 17 seconds he finished behind winner Nigel Mansell.

Tthe real heartbreak came in the Canadian Grand Prix, when Warwick drove superbly and was leading the wet race, only to have his Cosworth engine fail on lap 40. Reliability issues plagued Warwick's season and cost him good finishes in other races as well, resulting in only 7 points for the season, the last of his 3 years at Arrows.

For the 1990 season, 4 years after Senna's veto, Warwick finally drove for Lotus. But the glory days of that team were over and Warwick ended the season with a meagre 3 points tally. His greatest achievement of the season happened at the 1990 Spanish Grand Prix where his team mate Martin Donnelly suffered a severe crash leaving Warwick to help morale at the team by qualifying in the top 10 only for the gearbox to fail 10 laps from the end.

Warwick also competed successfully in sports car racing, winning the World Sportscar Championship in 1992, and was part of the Peugeot team which was victorious at the 24 hours of Le Mans race that year. He drove sports cars for Jaguar in 1986 and 1991.

Following a 3 year sabbatical, Warwick returned to Formula One in 1993 to drive for Footwork, but managed to score only 4 points. Unable to secure a drive for the following season, he retired from Formula One.

Warwick raced in the British Touring Car Championship (BTCC) after retiring from Formula One, driving for the Alfa Romeo works team in 1995. Despite the team's dominating the previous year, their car was underdeveloped this time, leading to a poor season.

After a year out of racing, he co-founded the 888 Racing team that took over the running of the works Vauxhall 1997 BTCC entry, as well as owning three car dealerships in Southampton and Jersey. Originally set to be team principal, it was decided he would drive one of the cars alongside established Vauxhall driver John Cleland, winning a wet race at Knockhill in 1998. He retired from racing at the end of the year, but continued his involvement in the team for another 3 years.

Warwick now writes his F1 blog on the Sports social network champions365.com and operates a Honda franchise in Jersey

He ended his Grand Prix career with a total of 71 Grand Prix points, from 162 entries, including four podiums.

Peter Whitehead
World Championship Years Active: 1950 – 1954
World Championship Teams: Ferrari, Alta, Cooper

Peter Whitehead was born on the 12 thNovember 1914, in Menston, in the Yorkshire part of England, and was able to fund his racing largely through the family wealth, gained from the wool industry. He began racing at the age of 20 in 1935, initially racing an Alta before buying an ERA B Type in 1936. Whitehead took the ERA to Australia in 1938 while touring on business, where he won the 1938 Australian Grand Prix and the 1938 Australian Hillclimb Championship.

Peter Whitehead is notable as the first person to whom Enzo Ferrari ever sold a Formula One car : a Ferrari 125 and for being the first driver to win a motor race on the Mount Panorama Circuit.

Whitehead teamed with Peter Walker to win the 1951 24 Hours of Le Mans, in a Jaguar. In July 1952 Whitehead qualified his Alta 2nd to Harry Schell for the Grand Prix of Rouen. In July 1953 Whitehead won a 12-hour endurance race together with Stirling Moss, at Reims, driving a Jaguar. In 1954 Whitehead and Ken Wharton piloted a new model 'D' type Jaguar to win the 12-Hour Race of Reims on 4 July.

Whitehead's last great performance was at Le Mans in 1958 where he came second in an Aston Martin, sharing the driving with his half-brother Graham Whitehead. A couple of months later Peter and Graham were competing together in the Tour de France, when their Jaguar crashed off a bridge into a 30-foot ravine at Lasalle, after overturning twice. Graham was badly injured, but Peter was killed instantly

During his World Championship carrer, Peter Whitehead was entered into twelve Grand Prix, finishing on the podium once, socring four World Championship points.

Reine Wisell
World Championship Years Active: 1970 – 1974
World Championship Teams: Lotus, BRM, March

Reine Wisell was born in Motala, Sweden on the 30th September, 1941. He won the Swedish Formula 3 Championship in 1967 and three years later he made the big step and signed with Team Lotus who was the best team that year.

In the 1970 United States Grand Prix in Watkins Glen, Wisell raced for Lotus who made their return in the championship after Jochen Rindt's death at Monza. Rindt's death caused his teammate John Miles to retire and Wisell replaced him. His first grand prix was the best in his career as he achieved a third place finish, trailing only his teammate and future champion Emerson Fittipaldi and Pedro Rodríguez and finishing ahead of title contender Jacky Ickx. This result was Wisell's best, as the subsequent years were not so good for him, and he retired after his home grand prix in 1974

In his first race at Watkins Glen Wisell finished third but the achievement was overshadowed by the fact that it was young Fittipaldi's first GP victory. It was enough to impress the team however and Wisell was re-signed for the 1971 season but Fittipaldi emerged as the stronger driver and at the end of the season Wisell moved to the Marlboro-supported BRM team. At the end of the year he was recalled briefly to Team Lotus but thereafter he faded from the F1 scene and did only occasional F1 races in the 1973 and 1974.

Despairing of the single-seater scene, Wisell signed to drive a Porsche in the European GT series in 1975 and won the title. That same year he took part in touring car events in a Chevrolet Camaro. Eventually, however, he dropped out of topline competition and turned his attention to teaching advanced driving techniques to his fellow Swedes although he continued to take part in occasional historic races when he was offered the chance.

He participated in 23 Formula One World Championship Grands Prix achieving 1 podium finish, and scored a total of 13 championship points.

Alexander Wurz
World Championship Years Active: 1997-2007
World Championship Teams: Benetton, McLaren, Williams

Alexander Wurz was born on the 15th February 1974 in Waidhofen an der Thaya, Austria. The second son of former rallycross champion Franz Wurz, young Alexander first tasted competition in the BMX World Championship, which he won in 1986 at the age of 12. This gave him an underlying physical fitness suitable for motor racing.

Like most Formula One drivers, Wurz's motorsport career began with karting. In 1991, Wurz drove in Formula Ford. In 1993, he switched to the German Formula Three Championship. During his time in Formula 3, Wurz famously crashed out of the lead at a race at AVUS in 1995 after a collision with the safety car.

For 1996, Wurz drove an Opel Calibra for the Joest Racing touring car team in the DTM. Also that year, Wurz, together with Davy Jones and Manuel Reuter, won the Le Mans 24 Hours and in so doing became the youngest ever winner of the 24-hour race. He still holds the record to this day.

Wurz's Formula One debut was at the 1997 Canadian Grand Prix for Benetton filling in for fellow Austrian Gerhard Berger, who couldn't race due to illness. Wurz impressed with a podium position in his third race (1997 British Grand Prix) before returning to being a test driver upon Berger's return to the cockpit at the German Grand Prix, which Berger won.

However, Wurz was rewarded with a full-time race seat for the 1998 season with Benetton and spent three more seasons at the team, partnered each year by Giancarlo Fisichella. A strong start to 1998 suggested a bright future, but the three-season stint at Benetton turned out to be a disappointment.

Toward the end of his Benetton time, Fisichella produced better results, although in 1998 Fisichella had one point less than Wurz, finishing 9th whereas Wurz finished 8th in that Season with 17 points (together with Heinz-Harald Frentzen, who finished 7th.) and five 4th places.

One notable race was the 1998 Monaco Grand Prix, where he was running 2nd ahead of Michael Schumacher for a brief period. His hopes of a podium finish were ruined when Schumacher tried to pass through at Loews hairpin, but collided together with him and like Schumacher's Ferrari, his suspension broke, causing him to spin off and crash at the Nouvelle Chicane exiting the tunnel. He retired and Schumacher finished 10th in the end after the German pitted for repairs.

In 2000, Wurz returned somewhat to his cycling roots, starting an MTB team with countryman Markus Rainer. The team, Rainer-Wurz.com, is currently sponsored by sponsors McLaren, Siemens, and Cannondale amongst others. They are multiple World Cup winners.

In 2001 he took on the role of third (i.e., test) driver for McLaren. In April 2005, with Juan Pablo Montoya injured, Wurz drove for McLaren in the 2005 San Marino Grand Prix, finishing fourth in the race, but taking third place after both BAR-Honda drivers were disqualified. This gave him a unique record, as no other driver has had such a long gap between podiums as Wurz, who went eight years without one. His drive at Imola was all the more notable because he was still not comfortable in the car, and at times had to drive with one hand.

In 2003 he was strongly linked to a race seat at Jaguar, where the under-fire Antônio Pizzonia was struggling. However, McLaren were struggling with their abortive new car and blocked the move to retain Wurz as a development driver. Jaguar then decided to give Pizzonia more time to prove himself, before drafting in Justin Wilson.

Alexander Wurz signed a deal with WilliamsF1 to become the team's official test and reserve driver at the beginning of 2006. He drove the third car at all Grand Prix Fridays in 2006. It was announced on 3 August 2006 that Wurz would replace Mark Webber as a race driver at Williams for the 2007 season. This was Wurz's first full time race drive since 2000, and his team mate was Nico Rosberg.

At the Monaco GP on 27 May 2007, Wurz scored his first points for the Williams F1 team, finishing in 7th place after qualifying 11th. He came 3rd for the 3rd time in his F1 career at the Canadian Grand Prix on 10

June 2007, staying out of trouble from 19th on the grid in an action packed race. He nearly repeated this at the European Grand Prix, but just didn't make it past Mark Webber at the final chicane. That race turned of to be Wurz's last points finish and especially from now on, team mate Rosberg distanced him. On October 8, 2007 Wurz announced his immediate retirement from Formula One, meaning that the 2007 Chineese Grand Prix was his final race.

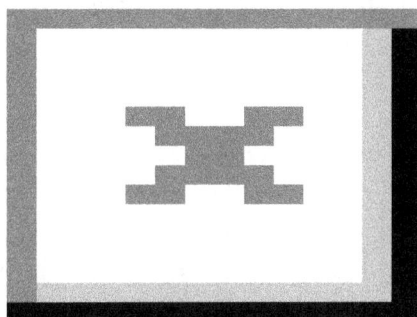

Wurz in his final F1 race, the 2007 Chineese Grand Prix

Wurz was the Honda F1 test driver for the 2008 Formula One season, a role he kept on the transition to Brawn GP in 2009.

Wurz then signed with Peugeot to be part of their driving squad for the 2008 24 Hours of Le Mans and he also participated 1000km of Spa in the Le Mans Series.

In 2009, together with Marc Gené and David Brabham, he took outright victory in the Le Mans 24 Hours, driving a works Peugeot. The 13-year gap between Wurz's victories is the largest in the event's history.

Together with his victory in the 2010 12hrs race of Sebring with Marc Gené and Anthony Davidson and his victory of the 1000 miles race of Road Atlanta with Stéphane Sarrazin and Franck Montagny in 2011 it made him win the 3 big Sportscar Classic Races in a Peugeot 908. Wurz continued to race for Peugeot Sport Total through 2010 and 2011, though no further Le Mans wins were forthcoming.

For the 2012 Formula One season, Wurz rejoined the Williams F1 Team, this time to guide the team's inexperienced drivers Bruno Senna and Pastor Maldonado. Toyota Motorsports alos announced Wurz as one of their factory drivers for the companies planned return to the 24 Heures du Mans in 2012, driving their new LMP1 Hybrid Prototype alongside Nicolas Lapierre and Kazuki Nakajima. A role he continued with into 2013.

Wurz is involved in many projects regarding Road Safety and Driver Education and Training. Together with his father he founded his own company Test and Training International, leader in the field of road safety and driver training working as well closely with the FIA Fédération Internationale de l'Automobile, since 2011 as an operating partner of the FIA Institute Young Driver Excellence Academy.

During his Formula One carrer, Alex Wurz competed in 69 Grand Prix, scoring 45 points and finishing o nthe podium three times.

BIBLIOGRAPHY

Cliff Allison: From the Fells to Ferrari, Graham Gauld; Publisher: Veloce Publishing Ltd; First Edition 2008

Ferrari the battle for revival, Alan Henry; Publisher: Patrick Stephens Limited; First Edition 1996

Ford Racing Century, Larry Edsall and Mike Teske; Publisher: Motorbooks International; First Edition 2003

Formula 1 Facts & Trivia, Anna O'Brien; Publisher: Parragon; First Edition 1999

Forza Amon!, Eoin Young; Publisher: J H Haynes & Co Ltd: Illustrated edition 2003

Go: The Bettenhausen Story : The Race Against a Dream, Carl H. Hungness; Publisher: Carl Hungness Pub: First Edition 1983

Inside Racing: A Season with the PacWest CART Indy Car Team, Paul Haney; Publisher: Motorbooks International; First Edition 1998

Racing Stewart: The Birth of a Grand Prix Team, Maurice Hamilton and Jon Nicholson; Publisher: Motorbooks International; First edition 1998

Stewart: Formula 1 Racing Team, David Tremayne; Publisher: J H Haynes & Co Ltd; First edition 1999

Team Lotus in Formula 1, Hartmut Lehbrink; Publisher: EarBooks; First edition 2011

The Concise Encyclopaedia of Formula One, David Tremayne and Mark Hughes; Publisher: Parragon; Second Edition 2002

The Encyclopaedia of Formula One, Tim Hill and Gareth Thomas; Publisher: Parragon; Third Edition 2009

The Great Encyclopaedia of Formula One, Pierre Menard, Bernard Cahier and Nigel Roebuck; Publisher: Chronosports; 2006

The Lost Generation, David Tremayne; Publisher: Haynes Publishing; 2006

1994 Indianapolis 500 Official Program; Publisher: Indy 500 Publications; 1994

WEBSITES

Autocoursegp.com

Crash.Net

Driver Database - www.driverdb.com

ESPN F1 - en.espnf1.com

F1 Rejects - f1rejects.com

GrandPrix.com

HistoricRacing.com

Indymotorspeedway.com

Los Angeles Times - articles.latimes.com/keyword/eddie-cheever

Mark Blundell - www.mark-blundell.com

http://s154140382.websitehome.co.uk/wpmu/mikeparkes/

Motorsports Hall of Fame of America - www.mshf.com

The National Midget Auto Racing Hall of Fame - www.worthyofhonor.com

Wikipedia – www.wikipedia.org

PHOTOGRAPHS

About The Author

Lloyd Bonson has been interested in cars since a young age and has spent all of his working life within the motor industry. From a production vehicle perspective he has been involved on many projects with Ford Motor Company, Jaguar Land Rover and Volvo Cars.

In motor sport Lloyd was part of the Woodcock Brothers Racing team which won the UK Formula Saloons Championship in both 2000 and 2001 and the John Danby Racing Team which won the UK Sports2000 Championship in 2003.

For six years Lloyd was the motor racing correspondent for Phoenix FM radio in Essex, as well as hosting a variety of other shows including a motoring show called 'Overdrive'. Lloyd has also presented a variety of television programs including the Ford Fiesta Championship, Porsche Club Championship and a one off special for Castle Combe's 60th Anniversary.

Away from cars, Lloyd loves rugby and is a proud supporter of London Irish; he is also a keen musician, singer, songwriter and amateur actor and is heavily involved with his local dramatic and operatic society in Essex, UK.

Also from the author

One Hit Wonders: The story of one off Grand Prix winners

Lloyd Bonson's first book, looking at the stories of drivers and teams with only one World Championship Grand Prix victory to their name.

www.stanhopebooks.com

facebook.com/stanhopebooks

Twitter @stanhopebooks